The Joaquín Band

The
Joaquín Band

The History behind the Legend

LORI LEE WILSON

UNIVERSITY OF NEBRASKA PRESS | LINCOLN AND LONDON

Chapter 3, "The Perspective of the *Los Angeles
Star* and *La Estrella*," was originally published as
"In Search of a Bandit," *Quarterly of the National
Association for Outlaw and Lawman History* 25
(January–March 2001) 1: 10–17.

Publication of this volume was assisted by The
Virginia Faulkner Fund, established in memory
of Virginia Faulkner, editor in chief of the
University of Nebraska Press.

Library of Congress
Cataloging-in-Publication
Data

Wilson, Lori Lee.
The Joaquín band: the history
behind the legend / Lori Lee Wilson.
p. cm.
Includes bibliographical references
and index.
ISBN 978-0-8032-3461-1 (cloth: alk. paper)
1. Murieta, Joaquín, d. 1853. 2. Outlaws—
California—Biography. 3. Mexicans—
California—Biography. 4. Frontier and
pioneer life—California. 5. California—
History—1850–1950. I. Title.
F865.M96W55 2011
364.3—dc22
2010047892

Set in Quadraat by Kim Essman.
Designed by Ray Boeche and Kim Essman.

Contents

Illustrations

Maps

Preface

My first encounter with Joaquín Murrieta was in a *Reader's Digest* book for kids about American legends and lore. His story came after Salem witchcraft history and lore and amid colorful depictions of pirate captains like Blackbeard and frontiersmen like Daniel Boone. Years later, when I read about Joaquín and his band in history books, I found a lack of consensus with regard to his existence. That bewildered me. I knew that the same was true of Robin Hood and King Arthur, but they came from a time of little documentation. Joaquín Murrieta, on the other hand, rode into legend a mere century-and-a-half ago, and out of a place and time that is exceedingly rich in primary sources. It seemed incredible that some historians had decided he has more in common with the fictional Zorro than with the historical Tiburcio Vásquez.

This provoked a more intense interest in Joaquín and band. I visited previously cited sources and found a few hitherto unexplored ones. I wanted to know more about the history out of which the legend came, and I found that the history relevant to Joaquín Murrieta reaches beyond him to include other outlaws with whom he had associated, some of whom outlived him. There were Claudio and Reyes Féliz, Bernardo and Francisco "Pancho" Daniel, Joaquín and Jesús Valenzuela, Juan Flores, Ana Benites, Antonia "La Molinera," Luis Burgos alias Joaquín, Luciano Tapia alias Lorenzo Lopez, John "Jack" Powers, Tiburcio Vásquez, and Procopio Bustamente, among others. Their histories have influenced Joaquín-related oral tradition, folklore, and legend. This history looks beyond Joaquín Murrieta to include these other outlaws, the sources that tell their stories, and the vigilantes who pursued them.

At the heart of the Joaquín legend there is a tale of revenge against the unjust. During my research I found that vigilantes and other posses were often motivated by a lust for revenge as well, after friends, fellow Masons, or countrymen were murdered. Indeed both the outlaws and their pursuers treated life as though it was cheap and excused their acts as justifiable, given the circumstances.

California's vigilantes sought to enforce the law in a lawless land and attempted to do so within the framework of American law and order by holding hearings, appointing juries, and passing sentences. But the result was almost always a death sentence that was hastily carried out. Occasionally vigilante posses did not bother to hold hearings but opted instead to lynch or shoot prisoners on the spot. So people on both sides of the law ended up killing innocent persons. Vigilantes excused their actions as necessary or pardonable when those actions were scrutinized and condemned. Bandits also sought pardon or praise for their actions when they insisted that their adversaries in law enforcement, or "the Americans," provoked them. ("Americans" here and in most cases throughout this book means white U.S. citizens who arrived in California after 1840. Those who arrive earlier became "Californios.") Both groups faced condemnation for their actions, although the outlaws duly earned more consistent condemnation than did the vigilantes or even the lynch mobs. This reflects the central difference between the two groups: bandits never claimed what they did was right or good. Vigilantes and lynch mobs did.

Moral condemnation of bandits and also of those who pursued them with deadly zeal begins with witnesses and continues in the pages of history, for we historians dig up the past in search of the truth. We interpret what we find in different ways, but we all set out looking for evidence of reported events. In doing so, we are, to some extent, hypocrites, in that very few historians would be comfortable recording and publishing events from his or her own life inclusive of misguided deeds and utterances that proved destructive. For some of us, researching history is an escape from present moral dilemmas, a withdrawal to a place and time where everything seems so much clearer due to the advantages distance and retrospect endow. And yet, to get at the truth, we must set aside those advantages and make some attempt to relate to those on whom we are about to pass judgment. We must take our own faults with us into the past in order to better empathize with and understand the authors of our sources and the famous and not-so-famous events and people they wrote about.

In legend Joaquín Murrieta is described as a good Mexican who went bad because of the abuses he suffered at the hands of unscrupulous Americans. Such ethnic-based abuses were indeed commonplace in gold rush California (though I found no evidence of good men turning bad because of it). Regardless of whether or not Murrieta himself suffered unjust treatment, this part of the legend does reflect a historical reality, with substantial evidence supporting it. Indeed, because so many Mexicans—including those born in California and called "Californios"—were abused, robbed, and cheated by North American immigrants, the legend of Joaquín Murrieta and band was given a permanent place in early California history. A hunger for justice permeates the legend as written by John Rollin Ridge, a hunger which historians have acknowledged was justified. Familiarity with the legend's storyline is essential to understanding how the author was influenced by what were to him current events and recent news. When he wrote the book he romanticized events but he was also influenced by his own life experiences as a Cherokee mestizo.

Acknowledgments

Many thanks for encouragement and a generous grant from the National Outlaw and Lawman Association, now called the Wild West History Association. Thank you, Joshua Reader, for sharing sources and giving me a guided tour of Joaquín country from Cantua Creek to Mariposa to Pacheco Pass. Thank you, Barbara McKee Pampanin, for introducing me to your cousin, Mary Jane Garamendi, of Chile Gulch, Calaveras County. Thank you Mary Jane for sharing local oral traditions your father passed down about Joaquín Murrieta. Mary Jane pointed out Golden Gate Hill and said that a woman who lived there in the early days ran a boarding house and that Murrieta and band stopped there more than once to get a bite to eat.

No historian could do without librarians! Many thanks to Sibylle Zemitis, John Gonzales, Ellen Harding, and other staff at the California State Library and to Angus Robertson and others at the University of Vermont's Bailey-Howe Library. Thank you Karen and Richard for hosting me while I availed myself of the collection at New York Public Library. At the Bancroft Library, David Kessler, Emily Balmages, Corliss Lee, and Naomi Schultz were wonderfully helpful. Special thanks also to Genevieve Troka at the California State Archives, to Peter J. Blodgett and others at the Huntington Library, Polly Armstrong at Stanford University Special Collections, Patricia Keats of the California Pioneer Society, and volunteer Peggy Zeigler of the California History Society. James F. Varley's well-researched book *The Legend of Joaquín Murrieta* proved a useful reference source. Luis Leal, William Secrest, and John Boessenecker responded to letters. Thanks to my family, too, for being patient with me while I researched and wrote this book.

> History
> is memory refracted,
> retold,
> a beam of light
> the scattered dust
> makes bold.

1. The Legend and History

The Life and Adventures of Joaquin Murieta, the Celebrated California Bandit, by Yellow Bird (Tsis-qua-da-loni in Cherokee, phonetically rendered "Chees-quat-a-lawny"), better known as John Rollin Ridge, was published in San Francisco in July 1854, one year after the California State Rangers brought in a head identified as that of Joaquín Murrieta. Ridge's book was a slender little volume with a soft cover of heavy yellow paper, signifying to book buyers in those days that here was a "blood and thunder" adventure full of violent action sequences interspersed with scenes of illicit love. (In all Spanish-language sources, the name "Murrieta" is consistently spelled with two r's. English-language newspapers often misspelled the name with only one r. John Rollin Ridge relied on these newspapers for source material.)

Nineteenth-century authors of yellow-covered books generally wrote hastily and usually published their work under pen names as did Ridge. Publishers printed them hurriedly (printing errors were common) and on cheap paper; buyers paid little for them and did not treasure them but passed them on to friends or traded them in toward other purchases. Very popular and often advertised in gold rush California newspapers, yellow-covered books were sold by booksellers in San Francisco as well as at trading posts near river crossings and at mining and lumbering camps.[1]

Joaquín Murrieta was a natural subject for the genre because his name had recently been in the news a lot. Heroes in such books were generally based on such persons, be they pirates, highwaymen, Indian killers, fugitives, mercenaries, buccaneers, or duelists. Though popular and profitable, yellow-covered literature was often denounced as worthless, immoral, sensationalistic, and a bad influence on young, impressionable minds. Among those who read them was John Rollin Ridge.[2]

John Rollin was born at New Echota, Cherokee Territory, in 1827 to Chief John Ridge and Sarah Bird Northrup, the daughter of New England–based missionaries whose school Chief John Ridge had attended. The Cherokee had been striving for two decades to observe the terms of a treaty signed by George Washington that promised them they could keep their land and live independently of the U.S. government as peaceful neighbors, if they became "civilized." The Cherokee women learned to spin and weave wool, and the men learned to farm. Hundreds of Cherokee farmers used African slave labor, as did their white neighbors in Georgia and Tennessee. Missionaries came and opened schools. Sequoya, a Cherokee warrior who observed an American soldier reading what looked like symbols on a letter from home, created a Cherokee syllabary and taught it to his people so that they could read and write. By 1827 the Cherokees dressed like whites, but they added their own splashes of native decorum. They owned horses and cattle, ran farms and orchards, and lived in log cabins or clapboard houses. So John Rollin Ridge grew up in a house and went to a school that had a missionary teacher, a school that his brothers, sisters, cousins, and neighbors attended, a school that the Georgia state government threatened to close because a few of the pupils were black. In Georgia it was against the law to educate blacks.[3]

Had the treaty with George Washington been kept, Ridge may never have gone to California or written about Joaquín Murrieta. But like so many other treaties, this one, too, was broken, though not until after George Washington had died. It was broken because a company of Georgians, including corrupt politicians, took part in what became known as the Yazoo Land Fraud. They claimed all the land belonging to the Cherokees, Choctaws, Chickasaws, and Creeks (or what is today northwest Georgia and all of Alabama and Mississippi) with the goal of selling it for profit. The government broke up the company but in doing so ended up paying the state of Georgia for the land and promising to remove all the Indians. Removal efforts began in 1803, with a few thousand Cherokees volunteering to relocate west of the Mississippi River. Those who stayed behind agreed to fight for the U.S. government against the Creeks when they rebelled. The government promised the Cherokees that in return for their allegiance, they could stay in their homeland. But Georgian settlers kept encroaching on Cherokee land, and the Georgia government would not allow Indians to testify in its courts against settlers who harassed Cherokee residents. When gold was discovered on Cherokee land, matters got worse.

Young Ridge and his siblings saw their home become crowded with displaced Cherokees. As chief of a clan, his father was obliged to open his property and home to those of his people whose homes had been confiscated, or looted and burned. Among them were widows and orphans, because men who resisted were flogged and hanged. On occasion women were also abused. The horror stories they told provoked Chief John Ridge to work hard, via diplomatic channels, to get U.S. military protection for his people. He and his cousin, Buck Watie (also known as Elias Boudinot), pleaded with President Andrew Jackson, but Jackson knew he presided over a young and shaky democracy that might break if it presumed to take military action against the Georgians on behalf of Indians. Jackson told them that, even though Supreme Court Chief Justice John Marshall had ruled in their favor, he would never enforce the ruling. The Cherokee had a choice: they could stay in New Echota and lose everything to the Georgians, or they could sign a treaty whereby they would be compensated for their losses and remove west, as had thousands of their countrymen, including Sequoya. That was when Chief John Ridge and his cousin gave up hope of saving their homeland.[4]

They shared what they had learned with Chief John Ross and others at a tribal meeting. Ross swore he would fight for their homeland to the bitter end. That was a popular stand, and he soon became Principal Chief. His first act as such was to censor the Ridge party to keep them from winning converts to the view that signing a treaty was best for the people. About 350 Cherokee families followed the Ridge party lead anyway and traveled to Indian Territory in what is now Oklahoma in 1837. John Rollin Ridge was ten years old at the time. Chief John Ross and thousands of his followers were forcibly marched west the following year on what became known, because so many died en route, as the Trail of Tears.[5]

Once settled out West, Principal Chief Ross made a grab for power over the whole Cherokee Nation. The western Cherokees, who had been living there for decades and had their own chief, and the Ridge party, which had willingly submitted to the western Cherokee governance, resisted. Ross's party responded by condemning the Ridge party for having signed the treaty, insisting that if they had not done so, the Cherokee would still have their homeland. Their leaders were slated by the Ross faction for execution.

On the night of June 22, 1839, twenty-five men burst into Chief John Ridge's home, dragged him outside and knifed him to death in front of his protesting mother, wife, and children. His father, Chief Major Ridge, was shot in the back and killed, and Buck Watie was axed to death. (Buck's brother Stand Watie escaped.) Twelve-year-old John Rollin Ridge never forgot that bloody night. He held John Ross responsible for the murders and wanted to kill him in revenge. He never got near Ross, who always traveled with about forty bodyguards. But as a young man of twenty-two, after he had married and settled on a ranch he had inherited, he shot and killed David Kell, one of Ross's men. Kell had stolen John Rollin's breeding stud and gelded it, and then he threatened young Ridge with a bowie knife.

After killing Kell, Ridge fled to Missouri where he tried to round up a party of white men to go with him to kill Chief Ross. The plot failed because the men wanted compensation, and Ridge had very little money. He went to his mother's house in Arkansas, where she had moved after her husband had been murdered. While he was there, his cousin Stand Watie urged him to stand trial, saying he was sure he could get him acquitted. Ridge was amenable to that idea until he learned how much it would cost him in legal fees. That was when he decided, in the spring of 1850, to join a party of Cherokees heading for California, leaving his wife and child with his in-laws.[6]

Like hundreds of others, Ridge hoped to solve his financial problems by panning for gold in California, but after mining for a year with poor results, he decided he would have to strike it rich by some other path. He went job-hunting in Sacramento and was hired as a correspondent for the *New Orleans True Delta*, which had an office there. That job gave him access to other newspaper offices in town where he read about Joaquín and his fellow outlaws. Two years later the California Rangers arrived in town with a head in a jar, identified as that of Joaquín Murrieta. Ridge

1. John Rollin Ridge, c. 1850. Courtesy of the California History Room, California State Library, Sacramento, California.

was not well at the time and probably did not see the head. He was burning with fever and suffering from an ulcer, it seems. But his young wife, on hearing that he was ill, traveled out to California and nursed him back to health. He then began to work with zeal on his book about Joaquín.[7]

The Life and Adventures of Joaquin Murieta was reviewed by a columnist for the *San Francisco Chronicle*. He said John Rollin Ridge's writing style was respectable—for an Indian, that is. The jab was aimed at Ridge's open pride in his Cherokee heritage, as demonstrated in his choice of pen name and as discussed in the publisher's preface. The publisher pointed out that Ridge knew what it was like to be born and raised on land that white people coveted because of the presence of gold. He also knew how it felt to kill a man who insulted him and threatened his life, and he knew what it felt like to desire bloody revenge against those who murdered a family member. It was these experiences that gave the author insight into his subject.

In an interesting twist that only history could produce, twentieth-century scholars list Ridge's book as the first American Indian novel ever published. American pride in American Indian accomplishments has at long last replaced contempt, but that laudable move also turned the legendary Murrieta into a fictional character, a myth. Lydia D. Hazera, Peter S. Christensen, Joseph Henry Jackson, María Mondragón, Alberto Huerta, and Luis Leal have all examined the literary merit and cultural significance of Ridge's depiction of Joaquín Murrieta. The author, they all say, identified strongly with his subject. He was a mestizo who witnessed the effects of persecution inflicted by whites, even as Ridge's own publisher had asserted.[8] His biographer, James Parins, interpreted Ridge's depiction of the avenging Joaquín Murrieta as a kind of dream fulfillment. His Joaquín died knowing that his enemies were dead. (As it turned out, so did John Rollin Ridge, John Ross having giving up the ghost fourteen months before Ridge died in October 1867.)

The Original Story Line

John Rollin Ridge knew that the California state legislature had hired rangers to hunt down no less than *five* bandits named Joaquín and their banded associates, so before telling Murrieta's story he wrote, "There were two Joaquíns, bearing the various surnames of Murieta, O'Comorenia, Valenzuela, Botellier, and Carillo." Murrieta was the famous brigand chief, he explained, and Valenzuela was "a distinguished subordinate" of his.[9] Both came from Mexico and looked enough alike to be mistaken one for the other, he wrote.

Ridge went on to describe Murrieta as a young Sonoran with large black eyes "kindled with the enthusiasm of his earnest nature," glossy black hair that hung to his shoulders, a well-shaped head, silvery voice, and cordial bearing, his features reflecting his combined Castilian and "Mexiques" (or Aztec) Indian heritage.[10] Ridge's own features likewise reflected his combined New England white and New Echota Cherokee heritage, but it was probably an illustration he saw in an April 1853 *Steamer Edition* of the *Sacramento Daily Union* that influenced his description of Murrieta.

Ridge wrote that Murrieta had first met North Americans in his homeland and that he had been favorably impressed. The young Mexican was "tired of the uncertain state of affairs in his own country, the usurpations and revolutions which were of such common occurrence," and so departed for Alta California in 1849 with the intention of making a new home among the North Americans there.[11] In the spring of 1850 he built a little home for his "heart's treasure—a beautiful Sonorian girl" whom Ridge belatedly identified as Rosita. The young couple prospered until "lawless and desperate men, who bore the name Americans but failed to support the honor and dignity of that title," ordered Joaquín to leave.

When he refused, they struck him a blow to the face, then they bound him and "ravished" Rosita.[12]

The distraught couple moved northwest, where they farmed in a little valley near the Calaveras River until again forced out by rude Anglo-Americans. They moved to Murphy's Camp where Joaquín dealt monte (a card game popular among Hispanic gamblers). He fared well until seen riding a stolen horse he had borrowed from his half-brother. He was arrested and flogged under the same tree from which his half-brother was hanged for horse-stealing.[13] All of this was influenced by an April 1853 correspondence published in the *San Francisco Herald* which referred to an "interview" or conversation with Joaquín Murrieta.

"It was then that the character of Joaquín changed," wrote Ridge. "Wanton cruelty and the tyranny of prejudice" had destroyed Murrieta's faith in Americans. Even though an American friend doctored his wounds and tried to calm his angry soul, it was of no avail. He disappeared, and soon afterward corpses turned up along side roads and in gullies. Joaquín had started a campaign of bloody revenge and ruthless murder, his first victims being the vigilantes who hanged his half-brother and flogged him. His violent reprisals soon attracted followers of like mind.[14]

Murrieta won the loyalty of a California war veteran named Manuel "Three-Fingered Jack" García, whom Ridge described as "blood-thirsty" and violent. Then there was the resourceful Joaquín Valenzuela who had served under "the famous guerilla chief, Padre Jurata" (Fr. Celedonio Dómeco de Jarauta) in Mexico during the war, as had Valenzuela's comrade in arms, Luis Vulvia (probably based on the outlaw, Luis Burgos).[15] Sixteen-year-old Reyes Féliz was a member of the band, too. Ridge identified him as the brother of Joaquín's mistress. There was one Claudio, whom Ridge described as being thirty-five, vigorous, dark-complexioned, sly, quick, and savage. There were also Pedro Gonzalez and Juan. Reyes Féliz had a sweetheart named Carmelita, and a woman whose name was never given seems to have been Juan's lover. Ridge mentioned an Anglo-Saxon bandit called "Mountain Jim" and a messenger and spy named Reis.[16] Several hundred other band members, matching descriptions given by Harry Love in newspaper interviews printed in August 1853, remained nameless foot soldiers and cavalry in Murrieta's legendary guerrilla band.

2. Joaquín Murrieta and Three-Fingered Jack in the style of Charles Nahl. Author's collection.

Ridge's Joaquín Murrieta is the guerrilla chief Harry Love spoke of, a Mexican whose scheme was to have his various banded associates loot California and cart all the gold and horses they stole to their headquarters at Arroyo Cantua, from where they would depart for Sonora, Mexico. This was the same plot that William Walker (popularly known in the 1850s as a freebooter or filibuster leader) and his supporters in the press assigned to Joaquín and his band in 1853. Walker was going south of the border, pretending he was going to liberate the people of Sonora when really he intended to subdue them and profit from the conquest. (After Walker and his filibusters failed, Henry Crabb led a filibuster campaign into Sonora in 1857.)

While the legendary plot was ostensibly underway, Ridge filled his book with numerous side adventures. For example, in the spring of 1851 he wrote that Joaquín was arrested at Santa Clara by the county sheriff—a man Ridge named Clark. This sheriff brought Murrieta before the magistrate, who fined him twelve dollars for his part in a row at a fandango house (a Mexican saloon where there was music and dancing, as well as gambling and drinking). While being escorted to his dwelling, where, Murrieta said, he had the money to pay the fine, he suddenly drew a knife, stabbed the sheriff in the heart, and escaped into the night.[17] A little later, near Marysville Sheriff Robert Buchanan attempted to arrest him but was shot and severely wounded. Murrieta and those with him then rode north into Butte County where, wrote Ridge, they stirred up the local Indians. The Indians rebelled against encroaching white settlers, but the American response was swift and brutal. All of this was based on newspaper accounts.

Murrieta and band then turned south, wrote Ridge. They rode along trails connecting mining towns in the Sierra foothills and by early spring of 1852 were camped near Mokelumne Hill. Joaquín went to a saloon in town to gamble. While there he overheard an American boast that if ever he came across Joaquín, he'd shoot him "quick as a snake." Young Murrieta jumped up on the monte table where he had been gambling and, revolvers in hand, shouted, "I am Joaquín!" He then dared the braggart to live up to his boast and, after firing a couple of shots, bolted out the door, leapt on his horse, and rode away under fire. He escaped without a mark, rejoined his band, and they continued southwest.[18]

On the road to Stockton he met Allen Ruddle, who, Ridge said, recognized Murrieta and threatened to turn him in. Murrieta shot him dead and continued on. He was with Reyes, Pedro, and Juan when they reached Rancho "Oris Timbers" (Orestimba), from which they stole horses and saddles, then rode south toward Arroyo "Cantoova" (Cantua). En route they were joined by Rosita, Carmelita, and another woman, and the bandits enjoyed an amorous moment amid wildflowers at Tejon, about a hundred miles northeast of the pueblo of Los Angeles.[19] That night the band was encircled and arrested by Chief "Sapatarra" (Zapatero) and his warriors, whom Ridge described as being armed with bows and arrows. The Indians confiscated the robbers' horses, garments, and gold. The chief then sentenced them to a light flogging and sent them on their way naked—except the women, who for modesty's sake, wrote Ridge, were allowed to keep their slips.

John Rollin Ridge described Murrieta as making light of this adventure—laughing heartily at his ludicrous ill luck—until they encountered a grizzly bear. Reyes Féliz was mauled. Joaquín left him in the care of Carmelita while he and the others went for help. They found it at Mountain Jim's ranch.[20]

Not long after leaving Jim's cabin with some provisions and borrowed clothes, the band split up. Reyes and Carmelita sought shelter at the home of a local ranchero. Juan and Pedro headed toward Los Angeles, but they were captured by Harry Love. Juan escaped and Pedro was shot and killed while attempting to do the same. Joaquín, meanwhile, went to Los Angeles alone and there shot and killed Deputy Sheriff Wilson, of Santa Barbara, who was asking too many questions about the band, Ridge explained.[21] He then wrote that Murrieta went to San Gabriel, where he killed General Bean, because he was seen as a threat to the band's horse-stealing operations. After that, Ridge has Murrieta and Claudio return north with about forty others. Reyes, Carmelita, and Rosita stayed in Los Angeles.

Ridge has Joaquín and band head for Calaveras County next, arriving in the winter of 1852–53, where Joaquín encountered and killed Joe Lake, who, like Ruddle, had recognized him and threatened to turn him in. (In both cases Ridge inserted a conversation in which Murrieta appealed to them, tearfully insisting he had no choice but to turn outlaw, as making an honest living had proved impossible, but neither of them was moved by this appeal, and both called on him to lay down his arms.)

After killing Lake, Ridge has Murrieta and band travel several hundred miles southwest again, where they stopped to rest at a mission in San Luis Obispo County. While they were there a sentinel came and informed them that Reyes Féliz had been hanged by Los Angeles vigilantes and that Carmelita had gone mad with grief, wandered into the woods, and died of hunger. While they were still mourning these losses, a vaquero rode up and warned Murrieta of the approach of an armed party of North Americans. The brigand chief immediately led his men to a ravine and prepared to ambush them. But the American party guessed the plot and approached from every side, putting up a mean fight. During the battle, Mountain Jim and twenty others were killed.

Ridge then sends Joaquín and band back across the San Joaquin Valley to Calaveras County. They murdered and robbed one German, three French, and numerous Chinese miners there. Once they had accumulated enough wealth, they headed to Stockton to celebrate their success. There Joaquín saw a poster offering five thousand dollars for his capture. He wrote on it in pencil, "I will give $10,000. JOAQUIN."[22] Even this act of bravado had its newsprint source.

Ridge next depicts Murrieta in true Robin Hood form as taking pity on a poor Greek ferryman and rescuing a damsel in distress whom Reis kidnapped while on a horse-stealing mission with Joaquín Valenzuela. Ridge also describes how Murrieta rescued Luis from the noose by impersonating a respectable American and offering a convincing alibi. All three of these events were undoubtedly influenced by fictional works Ridge had read, but he attempted to make them sound authentic by interweaving them with descriptions of events he had heard from one Jim Boyce.

Boyce recalled how Joaquín, in the spring of 1853, stopped to chat with some twenty American miners in Tuolumne County. To them he was just a friendly Mexican who could converse rather well in English. They invited him to join them for breakfast, but he declined, preferring to stay mounted, though he had casually hooked one leg around the saddle horn and was allowing his horse to graze. Boyce himself wasn't present, having gone down to the creek to fetch water for coffee. On returning, he recognized the Mexican and shouted, "That is Joaquín!" Everyone scrabbled

3. The legendary Joaquín in an engraving by Charles Nahl from *The Life of Joaquín Murieta, the Brigand Chief of California* (Police Gazette 1859).

for a gun while Murrieta threw his leg back over the saddle horn and spurred his horse down the ravine, across the creek and up the other side, riding precariously along a narrow ledge that cut across the face of a steep and jagged rock and put him within pistol range for several yards. Ridge depicts him as drawing his knife and defiantly shouting, "I am Joaquín!" as if daring the miners to shoot.[23] They did, but without effect. The dramatic scene warranted an illustration, one that Charles Nahl would render again in oil on canvas.

Near the end of his book, Ridge recounts in some detail what the *Calaveras Chronicle* and other papers reported concerning "Capt. Charles H. Ellas" (Ellis) and Justice Thomas Beatty's and Willis Prescott's pursuits of Joaquín and band during the spring of 1853. Ridge's retelling of Ellis's description of events is probably the most historically accurate section in the book. Joaquín escaped all three posses, but in the end the California State Rangers, led by Harry Love, caught up with him. Murrieta and Three-Fingered Jack were among those killed in a gun fight at Arroyo Cantua in July 1853, but Ridge credits Captain Harry Love with killing Joaquín, an assertion Love never made. Ridge also wrote that Captain Love ordered the head of Joaquín cut off and preserved because it was "important to prove, to the satisfaction of the public, that the famous and bloody bandit was actually killed, else the fact would be eternally doubted."[24]

On the last page of his book Ridge points out that the life of the young Mexican, Joaquín Murrieta, "leaves behind him the important lesson that there is nothing so dangerous in its consequences as injustice to individuals—whether it arise from prejudice of color or from any other source; that a wrong done to one man is a wrong to society and to the world."[25] This truth is why the legend has not only influenced a number of literary works but has entered various histories of California.

The Legend and Early Historians

Two more editions of Ridge's book came out after the author died, one in 1871, another in 1874, his widow having released them in order to supplement her meager income. In 1859 a plagiarized version was anonymously published by the *Police Gazette*. Titled *Joaquin Murieta, the Brigand Chief of California; A complete history of his life from the age of sixteen to the time of his* capture and death in 1853, the Gazette version added a couple of new adventures, changed a few names (Rosita became Carmela), and used more fluid prose that focused on telling a story. It left out Ridge's high moral talk about "prejudice of color" and "injustice to individuals" and made the white men in the story less onerous. Well-written and beautifully illustrated by Charles Nahl, the Gazette version was more widely circulated and was often reprinted. A modified version came out in French that depicted Joaquín as a Chilean instead of a Mexican. Spanish and Mexican renditions also surfaced. In spite of this, or perhaps because of it, the Gazette version was ignored by historians. It was Ridge's book that Bancroft and Hittell cited in their histories of California.

Hubert Howe Bancroft published California Pastoral in 1888. (California's colonial and Mexican history was rural and so came to be called the Pastoral Era, a name that evoked peaceful and picturesque mental images, which was how many Hispanic Californians remembered it.) He had an enormous library at his disposal, having collected thousands of sources from private California libraries, including religious, military, and governmental documents. He also collected narrative recollections or testimonios from California pioneers, Hispanic and otherwise. They dictated their recollections to Bancroft employees Thomas Savage and Henry Cerruti.[26]

In California Pastoral, Bancroft focused on California's Spanish colonial and Mexican eras, but in the last chapter he wrote about highwaymen who were active after 1850. Prominent among them were Joaquín Murrieta and Tiburcio Vásquez, both mentioned in the testimonios Bancroft used as sources. Murrieta and his fellow highwaymen, Bancroft argued, were not common criminals. Common criminals had been the focus of an earlier chapter titled "Crimes and Courts." For that chapter Bancroft had relied on court documents and military records provided by former Governor Juan Baptiste Alvarado. Alvarado judged numerous criminal cases in Mexican California from 1836 to 1842. Mexico's policy of using California as a penal colony had caused a sharp increase in crime in the 1830s. Among those Mexico sent were political prisoners and former guerrilla band leaders, but the vast majority were men that Californians referred to as cholos, meaning penal colonists who were generally darker-skinned than the average Spaniard.[27]

Although Bancroft mentions cholos again in his chapter about high-waymen, he primarily focused on those who became folk heroes. They became folk heroes to the common man and woman because, he argued, they were from among them, and in a way they were more honest than robber barons. "There seems to be a prejudice in some quarters against the profession of highwayman," he began sarcastically. "It has become the custom of our refined and discriminating civilization, when such a person is caught to kill him; for which reason many good men . . . have in consequence fallen into . . . meaner kinds of thievery." Ambitious businessmen, for example, who wanted to make a fortune learned to cheat and "to adulterate food, drink, and medicines; to filch a neighbor's good name; to blackmail . . . ; to accept a bribe . . . ; to make the poor pay an exorbitant price for bread . . . ; to build a railroad with the people's money and then . . . extract money from people's pockets through false representations and chicanery." Then there were the lawyers who "sell their services to defeat the ends of justice," Bancroft complained. America was full of men who "go unhanged" for such crimes. Worse, if one such fellow succeeded in "making sufficient money or fame" he was lauded as "a good and great man" even though he behaved like a rogue.[28]

This cruel reality motivated a popular affection for the highwayman, Bancroft argued. Robbers and highwaymen made no pretense about their intentions and, much to the delight of the common man, highwaymen often robbed the robber barons. True, Bancroft admitted, "neither Joaquin Murieta nor Tiburcio Vásquez were Robin Hoods," and true, "robbery is bad, but men will steal . . . and women, too, and children. At least there is something courageous in stopping a stage, . . . but in legalized stealing there is . . . nothing but cowardice and meanness." That was why, as he saw it, "our most famous gentlemen of the road . . . are as much entitled to a place on the pages of history, as those who become famous robbing within the bounds of conventionality."[29] Founders of railroads and banks were indeed crowned with laurels by early American historians whereas the men that built their railroads and banks were barely mentioned, if at all.

In sketching Joaquín Murrieta's life, Bancroft cited John Rollin Ridge's 1874 edition, but he also cited the testimonials of General Mariano Guadalupe Vallejo and Don Antonio F. Coronel. General Vallejo told Bancroft's employee, Henry Cerruti, that he missed the "Pastoral Era," or California as it was before the United States took over, even while admitting that the Americans had brought many good changes to Alta California. He had built an American-style house for his family, employed American winery methods, and, because the Americans brought many new imports to California, he was able to provide his daughters with a piano and other luxuries. But sometimes he retreated on horseback to the old adobe homestead and smoked a hand-rolled cigarette while watching the sun set. Sometimes he was lonely for the simple tastes of old Mexico.

Vallejo had been a rebel as a young man. He had called for independence from Mexico and rallied neighbors in northern California behind his cause, only to be taken prisoner by those he had thought were his allies: the American Bear Flag filibuster band led by John Frémont. The Bear Flag band robbed Mariano Vallejo and his brother of their jewelry and money, then locked them in jail. They also plundered Mariano's ranch and intimidated his wife and sisters. Vallejo's nephew, Ramón Carrillo, was incensed. A tall, uncommonly handsome, well-read, and articulate young man in his early twenties, Ramón was often described as an excellent horseman and gutsy bear hunter, skilled with revolver, sword, and lasso. Determined to relieve the fears of his aunt and cousins, in the spring of 1846 Ramón recruited a few followers, went scouting, and took four Americans prisoner. Two of Frémont's men, Thomas Cowie and George Fowler, were among them.

While on his way to Fort Sutter, where he intended to offer his prisoners in exchange for his uncles, Carillo crossed paths with Juan Padilla and his vaqueros. Padilla had been robbed of cattle and horses and was looking for two horse thieves. His vaqueros recognized Cowie and Fowler as the thieves. Because Padilla was older, he had seniority and demanded the prisoners be handed over. Carrillo begged Padilla to permit him to use them to get his uncles released, but to no effect. The prisoners were bound to a tree and left under guard while Carrillo and Padilla went into Padilla's ranch house for supper. Cowie and Fowler apparently attempted to escape. Bernardino García and his men recaptured them and, being incensed, tortured them to death. (The other two prisoners were shot dead.) Mariano Vallejo remembered that this García, called Three-Fingered Jack by the Americans, was reportedly killed with Joaquín

Murrieta at Arroyo Cantua.[30] (Bernardino Garcia was later identified as Emmanuel Garcia, the man who inspired the legendary Manuel Three-Fingered-Jack Garcia.) Unhappy about the fate of his prisoners, Ramón Carrillo went to Baja California and reported the incident to a Mexican general, saying it was at Padilla's prompting that they were executed. Meanwhile, war broke out between Mexico and the United States. When it was over, Ramón's uncles were released.

Ramón Carrillo was among the first to profit from gold diggings in 1848. Like other Californians, he hired local Indians and Sonoran immigrants to work claims while he rounded up and herded beef cattle to large mining camps, where the animals were sold and butchered on the spot. After losing his land in northern California to unscrupulous American land grabbers, Ramón Carrillo went south and settled on a ranch in Los Angeles County in 1859. He prospered, but in 1864 he was murdered. Northern California newspapers reported that he had been lynched, but Los Angeles papers said he was shot through the heart by a secluded assassin who used a rifle and aimed from behind.[31] The American press hinted that Ramón had been assassinated in retaliation for the deaths of Cowie and Fowler and that he had links to the Joaquín band, a claim Mariano Vallejo and his Carrillo in-laws vociferously denied in 1864. However in 1878, when interviewed by Cerruti, Mariano Vallejo said, "The majority of the young men that had so unjustly been dispossessed, thirsty for vengeance, took off to join the band of Joaquín Murieta and under the command of this fearsome bandit they were able to avenge some of the wrongs inflicted upon them by the North American race." He did not implicate family, but the remark suggests he would not have blamed his nephew if he was for a time associated with outlaws like Joaquín Murrieta.[32]

In addition to Vallejo, Bancroft cited Don Antonio Franco Coronel, who told him in a letter that his imperfect memory undoubtedly confused the order of events. He asked pardon for any errors and thanked Bancroft for taking an enthusiastic interest in California's Hispanic history. Bancroft, for his part, noted that of all the *testimonios* collected, he found Coronel's *Cosas de California* "full of valuable matter related in a clear and pleasant style, free from exaggeration or bias."[33]

4. Antonio F. Coronel. Seaver Center for Western History Research, Los Angeles County Museum of Natural History.

Coronel had mined for gold alongside Americans in 1848 and 1849. Like Ramón Carrillo, he employed a retinue of Indian and Sonoran laborers. Unlike Carrillo, he marked his camp with red piñons. One day a band of armed American miners came, tore down his piñons, swore at him, threatened him, and said the only banner allowed to fly in California was the United States stars and stripes. He broke camp and retreated to San Jose for the winter. While there, Coronel was enjoying a repast at a saloon when suddenly the lights were extinguished and Juan Padilla, who was also there, was set upon by a group of Americans who sought to avenge the deaths of Fowler and Cowie. Padilla survived the beating and Coronel nursed him back to health. He told Padilla he should do as Ramón Carrillo did and avoid saloons popular with the Americans.

Back at the mines in the spring of 1849, Coronel shared a claim on the Stanislaus River with Ramón Carrillo and Carrillo's Irish brother-in-law, Jacob Leese. It was a rich claim, and they prospered until a band of heavily armed Americans came. Their leader told Coronel, in broken Spanish mixed with English, that the claim was theirs—they had staked it first. Coronel recalled, "I was very excited and answered him harshly. Fortunately he didn't understand me, and with a moment to reflect, I realized the gold wasn't worth risking my life."[34] He broke camp and returned to Los Angeles, never to visit the mother lode again.

In spite of these experiences and their similarity to those suffered by the legendary Murrieta, Coronel did not see Joaquín Murrieta as an avenger or folk hero. He knew too much about the young thief to reach the kind of conclusion Vallejo had reached. As a resident of Los Angeles, Coronel was present when, in November 1852, American vigilantes investigated the shooting death of General Joshua Bean. He had served as an interrogator. "I didn't want to serve," Coronel told Thomas Savage in 1878. "I have always been against any measures that depart from legal precedent, but I was given to understand the committee was purely one of inquiry. Testimony would be taken and made public, so as to avoid any imputation of partiality on one side or the other." It was during the investigation, he recalled, that "the pursuit of Murrieta and his band had . . . begun." That thought led him to recall the Indian women whose testimony he heard. One of them was a young woman known as Antonia "La Molinera." (La Molinera means *miller's wife* and is the name of a flamenco dance and song inspired by the tale of the magistrate and the miller's wife in Gilgamesh.) "Antonia," recalled Coronel, was "a woman Murrieta was reputed to take with him dressed as a man." She said that the prisoner Cipriano Sandoval told her "San Cayetano is a good saint." Coronel's wife then explained to Thomas Savage that "Cayetano" is a word play on *callete*, Spanish for "shut up" or "say nothing." Sandoval was hanged with two others, though he was innocent, Coronel recalled.[35]

Coronel then confused the vigilante response to the Juan Flores and Pancho Daniel band in 1857 with that of the Joaquín Murrieta band in 1852, but then, they were the same band, according to Antonia. That which Coronel confused, chronologically, Bancroft decided not to incorporate and incorporated it into his history of Joaquín Murrieta and band. La Molinera, Coronel recalled, was in San Gabriel with Pancho Daniel either the night General Bean was killed (in 1852) or the evening Sherriff Barton and his posse were ambushed (in 1857). He also said that "the identities of Murrieta's band were learned" from La Molinera. "One of them was Flores. The first of the band to fall victim to popular justice, he was executed in Los Angeles even before the above mentioned" execution of Sandoval. But here Coronel was confusing Reyes Féliz with Juan Flores. Féliz was hanged a week before Sandoval, whereas the bandit Juan Flores was hanged in 1857. La Molinera was undoubtedly interrogated in 1857, as well as in 1852. The female informant, Coronel recalled, "was not a prisoner, but was kept in a house under guard in case one of the band might kill her."[36]

After mentioning Juan Flores, Coronel remembered how, sometime after that, "Pancho Daniel was caught, the second of Murrieta's men," and he was lynched [in 1858]. La Molinera said that by 1877 the whole gang was dead: "Some had been executed by popular justice, some by Murrieta . . . except for one who emigrated to Sonora." She also said that after Pancho Daniel "had seduced her away from Murrieta and left the band with her . . . Murrieta swore vengeance. . . . She turned him in, in self-defense," claiming it was she who told Harry Love's rangers where to look for Murrieta. She did it because she was angry that "her former lover had once sent a man named Vergara to kill her." Vergara deserted instead, so Joaquín "sent another man . . . but this one turned up murdered." Pancho Daniel killed him, she claimed.[37]

Coronel then remembered that Vergara had met with a violent death, too. As he saw it, men like Vergara, Daniel, Flores, and Murrieta deserved their fates. Those who escaped, he said, would face a divine judgment that was inescapable; for example, Dr. William Osburn, who had argued in favor of hanging Sandoval, though the evidence was flimsy. Osburn, Coronel recalled, had also been active during the hunt for Pancho Daniel [in 1857], and his actions at that time were despicable. "One or two of the Murrieta band," Coronel recalled, "were caught in San Gabriel by a civilian posse headed by Captain [Hilliard] Dorsey and Doctor Osburn. It was said these two cut off the head of one outlaw and displayed it as an object of scorn." Providence judged these men, as Coronel saw it, for Hilliard Dorsey was shot dead by his own father-in-law and Osburn suffered a stroke and became paralyzed from the neck down.[38]

Hubert Howe Bancroft left out Coronel's allusions to divine judgment, focusing instead on the perspective Vallejo had shared. The Californios, Bancroft insisted, saw Murrieta and other members of the band as having taken up brigandage "against the encroaching and heretical neighbor, the insolent gringo," and as having engaged in his own brand of "political privateering, religious crusading, and race revenge."[39] This was why outlaws like Joaquín Murrieta and Tiburcio Vásquez had become folk heroes and why they deserved mention in the pages of history, Bancroft argued. In effect he was validating the claim John Rollin Ridge had made in the opening paragraph of his book about Joaquín: "The character of this . . . man is nothing more than the natural production of the social and moral condition of the country in which he lived, . . . and consequently, his individual history is a part of the . . . history of the state."[40]

A decade later Theodore H. Hittell published a three-volume history of California in which he cited John Rollin Ridge's 1871 edition, but not because he saw highwaymen as robbers of robber barons or heroes of the common man, as had Bancroft. Instead, Hittell saw Joaquín Murrieta's story as a useful illustration of the social climate at the mines in the 1850s. It was, he argued, the Foreign Miners Tax of 1850 and frequent anti-foreigner mob violence that gave rise to outlaw bands like the one led by Joaquín Murrieta. Foreigners (immigrants to California from parts outside the United States), wrote Hittell, the majority of whom came from Mexico, were "thus rendered destitute of the means of purchasing food and clothing, they became desperate and were driven to theft, robbery and sometimes murder."[41] Provisions were expensive at the mines.

Some thieves banded together and rendezvoused in "the upper San Joaquin Valley, and particularly that portion of it west of Tulare Lake," wrote Hittell. Arroyo Cantua winds its way down from the San Benito coast range and empties into the San Joaquin River tules, or wetlands, around Tulare Lake (which, sadly, no longer exists). It was there, wrote

Hittell, that "Spanish-speaking vagabonds, whose ostensible occupation was running mustangs but whose real business was believed to be robbery and the protection of robbers," continued to be troublesome for decades. Vigilantes, rancheros, and lawmen led expeditions against them until, around 1885, "the country was cleared of the bandits and it became safe to travel through it."[42]

Though some of these outlaws had started robbing travelers before the discovery of gold, "the famous brigand chief, Joaquin Murieta," wrote Hittell, "and many of his bandit companions . . . were said to have been driven into their career of crime and blood by anti-foreigner persecution."[43] Hittell had read numerous sources indicating this was true, but he turned to Ridge's book to recount the life of Joaquín Murrieta because the legend was easier to live with than the truth. In fact there had been too many completely innocent victims of anti-foreigner abuse, but Murrieta and his band were not innocent. Hittell insisted, "It is not at all probable, judging from Joaquin's subsequent career, that he was ever anything but a vicious and abandoned character, low, brutal and cruel, intrinsically and at heart a thief and cut-throat." Even if he suffered at the hands of American persecutors, all that did was make him "worse than he would otherwise have been," and so his persecutors were not to blame.[44]

Hittell followed a synopsis of Ridge's account of the crimes and death of Murrieta with evidence supporting its accuracy. Caleb Dorsey's recollections as recorded in Herbert Lang's History of Tuolumne County, which was published in 1882, were cited. Lang said the bandit chief had been so romanticized that "almost no dependence can be placed upon the multitude of stories . . . which have gone the rounds of the press." For example Joaquin's "oath of undying hatred" for North Americans, or "Yankees," was without foundation. The Hon. Caleb Dorsey, Esq., a lawyer and sawmill proprietor at Sawmill Flats, "was, through a remarkable chain of events, brought into close relations with the noted robber and his band," even though he was an American. According to Dorsey, while it was true Joaquín "did evince on one or more occasions a decent respect for the laws of humanity and a regard for truth," the famous outlaw should not be remembered as an innocent victim of injustice who took revenge. Joaquín Murrieta robbed and murdered people "because his own bad passions impelled him," Dorsey insisted.[45]

Caleb Dorsey recalled first meeting members of the outlaw band in 1851. Alone and lost in the hills east of Columbia, in Tuolumne County, he decided to camp for the night. Worried about bears, when a party of Mexicans set up camp nearby and invited him to share their repast he gladly joined them. After eating they made music, a one-eyed man singing quite well, Dorsey recalled. Some time later that singer was arrested in Sonora Camp for horse stealing, and Dorsey was summoned to serve as defense attorney. His client told him that he and his party could have killed him and would have if they'd known who he was, but as they spared him, he should in return secure an acquittal or governor's pardon. If he did so, they would protect him from bandits. Dorsey got his defendant acquitted.

Of Joaquín Murrieta, Dorsey recalled he had been a monte dealer at Martinez, near Saw Mill Flat, in the early days. In the spring of 1852, when some crime Dorsey couldn't remember was committed and a Mexican named Joaquín was blamed, he and some friends went to a fandango house in Martinez to question people. At that time, he had no idea what Joaquín looked like, but soon he "fell into conversation with an ordinary looking Mexican, upon the subject of Joaquin's whereabouts, and was informed with most charming innocence that it was very foolish to attempt to arrest the brigand, as he would never be taken alive." Dorsey said he didn't care "how he was taken, alive or dead, for the Americans were bound to have him." He and his party left without any useful information, but he later learned that the young man to whom he had been speaking was none other than Joaquín Murrieta.[46]

Dorsey also recalled how Reyes Féliz was caught stealing a pistol. Constable John Leary of Columbia arrested him, then deputized Dorsey and another man to help him escort the prisoner to Sonora Camp, as he feared an attempted escape or rescue. Leary's fear was soon realized. They were ambushed by a band of Mexicans, and Reyes escaped, but his brother Claudio—whom Dorsey remembered as being a short, lithe eighteen-year-old at the time—retreated up a hill after being shot off his horse. Hotly pursued, "he emptied his two six-shooters at them," and suffered several wounds but failed to kill his assailants. Constable Leary "was about to blow the youth's brains out" when Dorsey stopped him. The posse took their new prisoner to Sonora where his wounds were treated and he was lodged in jail. Dorsey said Claudio promised to give him a fine horse with rich trappings in payment for services as defense attorney, but Dorsey also wanted him to swear "that the whole band should leave the county." Claudio promised and Caleb Dorsey got him a gubernatorial pardon.[47]

About a month later, Dorsey recalled he encountered members of the band in Mariposa County and was again invited to dine with them. After supper he went up the hill Claudio Féliz pointed out, the teenager saying the horse with "the rich trappings" was up there. While en route the lawyer suddenly came face to face with Murrieta, and both of them instinctively drew their pistols. But Murrieta put his weapon away and said, "We keep our word; you are safe, sir!" A year or so later Dorsey learned that "the notorious brigand fell by the hand of Capt. Harry Love." When two of Captain Love's rangers arrived with Murrieta's preserved head and exhibited it in Sonora Camp, county historian Herbert Lang said it was "inspected by Mr. Dorsey, who knew him so well in life, and . . . says now, unqualifiedly, that it was the head of the man whom he knew as Joaquin."[48]

Theodore Hittell left out Dorsey's testimony concerning the identity of the head, turning instead to state documents to recount the rangers' story. Then he added that "various stories" were circulating by 1898 to the effect that "the real Joaquin was never taken." But as far as he was concerned, "there can be little or no reasonable doubt that the man killed was the right one. . . . He at least gave no further trouble."[49] In other words, he viewed Dorsey and others who had positively identified the head as having in their favor the fact that Joaquín Murrieta's name never surfaced in valid news reports again.[50]

A few years after Theodore Hittell's voluminous state history was published, James Miller Guinn published an oversized volume of historical and biographical records in which he devoted only one paragraph to Joaquín Murrieta, but that paragraph was immediately followed by two more about the "metamorphosis" of Hispanics in California. "Before the conquest by the Americans," wrote Guinn, "they were a peaceful and contented people." He overlooked the penal-colony cholos Alvarado complained about and idealized the Pastoral Era of the early nineteenth century, writing that it was not until after "the discovery of gold that the evolution of a banditti began."

Not all Hispanic bandits were Mexican immigrants, wrote Guinn. Many had been born in California. (Solomón Pico, Juan Flores, and Tiburcio Vásquez were among these.) Guinn wrote, "The Americans not only took possession of their . . . government, but in many cases they despoiled them of their ancestral acres and their personal property. Injustice rankles; and it is not strange that the more lawless among the native population sought revenge and retaliation."[51] He too saw truth in the words John Rollin Ridge had applied to Joaquín Murrieta. However, lest his readers think he was excusing crime, Guinn added, "The plea of injustice was no extenuation for their crimes." Bandits could not justify murder as retaliation, because they went well beyond taking revenge. Had Joaquín, for example, attacked only his assailants, "it would have been but little loss, but . . . he made the innocent suffer with the guilty," and for that he deserved the fate he so readily inflicted on others.[52]

The Legend and Twentieth-Century Historians

For decades it was thought that all copies of the original 1854 edition of Ridge's *The Life and Adventures of Joaquin Murieta* were lost. Then one turned up in Connecticut and was reprinted in 1955 by the University of Oklahoma Press. The reprint included a lengthy introduction by Joseph Henry Jackson. Jackson began researching Joaquín Murrieta at about the same time Frank Latta and Walter Noble Burns were doing so. All three started with the legend as written by John Rollin Ridge, but they carried it in very different directions.

To Jackson, Ridge's book was a romance, a novel, a work of fiction, even though in his opening paragraph Ridge said, "I sit down to write somewhat concerning the life and character of Joaquín Murieta, . . . to contribute my mite to those materials out of which the early history of California shall one day be composed." His editor also asserted, in his preface, "The author has not thrown this work out into the world recklessly, or without authority for his assertions. In the main, it will be found to be strictly true." Such claims, Jackson argued, were part of the language of the genre. Ridge had simply taken a name that had been in the news recently—that part was "strictly true"—and developed a California folk-hero. Soon this hero became "a firm fixture in California's myth-ology—so firm it is considered historical truth by most Californians," wrote Jackson.[53] That was why it had worked its way into Hubert Howe Bancroft's *California Pastoral* and Hittell's comprehensive state history, Jackson insisted.

Jackson did not think much of Bancroft as a historian, but Hittell, he noted, had correctly tied the birth of the Murrieta legend to the 1850 Foreign Miners' Tax and persecution of foreign miners in general. More than half the foreign immigrants in gold rush California had come from Sonora, Mexico, as had Joaquín Murrieta. Persecution of the sort Murri-eta allegedly suffered really did happen—if not to him, then to others. There was also a very real and violent response among foreigners. Soon after the tax was enforced, outlaw bands formed and began to plague the gold-mining region. However, Jackson insisted, there were no Robin Hoods among them.

Jackson pointed out that Ridge's rollicking adventure story was obvi-ously composed of newspaper reports about various outlaws that were readily available to the Cherokee author. For example Ridge's depiction of Joaquín's murder of a sheriff named Clark, in San Jose, matches the details of the following clip from the *Sacramento Daily Union* of March 20, 1852:

> Murder in San Jose—The last number of the Visitor states that a horrible murder was committed in that place on Thurs-day last. It appears that a Mexican, named Montemeyor, had been arrested and brought before Mayor White for striking a woman. The Mayor, upon a hearing, fined the culprit, and at his own request, had permitted him to go under charge of Deputy Marshal Charles H. Smith (familiarly known as "Buck-skin" Smith), to collect the money to liquidate the fine. What conversation took place between the deputy Marshal and the prisoner on the way is not known, but when in the vicinity of the asequia [water fountain or irrigation canal] Monte-meyor was observed by two or three women to draw a knife and plunge it into the body of Smith, in the vicinity of the heart. Smith fell, and expired in a few minutes. The murderer made his escape.

Another story featured in several northern California newspapers in the spring of 1852 told of how a band of four Mexican horse thieves had been plaguing the Ione Valley and vicinity, in what was then part of Calaveras County. On April 5, 1852, Judge H. A. Carter discovered that one of his finest horses was missing. He and two cowboys, James Clark and James Corcoran (also spelled Cochran) tracked Carter's horse, which had a distinctive shoe, to an inn and boarding house at Willow Creek (now Wait's Station) and found the stolen horse corralled with others. A band of five Mexicans were dining inside. The posse enlisted the help of B. F. Moore, a black man who worked there. Moore and Clark entered the inn through the back door in hopes of catching the Mexicans off guard, but the Mexicans instantly snuffed the lamps and fired their weapons while charging out the front door. Moore killed one thief at the threshold. Clark was killed by another. Corcoran wounded one in the leg. Moore dodged a Mexican lasso while the wounded Mexican dodged Corcoran's lasso and was assisted in mounting a horse. Corcoran pursued them, but, as he was wounded in the thigh, he could not keep up. The horse thieves not only escaped, they managed to spook the stolen horses into running and then rounded up the majority of the animals while in flight. Carter's race horse was left behind.[54]

Three weeks later, the *San Joaquin Republican* reported, "One of the Mexican horse thieves who killed Mr. Clark . . . was arrested at Jackson Monday last. . . . He gave his name as Joaquin, and is doubtless one of a large band of rascals who infest this county. He was sent to . . . the scene of the murders, where, it is supposed, he will be summarily dealt with."[55] News reports like this, or imperfect recollections of them, helped shape Ridge's account of the California adventures of Joaquín Murrieta because that was the nature of the genre in which he wrote, argued Joseph Henry Jackson. But it was also why Ridge's version of the legend had some credibility to Bancroft and Hittell.

Although some later historians would quote Jackson selectively and claim that the gold rush outlaw named Joaquín Murrieta never existed, Joseph Henry Jackson never made such a claim. Instead, he argued, correctly, that the character in the legend is based on several outlaws, Murrieta among them, and that the only reason Murrieta's name stood out was because he was one of the Joaquíns listed in the state legislature's

ranger bill. When the rangers brought back a head it was repeatedly identified as that of Joaquín Murrieta. As to whether or not that head was correctly identified, Jackson cited a newspaper correspondence sent from
Los Angeles to the *San Francisco Alta* in August 1853, which insisted it was
really the head of Joaquín Valenzuela. He also quoted an editorial response to said correspondence that called the whole Joaquín "hysteria"
into question: "Sometimes it is Joaquin Carrillo that has committed all
these crimes; then it is Joaquin something else, but always 'Joaquin!'"[56]
Such remarks, argued Jackson, undermined the historical reliability of
Ridge's sources, but then, he admitted, Ridge's book was never really
meant to be a history or straight biography. California needed a folk
hero and Ridge provided one. The Joaquín legend entered state history
because history must have its myths!

While Jackson ripped the legend out of history, called it fiction, and
then stuffed the legend back in as a kind of panacea, Walter Noble Burns
sought to contribute to the legend and further solidify its place in history. Burns admitted he was dealing with a folk hero, one about whom
people still argued with regard to his appearance, behavior, and fate. In
an effort to smooth over differences in descriptions of Joaquín Murrieta, Burns carefully constructed an image that paid homage to all. Murrieta, he wrote, was a "handsome young fellow with black eyes and black
hair but with a face of ivory pallor such as you might have expected if his
hair had been golden and his eyes blue. Of medium height, well set up,
athletic. An hidalgo touch in his grave dignity, his punctilious politeness and his air of proud reserve."[57] Some old-timers Burns interviewed
lived in Calaveras County. One insisted Joaquín was tall. Another said
he was on the short side. Many claimed he had light brown or blond hair
and dark blue eyes, not the black eyes and hair assigned to him in legend and literature. However everyone agreed that the outlaw's skin color
was on the light side for a Mexican and that he had a mustache. Burns
exploited areas of agreement like this.

For example he discovered that "old timers who knew him and who
disagreed on the details of his career, were in unanimous agreement on
. . . his original character."[58] Joaquín, they all said, had been a frank, honest, industrious, and agreeable young man with a sense of humor and
even temper. It was not until after he suffered persecution at the hands

of drunken Americans that his soul darkened. Burns then recounted the *Gazette* version of the legend in which Murrieta's young wife (instead of his mistress) dies after her assailants have had their way with her. He followed this tragedy with a description of how Joaquín was flogged and his half-brother hanged, but this time he cited neither the Ridge nor *Gazette* versions of the legend. Instead he based his dramatic account of the flogging on a typescript provided to him by Frank Marshall.

Frank said he had the story from the diary of his father, Ben Marshall, who had been constable at Murphy's Camp in 1850 and Calaveras County Sheriff in 1851. It was in 1850, he said, that Joaquín worked at Murphy's as a monte dealer. Frank said he had type-copied his father's diary, admitting he had seen fit to edit the original, which had since been lost. According to his account of events, when his father, Ben Marshall, learned that a blue tent where young Murrieta worked as a monte dealer had been pulled down by a gang of rowdy American gamblers, he intervened in time to stop the Americans from assaulting Murrieta. A year later Ben was less successful when a lynch mob was excited into a frenzy by a merchant named Bill Lang. Lang accused Joaquín of stealing the mule he was riding. He said he had borrowed it from his brother, Jesús. Jesús was fetched, and he said that he had bought and paid for the mule and that Lang had sold it to him, but Jesús could produce no bill of sale. Jesús was dragged to the hanging tree. Joaquín fetched Ben Marshall, who, however, could not stop the lynching, but he did persuade the mob to show mercy on Joaquín—if a flogging can be considered more merciful than hanging.[59]

By depicting the Murrieta brothers as being entirely innocent victims of a lynch mob—something Ridge had refrained from doing—Burns changed the tone of the legend. Murrieta could not be viewed as Herbert Lang and Theodore Hittell had depicted him and as Caleb Dorsey remembered him: criminally inclined even before he came to California. The prevailing oral tradition about Joaquín Murrieta that Burns encountered in the economically failing gold rush towns of California during the Great Depression was that Murrieta was a good man who suffered grossly for no good reason; he smoldered with rage, and that rage corrupted his soul. He took bloody revenge, and the act of murder changed him forever. He became a gold rush Al Capone.

Walter Noble Burns's sources included old newspaper reports and late-nineteenth-century histories that mentioned Caleb Dorsey and Antonia La Molinera. Like John Rollin Ridge, Burns depicted Murrieta as leading a kind of guerrilla war which made life so precarious in California that the state dispatched Captain Harry Love and his rangers to break up the band. They succeeded, ambushing and killing Murrieta and several others in a gun fight at Arroyo Cantua.

The story ends there, but as Burns encountered numerous reports of alternate endings, he closed with a chapter titled "Strange Tales." In it he recounted various claims to the effect that Murrieta had escaped the rangers and died of old age in Sonora. There were those who saw a white-haired Mexican in the late nineteenth or early twentieth century looking for buried treasure. When questioned, he said he was Joaquín Murrieta. "The terrible Joaquin Murrieta of the old days has become a tale told in the twilight or a song sung to a guitar," wrote Burns in his closing sentence. His book, *The Robin Hood of El Dorado*, was so popular MGM Studios made it into a movie.

Meanwhile Frank Latta, a high school history teacher who had been skeptical about the historical value of the California oral tradition surrounding Joaquín Murrieta, changed his mind after meeting José Antonio "Tony" Águila. Águila was a Yokuts vaquero who grew up at Rancho Orestimba. He told Latta of conversations he'd heard about how the Murrieta band stole horses and saddles and were pursued all the way to Tejon by Mexican ranchero Yrenero Corona, for whom Águila's father worked.[60] The vaquero's account supported what Ridge had written concerning the stealing of horses from Rancho Orestimba, which in turn was based on 1852 newspaper accounts.

It suddenly occurred to Latta that no one had interviewed California Indians living on the Tejon Reservation and asked them what they knew about the encounter with Joaquín Murrieta and band. On July 7, 1933, he drove south to do just that. The people he met—formerly called "Tejon" and "Tulare" Indians—identified themselves as a mix of Yokuts, Chumash, and mission Indians known as Luiseño, Gabrielino, and so on. Latta knew he would not find any of those who had actually captured Murrieta, "but their descendants would be there and surely they would be able to tell me something," he wrote.[61] He stopped at Bakersfield on the way and spoke with José Jesús Lopez, a Yokuts Indian. Lopez suggested he look up Chief Juan Losada and tribal elders Ignacio Montez and José Juan Olivas.

Chief Losada sent Latta to Ramón Ynjinio, but Ramón said that his father had nothing to do with the capture of Murrieta. He sent him on to Olivas. After lunch, Olivas received his guest.

> It was very formal—I might have been a U.S. Commissioner getting a treaty signed. A chair was provided for me at the middle of one side of the table and another chair for Juan directly opposite. A step-daughter, good looking and very intelligent, sat beside Juan and interpreted for us. Although I believe that Juan understood all I said, and I understood most of what he said in Spanish, all was fed through the interpreter. . . . We got started on the local Indian language and the Indian names of the local landmarks. We spent about two hours on those topics before I switched to Murrieta.[62]

Olivas said he had first heard about the capture of Joaquín Murrieta from his father, who was at La Centinela when the bandits arrived.

> We called it La Centinela because it was the vaquero camp where the Indian vaqueros watched the stock that fed on that range. There was a pozo and ciénaga [spring and grassland] there. . . . It was on the plains south of where Arvin is now. There were five or six big cottonwood trees there. . . . I heard my father tell lots of times how they captured Murrieta. . . . The vaqueros were cooking their supper when they saw some people coming [on] horseback on the north trail. . . . There were two men ahead of the rest. My father invited these . . . to eat with them. They got off their horses."[63]

But when the other bandits caught up, they charged into the vaquero's horses and scattered them, then turning on the Indians, beat them with *riatas*. The Indian vaqueros went to recapture their mounts, but on returning found that the rude newcomers had joined the other two and eaten the entire supper, leaving nothing for their hosts. Angry, Olivas's father went to report the incident to Chief Zapatero. The chief sent him

back with about a dozen men, two of them his sons. "They took with
them all the guns they had," said Olivas, and then waited for the night.
Meanwhile Santiago Montez, who had also gone for help, brought back
a party of twenty-two Indians. By the light of the moon they approached,
snaking quietly through the grass "on their bellies about two hundred
yards. . . . The bandidos' horses were tied to the trees. The bandidos were
all asleep about 50 feet away. They didn't make their beds down under
the trees. You can't do that. . . . The pah-hah-wéh-uhs will eat you up."[64]
Pajaroellos, in Spanish, means "ticks."

While some of them crept up to the horses and began leading them
away, others poked gun muzzles into the ribs of sleepy bandits, then began stripping them of whatever they fancied, after which they bound them
hand and foot. "There were three women and five men. . . . One woman
yelled and fought and broke away, ran off in the dark. She didn't have one
piece of clothing. Everybody left the bandidos tied up on the ground and
went to divide the things. . . . That took until after sunup." The traditional
way of dividing loot was by lots. When they returned for their prisoners
at dawn, they were gone. "My father," said José Juan Olivas, "thought that
the woman that got loose came back and untied them."[65]

Latta mentioned how Ridge had written that the Indians took the robbers to Chief Zapatero, who had them whipped. Olivas said that never
happened. Curious about the loot, Latta asked what they took from the
robbers. Olivas said there were about fifteen horses, some of which a
Mexican ranchero from the north claimed, along with some saddles. As
for the other goods, his father got "a fine pair of spurs that . . . had some
silver and some gold on them," which he kept until too infirm to ride.[66]
Another vaquero, named Santiago Montez, got a fine gold watch with a
chain that had square pieces of gold ore attached to it. Losada's father
got a pair of spurs, as well as "a good revolver and a black silk scarf that
. . . was about a foot wide and four feet long. It had a heavy silk fringe on
each end." Ramon Ynjinio's wife's mother was given three gold nuggets
and two women's rings, his wife's father having been the one who participated, as Latta soon learned.[67]

Frank Latta cited these oral histories as primary sources that tended to
prove the historical reliability of an event described by John Rollin Ridge.

He then spent the next fifty-plus years collecting more interviews, the bulk of them with Murrieta relatives in Sonora. These were compiled in his book *Joaquín Murrieta and his Horse Gangs*, which was published by his daughter in 1980. Though legend played a part in his interpretation of events, Latta ended up telling a very different story. He described Murrieta as a handsome Sonoran mestizo with light brown hair that tended to curl, dark blue eyes, light complexion, tall and lanky, who counted several brothers—other Joaquíns among them—as band members. He also claimed that the rangers did not kill Joaquín Murrieta at Arroyo Cantua, but that he died a year later of an infected wound he suffered in another gun fight with lawmen and was buried in secret, in the dirt floor of an adobe hut—with his head still attached.[68] Rich in black and white photographs and facsimile reprints of documents, including quite a few 1853 *San Joaquin Republican* newspaper clips, Latta's book remains a fascinating compilation of selections from his voluminous oral and written history collection. It is a unique work that remains valuable even though parts of the narrative do not stand up to scrutiny.

Several contemporaries of Frank Latta took an interest in Joaquín Murrieta in the 1960s because of the Civil Rights Movement. A Mexican movie about Joaquín Murrieta and his guerrilla war came out in 1961. A year later 20th Century Fox came out with one, and two years after that a popular spaghetti western version was produced in Spain.[69] Meanwhile scholarly interest in Joaquín spiked after the Chicano Movement in California embraced Joaquín Murrieta and Tiburcio Vásquez as examples of those who fought injustice in early California. The Chicano view of Joaquín shaped the research of professors Leonard Pitt and Stan Steiner. But freelance historians like William B. Secrest, Remi Nadeau, and James F. Varley took an interest in the subject for another reason: they wanted to know if there was any truth to the legend. All three decided there was, but there was also a lot of fiction.

Secrest was the first to publish a history of Joaquín and band based on documentary evidence. At the time he was digging up sources, Cesar Chavez was forming the United Farm Workers union not far south of where Secrest lived. Secrest's pamphlet, *Joaquin, Bloody Bandit of the Mother Lode*, came out in 1967, the same year Rodolfo "Corky" Gonzales

5. "I am Joaquin!" Ink wash illustration by Pierre Boeringer, 1895. Courtesy of the California History Room, California State Library, Sacramento, California.

published *I am Joaquín! Yo soy Joaquín!*, an epic poem which was distributed among Chavez supporters as a kind of anthem.[70] While Gonzales's poem used Joaquín's legendary persona to express what it felt like to be a mestizo from Mexico living in North America, Secrest's pamphlet depicted Joaquín and band as violent and dangerous. Chicanos in the Civil Rights Movement longed to stand up and be counted as Joaquín appeared to do when he jumped on a table and shouted his identity, defying those who would silence him. They were more interested in the legendary figure than in the history behind the legend.

In 1973 Secrest published another pamphlet: *The Return of Joaquin, Bloody Bandit of the Mother Lode*. This time his purpose was to trace "the curious saga of Joaquín's head." After sharing his findings, he said he did not know for sure whose head the rangers exhibited. There was no way to prove its identity because the head was destroyed in the San Francisco earthquake of 1906. "In the end," he wrote, "it boils down to this: enjoy the story and make up your own mind."[71] Though he was inclined to believe the evidence provided by the rangers and supported by Caleb Dorsey, William Secrest was not interested in arguing against apparent evidence to the contrary.

Remi Nadeau, in his book *The Real Joaquin Murieta*, reached many of the same conclusions Secrest reached, but he did more research and featured prominently a *Sacramento Daily Union* newspaper report in which Bill McMullen described his pursuit of Joaquín Murrieta in mid-February 1853. James F. Varley expressed skepticism about McMullen's account in his book, *The Legend of Joaquín Murieta, California's Gold Rush Bandit*. Varley dug deeper than Nadeau and Secrest (with the help of what was then a new research aid: inter-library loan). The result is a history rich in new details. He found, for example, that Claudio Féliz, brother of Reyes Féliz, played a prominent role as a band leader and that it was he and his band that committed many of the early crimes assigned in legend to the Joaquín band. This and other fascinating details were revealed when he found the confession of "Theodor Basques" (properly spelled Teodor Vásquez), which Varley reprinted in full as an appendix. The confession was printed in the (Benecia) *California State Gazette*, February 21, 1852, which had copied the story from the *San Jose Weekly Visitor* of February 14, 1852. Teodor was a Sonoran youth from Hermosillo who was arrested in San Jose in the fall of 1851, tried after the new year, found guilty of horse theft, and hanged on January 30, 1852. His confession included the names of a dozen Sonoran band members, a Chilean, and several Anglo-Saxons whose names were not printed. Aside from his own crimes, Teodor listed numerous murders and robberies that occurred between December 1850 and December 1851, which he attributed to Claudio Féliz and band.[72]

Among those Teodor named were Claudio's younger brother Reyes Féliz, the teenage Francisco "Pancho" Daniel and his brother Bernardo, and "Joaquin Gurrieta" [sic]. He did not mention Joaquín Valenzuela or Luis Burgos alias Joaquín, but he did mention Jesús Senate, a Californio outlaw who rode with Luis Burgos and was killed with him in 1854. Another Californio he mentioned was called "San Lorenzo" of Santa Clara. It was in the vicinity of Santa Clara that a Lorenzo Lopez—who had "J. C." (Joaquín Carrillo?) tattooed on his arm—was arrested in 1858. He was identified as a member of the Pancho Daniel band.

James Varley used Teodor's confession as an outline from which he could look up crime reports referred to by the condemned prisoner, many of which Claudio Féliz had boasted about while in jail with Teodor. Féliz escaped by using a penknife he kept in his boot to file through the irons that held him and then dig his way out. He invited Teodor to escape with him, but the latter preferred to face his fate, perhaps because he was afraid of Claudio.

According to Teodor, the Féliz band formed in the fall of 1850. Claudio had boasted of robbing three Americans at a ranch called Abra in company with six other bandits. He also went to John Marsh's ranch in December and, with thirteen others, robbed the place of everything of value. Marsh asked how many men were in their party and Claudio lied: 150 he said. The ranch occupants were bound and gagged and left alive in a house that was set on fire. (They managed to escape the building.)

In the spring of 1851, Claudio and Reyes Féliz, Joaquín Murrieta, and others stole horses, sold them, and lost all their money gambling. In June, Claudio and several American outlaws stole a safe from a business in Camp Seco, but they had to throw it in a pit and flee before they could break it open. One of the American thieves, Charles May alias David Hill, was captured and lynched. Shortly after that Claudio and three other Sonorans, Joaquín and Reyes likely among them, dressed handsomely in vaquero attire and attended a fandango dance at a town called Sonora that was near Marysville in Yuba County. There were several towns in gold rush California called Sonora: one in Yuba County, one in Tuolumne County, and one near Los Angeles. All of them were founded by immigrants from Sonora and Sinaloa, Mexico. The next day they committed a string of robberies, lassoing their victims and dragging them before stabbing and shooting them.

Historian James Varley pointed out that these crimes appear in Ridge's book and are attributed to Joaquín Murrieta as acts of revenge. But the real intent, according to Claudio's remarks to Teodor and according to newspaper reports of the day, was simply to pocket someone else's money. Varley also noted that Ridge gave Joaquín credit for shooting the sheriff of Marysville in November 1851, but Claudio boasted to Teodor that it was he who shot Sheriff Robert "Buck" Buchanan of Yuba County. Buchanan and a deputy had been investigating a tip and approached a cabin with a fenced-in yard. Buchanan decided to take a closer look and climbed over the fence, but a dog sounded the alarm and armed Mexicans suddenly appeared. One ordered the sheriff to retreat, which he did, but his clothing got caught on the fence, and while he struggled Claudio shot him in the small of the back. Buchanan survived, but his wound made life excruciating.[73]

Claudio also told Teodor that he and his band fled to Camp Seco, Calaveras County, after that but instantly became suspects in a recent murder and were chased away. Manuel Peña was wounded while they were in flight. They next went to Sonora, Tuolumne County, but were again chased away by Americans. From there they went through Mariposa County to San Jose, where Claudio was arrested. He said he wanted to kill Marshal Whitman of San Jose for arresting him. He also wanted to kill John Frémont of Mariposa County, presumably because he, too, had once arrested Claudio.

A couple of months after Teodor hanged, Claudio, who had escaped, rescued his brother Reyes, as described by Caleb Dorsey. After Dorsey got him pardoned and released, Claudio retired to a Mexican mining camp in Mariposa County, where Dorsey visited him. He renewed his promise to Dorsey, saying he had reformed, but in September, when recovered enough from his wounds to ride again, Claudio led a band of six or seven Mexicans who robbed Chinese and Americans in Calaveras County, then headed across the San Joaquin Valley toward Monterey after hearing a rumor to the effect that his brother was in jail there. The rumor proved false. He learned that his brother and Joaquín Murrieta were in Los Angeles, so Claudio and band turned south, stopping at a fandango house in Salinas for the night. En route he and his band had stripped a poor, honest countryman of his serape and trinkets in Monterey. The indignant victim ignored any threats they uttered and complained to Justice of the Peace Henry Cocks. Cocks, who had married into the Californio family of Francisco García, led a posse of Californio in-laws and neighbors to the fandango house known to be popular with bandits. They surrounded it and Cocks called upon Claudio to surrender. Instead the bandits snuffed the lights and charged out the door firing, counting on night dark to cover their retreat. Claudio, however, ran directly into Cocks, who seized him by the wrist, forcing him to drop his gun. He surrendered, then, feigning injury, stooped and drew a boot knife. Cocks saw the blade wink in the moonlight and fired point blank, his nineteen-year-old prisoner dying instantly. Three other gang members were also shot; two of them died.[74]

The history of Claudio and band surfaced in James F. Varley's research, but the history of Joaquín Murrieta remained difficult to trace. For example, Varley found numerous accounts of Joaquín having a scar on his face, but that scar was described as inflicted by a bullet, a knife, or a blow, and as being deep, long, or small, but always on the cheek. He also found that contrary to legend, there was no evidence of a large, well-organized band of Mexicans, nor did Mexican outlaws plot to loot the state of California and escape south of the border with their treasure. Instead, Varley discovered, early California outlaw bands of Mexicans, Americans, and foreigners constituted an assortment of "loose-knit" autonomous companies that sometimes banded together and that numbered anywhere from two to twenty strong per company.

Nonetheless, Varley noted, some of what Ridge wrote about the Murrieta band was supported by evidence. For example outlaws did use sentries and spies on occasion, and bands did roam from Yuba to San Diego counties. They traveled with surprising speed, and this mobility provided them with a degree of anonymity. They also killed countrymen they believed guilty of betraying them, and they targeted lawmen on occasion.

Regarding Murrieta's reported fate at the hands of the rangers, Varley wrote that "the capture and beheading of the man supposed to be Joaquín Murrieta had absolutely no impact in ameliorating California's plague of crime."[75] As to whether or not the rangers' evidence was genuine, James Varley, like William Secrest, remained noncommittal. As Varley saw it, if it was Murrieta's head, his passing did not slow down or stop crimes of the sort he and his band had committed at the mines and elsewhere. And after all, several other outlaws, Pancho Daniel and Joaquín Valenzuela among them, did continue to rob and sometimes kill miners, travelers, keepers of lonely roadside inns and stores, and occupants of isolated houses and ranches.

Secrest, Nadeau, and Varley did not work in university settings, unlike Raymund F. Wood, Leonard Pitt, Thomas Gordon, Stan Steiner, and Alberto Huerta, SJ. Raymund Wood had doubted the existence of the legendary outlaw, Joaquín Murrieta, before the diary of Albert K. Owen was brought to his attention. Albert Owen mentioned Joaquín Murrieta in an entry dated November 3, 1872. Owen was in the city of Hermosillo, Sonora, at the time, on business. He said that a popular tragic opera about Joaquín had excited intimidating anti-American sentiments among a formerly friendly people. While talking about it with a Sonoran acquaintance, he was informed that this was because Murrieta came from the district of Hermosillo. Indeed two of his brothers still lived in Buenavista near the Yaqui River, south of the city.

Wood also discovered that a 1919 Mexican version of the legend, *Vida y aventuras del mas celebre bandido Sonorense, Joaquin Murrieta*, featured a photograph of three Los Angeles residents, the middle-aged daughters of Antonio Murrieta, brother of the famous bandido.[76] He also mentioned Frank Latta's interviews with David Murrieta and his brothers, who said that their father was a cousin of the famous Joaquín, and he cited a December 1852 *San Francisco Alta* article which named "Joaquin Murieta" several times in testimonies given by Reyes Féliz and others. All of this convinced him that an outlaw by the name of Joaquín Murrieta did exist in gold rush California, and he was from Sonora.

Leonard Pitt agreed that there was a man behind the myth but argued that the legendary character was the real Joaquín Murrieta. To him, Joaquín's legend reflected the prejudice and violence at the mines. Ridge's comments about the effects of prejudice were true, Leonard Pitt pointed out in *Decline of the Californios*, and that truth was what made the legendary outlaw worth mentioning in the context of California history. Murrieta was a useful example of how a people see their own suffering as the basis for a good story with which they could empathize. They might even use that story to mobilize toward social and political change. Pedro Castillo and Albert Camarillo agreed. They wrote a book about California bandidos featuring Joaquín Murrieta, Solomón Pico, Juan Flores, and Tiburcio Vásquez. Presented as folk history, the book claimed relevance to the Chicano Movement in that Chicanos in California shared with these legendary bandits a continuing theme of unjust treatment and the anger it ignited.[77]

Thomas Gordon focused on Joaquín Murrieta as a popular character in both Chicano *and* Anglo-Saxon folk tradition in California.[78] He divided the folklore he collected into three categories: the Anglo-Saxon view of Joaquín as a light-skinned romantic Robin Hood or Zorro type; the less prevalent Anglo-Saxon view of Joaquín as a dangerous criminal who lived and died violently; and the Latino view of Joaquín as "an avenging angel" and guerrilla rebel chief at war with the Americans and their capitalist tendency to tred on others for the sake of a quick profit.[79] In spite of his skepticism, Gordon did try to unearth evidence of the man, but all he could find was a tax assessment record for March 1863 of property belonging to "Murieta-Yndart & Company," which included a ranch and butcher shop in San Andreas, Calaveras County. If this Murrieta inspired the folk tales, he argued, he clearly had nothing but a name in common with the legendary outlaw.[80]

Like Gordon, Stanford professor Stan Steiner focused on folk traditions about Joaquín Murrieta, but like Leonard Pitt his perspective was shaped by the Chicano Movement. He therefore leaned toward Hispanic sources. Finding little in print, he took to the road in search of unwritten oral tradition about the Joaquín band.

Steiner was much more skeptical than Frank Latta, and the results of his wonderings reflect that. For example when he got lost on dirt roads in the vicinity of Quartzburg and Hornitos on an unbearably hot summer day, he stopped and knocked on the door of a house to ask for a drink of water, and Mrs. Lee Sanchez answered the door. She invited him in, gave him a drink, and asked him what he was looking for when he got lost. On hearing of his interest in Joaquín Murrieta, she instantly shared her family's oral tradition on the subject. Steiner's skeptical expression provoked her to fetch a marriage certificate proving her grandmother had been "married to a man whose name I recognized as that of a lieutenant of Murieta," wrote Steiner. "All history is not in your books," said Mrs. Sanchez.[81] Though impressed, Steiner did not view her evidence in the same way she did. "Memories of the past often contradict not only one another but themselves," he wrote. "They are difficult to grasp and hold onto. But written histories may be as elusive."[82] A marriage certificate may be evidence of a family relationship to one of Murrieta's men, or it may be evidence of a family oral tradition built on the *belief* that said relationship existed.

Steiner also spoke to Arnold Rojas. "The legend of Murrieta begins with his baptismal paper," Arnold told him, adding that such a record did exist: "Dated 1830 and located in the old church of Alamos, a city in Sonora, the document says he was the son of 'Joaq. y Rosalia Murieta'. His father worked in a silver-mining camp of the Mayo Indians near Varoyeca."[83] So Stan Steiner drove down to Alamos, Sonora, and tried to find Murrieta's baptismal record, but all he could find was the baptismal record of a boy whose father had the same name as Murrieta's brother Antonio. He asked the priest if it was a record of a relative of "el pistolero" (the highwayman). The cleric walked away without saying a word. "But the limping porter of the cathedral came over to me," wrote Steiner, "and whispered in my ear: 'Sí, señor. It is the family of Murieta.'"[84]

Before returning to California, Steiner stopped at an Indian village called Cucurpe in northern Sonora. There, according to Arnold Rojas, Murrieta died of old age and was buried in 1878. Steiner asked a local Indian where Murrieta's grave was. The Indian led him to a pile of rocks inside an old mission cemetery and said, "Aqui!" (Here!). The Stanford professor asked how he knew that was where the famous pistolero was buried. The man grinned and said, "When the owl hoots the Indian dies. This may not be true but it happens."[85] In other words, the Joaquín Murrieta legend may not be true, but the events in the legend happened.

In 1976 Steiner sent an unfinished manuscript to his publisher; El Patrio: The Untold History of Joaquín Murrieta came back to him a year later. The publisher's letter said that it was a work of fiction, not a study in social history or folklore. However a book with a similar title was published in Mexico a decade later. The author was Manuel Perez Rojas, a high school teacher from Mexicali, Baja California. Rojas embraced the guerrilla chief image of Joaquín Murrieta. His book was largely about his search for genealogical evidence proving Joaquín Murrieta was indeed from Sonora. Church records at Alamos, Hermosillo, Ures, Real de Los Alamos, Arispe, and La Colorada proved disappointing. There were lots of Murrietas but no Joaquín Murrieta born between 1825 and 1832. Finally, at the district of Altar (where David Murrieta and his extended family lived), Rojas found a baptismal record on which Joaquín Murrieta and Carmen Féliz were "padrinos" (godparents) to the infant daughter of Miguel Vega and Dolores Ramírez, baptized on December 10, 1849. It was a very exciting find as the 1859 *Police Gazette* version of the legend said that Joaquín's wife's name was "Carmela Féliz." Carmela is a variation of the name Carmen (much like John and Jonathan, in English).

Rojas published his findings in *Joaquín Murrieta, El Patrio, el "Far West" del Mexico cercenado*.[86] He depicted the historical Joaquín Murrieta as a Mexican guerrilla-war revolutionary, asserted that the famous guerrilla chief was the son of Juan Murrieta and María Juana Orozco of Hacienda de Alamito in the district of Altar, and claimed that Carmen Féliz was his wife. His book started a debate among Chicanos over whether Joaquín Murrieta was a real man and whether or not it mattered. The almost unanimous conclusion reached at a conference held in Baja California was that he was real, he came from the Murrieta clan in Sonora, he went to California during the gold rush, and while there he undoubtedly encountered prejudice and persecution. The rest was speculation. To some he was a *bandolero* or revolutionary, to others, a *social bandit*. To Albert Huerta he was a *vendido*—someone who plays the part of a hero even though he wasn't heroic.

The term "social bandit" was coined by Eric Hobsbawm in his book *Bandits*.[87] Hobsbawm defined a social bandit as someone who has been outlawed or exiled by a dominant group because he is not one of them. He then begins to rob and even kill members of the dominant group, with or without a band of followers. Such bandits always surface in rural settings amid a desperately poor and oppressed people who idealize them even though the bandit never shares his booty with them.

The Chicano interpretations of Joaquín's history troubled historian John Boessenecker. He published an article repudiating claims to the

"...and to all those who died, scrubbed floors

6. "Last Supper of Chicano Heroes." Mural in the dining hall of Casa Zapata at Stanford University. Photograph by the author in 1999.

effect that the historical Joaquín Murrieta, or any of his fellow outlaws, were revolutionaries, guerrilla rebels, or even social bandits, though he did admit that Juan Flores seemed to come close when his band ambushed a sheriff's posse in 1857. The Joaquín band, Boessenecker pointed out, mostly victimized Chinese miners and even robbed and murdered their own countrymen. What was more, Americans were among the outlaws with which they associated. Hispanic bandits and gang members in the 1850s were not "patriots" at war with American authorities, Boessenecker insisted, nor did they defend their countrymen when American mobs seized property and exiled whole populations.[88] Instead they fanned the flames of prejudice and racism by exciting vigilante actions with their crimes against humanity.

Albert Huerta agreed. He, too, saw Joaquín and his fellow bandits as unworthy of hero status. The historical Joaquín Murrieta was neither a good role model nor a real hero, but his legend was a good source of inspiration to writers of literature and to common people swapping tales around a camp fire. He had become a hero to the people, although he did not merit it.[89]

His undeserved hero status won Joaquín Murrieta the most votes in an informal survey of 1980s Chicano students and 1960s Chicano activists. Asked to list the top thirteen Chicano heroes, they came up with about fifty names, with Murrieta making an appearance on every single list. The survey was taken with a view toward portraying Chicano heroes in a mural. No one wanted to give the legendary California outlaw the central seat in a "Last Supper" mural. He was instead relegated to the seat farthest to the left of Che Guevara, who sits at center with Death standing behind him and the radiant Virgin de Guadalupe floating above Death.[90]

Problem with Interpreting the Past from a Present-Day Vantage

As has been seen, the historical Joaquín Murrieta remains ubiquitous, in spite of very thorough research. Part of the reason is that Chicano scholars and freelance historians alike have encountered confusing, inconsistent, and contradictory newspaper reports and recollections. That is not surprising. The news media today still gives inconsistent and contradictory coverage, and commentators argue about the news and question each other's integrity.

Newspaper editors in the 1850s were aware of their vulnerability. Their sources were hired correspondents, travelers, express riders, the columns of newspapers from other towns and cities, and private letters. These overlapped and sometimes disagreed in particulars. One correspondent would refer with urgency to an event that took place "Thursday last," an event which another correspondent said took place "on Monday last." Editors overlooked these differences and saw one as a confirmation of the other, because both spoke of the same event or sequence of events. The order of events remained more or less chronologically the same, even though starting dates varied. Often details also varied. Although none of this seems to have troubled readers in the 1850s, it has proved to be a chronological problem for historians.

Editors in the 1850s tended to trust informants they knew more than they trusted others. They also tended to trust one another and often reprinted clips from each other's papers in spite of political differences. Only occasionally did they print news items or letters which they were not willing to vouch for. In such cases they printed disclaimers, followed up with corrections, or informed their readers that they had heard reports of a questionable nature which they deemed unworthy of publication.

James F. Varley relied heavily on newspapers, as there is very little else available about the Joaquín band. He even made an effort to become acquainted with the character of selected editors, correspondents, and writers of memoirs and recollections, then tried to judge how honest they were and, by extension, how trustworthy they were as historical sources. However he overlooked Spanish sources. He also did not weigh how much an editor's or gold rush pioneer's political and cultural background shaped their point of view. When writing about Mexicans, for example, 1850s newspaper editors used words that reflected their different points of view, based on existing preconceptions and prejudices. Spanish language newspaper editors, for example, frequently clipped and reprinted news from countries south of the border, while English language editors featured news from the eastern United States. The direction one faced when thinking of home exposed one's point of view.

If today current events and news commentaries contain all kinds of judgments, joking innuendoes, hidden agendas, and references to fictitious and real figures from popular culture, the same was true in the nineteenth century. And if today FOX NEWS and CNN report the same event from entirely different political platforms, the same was true in gold rush California. In the 1850s there were Democrat- and Whig Party–affiliated newspapers, as well as independent newspapers influenced by the political leanings of editors. All of this had an effect on Joaquín-related news in 1853 because it was an election year for state offices in California. That was also the year William Walker and his friends in the press were busy raising funds and winning over recruits for a filibuster or privately funded and illegal military invasion of Baja California and Sonora.

Henry Crabb, who was running for a seat in the state assembly that year, would lead another filibuster expedition into Sonora in 1857. Joaquín-related news was exploited by politicians and those who invested in filibuster campaigns. That exploitation and other forces that shaped what was written about the Joaquín band in newspapers and diaries helped this author to reach a new understanding of the history of the Joaquín band, the history behind the legend.

2. Joaquín and his Countrymen as Depicted in Diaries

The American belief in a divinely commissioned call to push west, described as "a manifest destiny" by journalist John L. O'Sullivan in 1845, fueled tension between the United States and Mexico, tension which exploded into war in 1846. The two-year-long war ended with the signing of the Treaty of Guadalupe Hidalgo. The treaty provided Mexico with badly needed funds in return for a swath of thinly populated land on Mexico's northwestern frontier, which included Alta California. Mexicans in these territories would become U.S. citizens. The treaty also included a provision by which the U.S. military promised to make every effort to stop North American freebooters from leading filibuster campaigns into Mexico.

During the war, U.S. troops had marched all the way to Mexico City. Soldiers, officers, and congressmen from the South urged the United States to lay claim to all of Mexico, but the majority in Congress were not inclined, and the president was not willing, to subjugate a people who did not want to be ruled by conquerors. The very notion of empire-building stood at odds with the principles of democracy. However the United States government did covet the land that John C. Frémont and other American explorers had mapped and described in books, the same land that was purchased through treaty.

Frémont had attempted to seize Alta California and establish an independent republic by means of a filibuster campaign in June 1846 that became known as the Bear Flag Revolt, before he learned of the U.S. war with Mexico. He and his men joined U.S. forces in California when they arrived a month later. Mexico did not send any reinforcements to California, leaving the sparse military there to defend the territory on their own. They met with success until January 1847, when more American reinforcements arrived. With a combined force of 660 men, the Americans defeated the Californios in a series of battles that ended with a truce.

California was coveted even before gold was discovered because of the usefulness of her Pacific shore bays to seafaring trade, because of the agriculturally rich soil and gentle weather, and because of the abundance of sulfur, mercury, lumber, and other exploitable resources. Alta California was but thinly populated in 1847, so it would be easy to Americanize. At least that was the expectation. Then gold was discovered.

News of the gold discoveries in northern California reached Sonora, Mexico, early in 1848. Thousands of Sonorans had already migrated to Alta California to escape Apache raids and severe drought. News of gold greatly increased the number of Sonoran caravans headed north. There were so many Mexicans at the mines in 1849 that a fear arose among the North Americans to the effect that the Mexicans, by virtue of their numerical presence, would make it difficult to establish a U.S. territorial government there. This fear of Mexicans and jealousy of Sonorans, who were competent miners, shaped events leading to the formation of Mexican outlaw bands.[1]

Eyewitness accounts bring to life the southern mining district where Joaquín Murrieta and the Féliz brothers, Claudio and Reyes, first panned for gold.[2] Hundreds of men and women, mostly Americans, kept journals and diaries. Whether written privately or with plans to publish a book, diaries offer vivid, personal perspectives that bring events to life and provide a peek at the history behind the legendary Joaquín band. They expose a colorful reality, a past that details moments of harmony and tension between Hispanics and Anglo-Saxons. The post-war atmosphere left Americans in a haughty mood and Mexicans feeling resentful. Diaries reveal when it was that companies of miners from Sonora were first described as bands of guerrillas led by a guerrilla chief—a title that was given to the legendary Joaquín Murrieta.

Immigrants from Sonora and from the Californio ranches mined for gold along the Mokelumne and Stanislaus rivers and their tributaries beginning in the spring of 1848, according to Antonio Coronel. Coronel also recalled that Joaquín Murrieta was first seen in Los Angeles in

7. William Perkins, c. 1845. Pencil sketch by the author.

early 1849, when he was about eighteen years old, and that he arrived with a Mexican *maroma* company—rope dancing circus performers—for whom he worked as a horse trainer. Doubtless the whole maroma company pressed on toward the gold-rich foothills of the high Sierras in the Stanislaus River valley that year. Murrieta and the Féliz brothers were in the vicinity of Sonora Camp (which later became a town) in the summer of 1849, according to Caleb Dorsey. They met Chileans and other Hispanic miners, as well as a company of Irish and some French and other foreign immigrants, all coexisting with an ever-growing number of North Americans.[3] Among the North Americans who visited or settled near the Stanislaus River were Thomas Butler King, Bayard Taylor, William Perkins, Alfred Doten, and Enos Christman. The last four kept diaries.

Canadian-born William Perkins, who was fluent in Spanish, traveled through Mexico on his way to California in 1849. He wrote of how "large numbers of Sonoraenses with their families and stocks of native merchandise, embarked in small vessels" at the port city of Guaymas, Sonora, and sailed, as he did, to Monterey, California. From there they made their way to the gold fields on the Stanislaus River and built "Campo de los Sonoraenses, afterward changed to Sonora."⁴ Perkins described the location of the Tuolumne County camp that became a town called Sonora as "situated in a valley of about two miles . . . in length, and about half a mile in breadth . . . [fringed with tree-covered mountains] around the bases of which a good level road runs. A water course, dry in summer but a torrent in the mid-winter months, divides the town into two parts." Because the Sonorans had been working there the previous year as well, Perkins observed, "the first placers . . . had been very thoroughly worked . . . pits and diggings, already deserted."⁵

Thomas Butler King, U.S. Customs Agent, visited the southern mines with Bayard Taylor in August 1849 and afterward wrote a lengthy letter to John M. Clayton, U.S. Secretary of State, describing what he saw: "At a place called Sonorian [sic] Camp it is believed there were at least ten thousand Mexicans. Hotels, restaurants, stores and shops of all descriptions, furnished whatever money could procure. Ice was brought from the Sierra, and ice-creams added . . . to luxuries. An enclosure made of the trunks and branches of trees, and lined with cotton cloth, served as a sort of amphitheatre for bull-fights."⁶ It was like stopping at a mining town in a foreign country, and he found that troubling. King was among those who vocalized an American fear of the large Mexican population in California, but he also disliked seeing hundreds of miners from other countries as well.

William Perkins initially felt at home among the diverse people at Sonora town. He, too, noticed that Spanish-speakers outnumbered other language groups, but Hispanics were a divided group, having brought with them a tendency to observe class lines as if still in Mexico or Chile. Class lines were evident in attire.

> Some [Mexicans] wore only drawers [ankle length white cotton pants] a shirt and zarape [striped wool blanket], with a huge sombrero hat, black outside and lined with green, the crown decorated with large patens of silver, round and convex. Others,

8. "Joaquin Murieta: The California Bandit," engraving by Anthony and Baker, *The Life and Adventures of Joaquin Murieta* by John Rollin Ridge (1854).

more the vaquero dress: a leather jacket, double, with an outer surface scalloped out into fantastic patterns, showing red or blue figures on the under leather; half-tanned leather trousers open down the leg on the outside, and adorned with rows of silver buttons; inside, a pair of white cotton drawers, very wide and loose, and the leg encased to the knee in botas [wraparound leather shin guards] ornamented in the same manner as the jacket. In their botas is stuck the knife, the handle of which projects along side of the leg, and, when the man is mounted, is most conveniently at hand.[7]

As a horse trainer, Murrieta would have sported vaquero attire, and indeed that is how he appears in early illustrations. The Féliz brothers also favored vaquero attire.

As for American miners like Alfred Doten, Perkins described them as wearing "thick pantaloons, heavy boots worn outside the trousers, a red or blue flannel shirt also worn outside and gathered round the waist by a Chinese banda or silk scarf, or black leather belt, perhaps both; and in which a colt revolver was invariably stuck."[8] Perkins and his Chilean business partner Ramón Navarro preferred business attire: dark pants, white shirts, silk ties, a vest, jacket, and any of a variety of hats. Perkins also carried a pistol, tucked within easy reach. American six-shooters fascinated young Mexicans like Murrieta and Claudio and Reyes Féliz. The weapon and its ammunition were readily available at American stores that doubled as inns and bars.

William Perkins and Alfred Doten both enjoyed the fact that in Sonora town there were "numbers of the gentler sex," nearly all of them Hispanic. Perkins wrote that when they walked and danced, Mexican women seemed to float. Some made good money selling "the national dish of meat and chili pepper, wrapped within two tortillas of wheat flour or Indian corn, a delicacy for which the Mexican . . . would sell his birthright."[9] A Sonoran woman working for Antonio Coronel made very good money selling tamales in her free time. Women also worked as laundresses. Mexican women would play an important part in the history and folklore about the Joaquín band.

On weekends Sonoran miners celebrated life by indulging in music, dancing, and gambling. Alfred Doten, who played the violin, loved "striking up a ditty" with Mexicans, Chileans, Frenchmen, and Scots. The Mexicans, wrote Perkins, played well on "drums, guitars, fiddles, and . . . the little Mexican lute," which had a high, metallic voice. Their music never disturbed "the ruffian looking American gambler, or the easy, careless Spanish player, who puts down his four, five, or ten ounces on a card and loses or wins with admirable equanimity of temper."[10] The most popular game was monte. Perkins called it the "national game" of Mexico. Joaquín Murrieta had a weakness for monte, as did many of his countrymen.

While Perkins and Doten enjoyed living and working around Sonoran and other foreign miners and merchants in 1849, Bayard Taylor, who accompanied Thomas King to the southern mines for a couple of months in August and September of that year, marveled at the industry of Mexican miners and the lack thereof among the Americans. The Mexicans worked tirelessly under a burning sun, uncovering up to ten or twenty dollars-worth of gold a day. They used a variety of tools, including wooden shovels and rude hand-made cradles used for separating gravel from the sand that was rich in small nuggets and gold placer (flakes that were smaller than nuggets but larger than specks). Shallow wooden bowls called *bateas* were used to wash away the sand under which the heavier gold was hidden. Yaqui Indians from Sonora used the dry-mine method: shoveling gold-rich dirt onto blankets and winnowing it by tossing the dirt in the air, the lighter, worthless matter floating away in clouds of dust while the gold ore and other heavy minerals sank back onto the blanket. The Indians were filthy from head to toe and were looked down on by Americans and even by their fellow Mexicans— excluding gamblers like Joaquín Murrieta.

If a miner was very lucky, he did not wait until the weekend to gamble. Bayard Taylor saw, at one mining camp, "at least a dozen monte tables, all of which were frequented at night by the Americans and Mexicans. The Sonorians [sic] left a large portion of their gold at the gaming table."[11] Alfred Doten was one of the Americans who liked to play card games with Mexicans on occasion. William Perkins frowned on gambling, but he liked to visit gambling dens to watch women who gambled or sang and danced as entertainers. Wherever there was gambling there was a bar serving drinks and Mexican men and women smoking

9. Panning for gold in the Stanislaus River. Lithograph by J. D. Borthwick, *Three Years in California* (1857).

hand-rolled cigarettes. Indian boys wound their way between the tables and spectators selling ice they had brought down from the mountains in buckets balanced on their heads.

Given the availability of liquor and the popularity of gambling, sudden conflicts sometimes arose, occasionally ending with deadly force. However this was rare in 1849.[12] Perkins marveled at "the almost perfect security with which people leave merchandise exposed night and day," even while they drank and gambled. Though thefts did occur now and then, no one worried much about thieves. Bayard Taylor said that this was because when a man was caught stealing and was shot, the shooting was viewed as an acceptable way to maintain law and order. It was not murder to shoot a thief, it was instant justice. Perkins recorded how "three Mexicans and one white man have been killed in street fights; but we have not yet heard of a single cold-blooded murder having been committed. . . . The laws, such as they are, have been respected."[13] The alcalde at Sonora town was an American of Scottish descent. The Mexican-style official served as town mayor, police chief, and judge, delivering sentences without calling for a trial by jury.

Though some semblance of law and order was kept at the mines, Bayard Taylor saw trouble brewing when he visited Columbia and noticed that too few Americans there were as industrious as Alfred Doten. Instead of mining, they took up trade, opening stores and selling goods brought from San Francisco, but there were so many stores in Columbia that prices fell. In an effort to make up losses, storekeepers turned their stores into combination inns, bars, restaurants, and gambling dens. Others targeted prosperous foreign miners and businessmen, passing edicts evicting them and then confiscating their property.[14] Taylor did not approve of such lazy and ruthless measures, but he did believe, as did Thomas Butler King, that there were too many Mexican miners.

The North Americans at Columbia complained to Taylor and King that the Sonorans had taken possession of "the best points on the Tuolumne, Stanislaus and Mokelumne Rivers," and for that reason their own efforts at mining had proved fruitless. At first, these capable Mexican miners "had been suffered to work peaceably," wrote Taylor, "but the opposition finally became so strong that they were ordered to leave. They made no resistance, but quietly backed out and took refuge in other diggings. . . . At the time of my visit . . . they were leaving the country in large numbers." According to William Perkins, the exodus of Mexican miners had to do with the weather. Sonorans packed up and left, he wrote, because they were "fearful of the cold in these high latitudes, and made their way to diggings further south, about Mariposa and King's River" in what became known as Mariposa County.

After the Sonorans left, weekends were quiet and dull. Perkins missed the music Mexicans had made every weekend and on some weekdays as well. So did Alfred Doten. Doten took off for San Francisco and worked as a musician there for about a year, returning to the mines in the fall of 1850. Meanwhile Perkins watched Sonora change into an American town. During the winter "Yankees . . . destroyed everything in the shape of romance," he wrote. "The *ramadas* or brush houses and the gay tents were all pulled down and ugly adobe or rough-hewn log huts were erected in their stead." The trees that hemmed the town were felled, and the "fronts of the habitations, once gay with streaming flags and decorated branches, were changed to the gloomy looking architecture typical of the American frontier."[15]

The Americanized Sonora was what Alfred Doten returned to in the fall and what Enos Christman found when he moved there in September of 1850. Christman set up shop for the *Sonora Herald*, a newspaper that editor John White had founded. Christman printed a little history of Sonora in the paper and described the changes brought about when the local alcalde was replaced with the more complex American town government, supported by higher taxes.

The Foreign Miners Tax and its Ugly Aftermath

Bayard Taylor saw the expulsion of foreign miners in 1849 as a spontaneous act of envy and greed committed by rowdy, lazy Americans, but Thomas Butler King saw such expulsions as acts of nationalistic protectionism. King's letter to the U.S. Secretary of State complained about how "more than 15,000 foreigners, mostly Mexicans and Chileans, came in armed bands into the mining district, bidding defiance to all opposition, and finally carrying out of the country some $20,000,000 worth of gold dust, which belonged by purchase to the people of the United States." King proposed selling mining permits to American emigrants for sixteen dollars each, permits that foreigners would not be allowed to purchase. He insisted that "this system of permits will make all who purchase them police officers, to aid in excluding from the mines all who are not entitled to, or who do not procure them." His proposal was being discussed by California's first politicians at the time he wrote his letter.[16]

American citizens gathered in San Francisco on February 12, 1850, and voted to dissolve the Mexican governmental and judicial system in California. California's leading citizens then drafted a state constitution, drew county lines, and ordered a census taken. Elections were held in March. American and Californio men voted for the first American governor, lieutenant governor, senators, assemblymen, mayors, county judges, district attorneys, town and city sheriffs, and justices of the peace.[17] Sonora town became the capital of Tuolumne County.

For Mexican immigrants like Joaquín Murrieta, these changes went largely unnoticed until the new state legislature passed the Foreign Miners' Tax Act in April 1850. The new law taxed foreign miners twenty dollars each per month to work mining claims. The year 1850 proved a slow one for miners. They were uncovering about two to four dollars worth of gold a day, all of which they spent on daily rations. The tax was exorbitant, but it was enforced all the same. Resistance was anticipated, so the legislators also granted American miners permission to assemble militias and support their sheriffs in enforcing the new law.

Lorenzo Besançon of New Orleans was appointed tax collector in Tuolumne County in spite of his reputation for siphoning funds when employed by the state of Louisiana. He quickly posted notices throughout Tuolumne County in May announcing that the new law would be enforced forthwith. Foreigners in the county converged on Sonora town and protested. They wanted the law to be redrafted. They were not opposed to the tax per se, but they complained that it was too high and that it was being enforced too hastily. They asked Tuolumne County Judge Anson Tuttle to give them three months notice and to reduce the tax to a manageable five dollars per month, a suggestion William Perkins supported. Although sympathetic, Tuttle said he did not have the authority to redraft state laws, but he urged them to draft a petition and collect signatures, then carry their complaint to the state supreme court. He could not prevent tax collectors from doing their duty, but he could get a stay on the law beginning in June for however long it took them to get a court hearing. William Perkins and his business partner signed the petition.[18] A delegation of foreign miners then carried the petition to San Francisco and sought a lawyer to represent them.

There were only about two hundred Americans living in Sonora in May 1850, many of them belligerent drinkers and gamblers from nearby Columbia. Mexicans and other foreign-born together numbered around two thousand, a number that was augmented by the arrival of protestors. Judge Tuttle and Sheriff George Work enlisted the support of some responsible Americans in keeping the peace. In spite of expressions of sympathy, tensions were high. Perkins wrote that a riot almost broke out when an American elbowed his way through a crowd in a bar and bumped into a Mexican who turned on him and drew his pistol. A correspondent for the *San Francisco Alta California* made no mention of a pushy American and quick-drawing Mexican. He wrote that things grew wild after a Chilean became unruly, insulting Americans and making threats (perhaps with a pistol in hand). Sheriff Work arrested and disarmed him with some difficulty. While he was taking the Chilean to jail, a Mexican accosted the sheriff and asked him if he intended to enforce the tax law in like manner. Work answered in the affirmative, probably adding that it was his duty. The Mexican decided it should not be so and drew his knife. An American bystander saw him draw and did likewise, slashing the would-be assailant's neck so deep that he nearly severed the head. The victim's friends immediately surged forward, threatening revenge. A well-armed group of drunk North Americans egged them on, but Anson Tuttle and George Work boldly placed themselves between the two parties and managed to calm the crowd enough to prevent a general melee. Worried that another episode might accelerate tensions beyond control, Tuttle sent messengers to Stockton and San Andreas asking for reinforcements.[19]

Tension held the night captive. William Perkins couldn't sleep. He remained armed and alert to possible arson and riots all night long. It was with relief that he heard, early next morning, the sound of fife and drums playing an American tune. The foreigners dispersed as an American militia force of some five hundred footmen and cavalry from Stockton and San Andreas marched into town. Lorenzo Besançon selected a bodyguard of about fifty cavalrymen, then set out to collect taxes, even while foreigners scrambled to pack up their belongings and leave. Perkins noticed that not a few Sonoran miners chose to hide in the mountains instead and wait for the collector to leave. This was something they had learned to do back home in Mexico to avoid conscription into unpaid gubernatorial militias.[20] Given the Féliz brothers' and Joaquín Murrieta's knowledge of the mountainous terrain in the southern mining district, which they and their confederates in crime used to their advantage when fleeing law enforcement, it is highly probable that they were among those who took to the hills in May 1850.

It is not known at what point in time that Joaquíns Murrieta and Valenzuela, Bernardo and Francisco "Pancho" Daniel, Claudio and Reyes Féliz, and other young men started stealing horses and mules, committing highway robbery and murder, and burglarizing homes and businesses. But there is ample evidence that the first bands of thieves to hit the mining districts struck hard and fast in August 1850. This was after the foreign miners petition had made it to court. San Francisco attorney Solomon Heydenfelt took the case before the State Supreme Court, where it was thrown out on grounds that the appellants had no constitutional rights in California as they were not U.S. citizens. The judge sent them to their District Court of Appeals, which heard their case and ruled in favor of the state legislature's tax law. A gleeful Lorenzo Besançon, who had not collected any taxes in June and July, took a band of about a dozen armed men and began collecting taxes from anyone who did not look like a white North American, including those who had acquired papers showing they were American citizens. Their papers were destroyed and three months worth of taxes collected, in material goods when gold was insufficient. Those who could not pay were arrested.[21] A fear of renewed trouble in Sonora town caused the North American citizens there to pass an edict on July 21, 1850, requiring all foreign-born residents "not engaged in permanent business and of respectable character" to leave the area within fifteen days. Those who were "respectable" were required to defend themselves before a committee and hand over their firearms. Hundreds of Sonorans and other foreigners packed up and left.[22]

On August 11, 1850, Enos Christman wrote, "Great excitement existed along the road on account of the horrid murders. . . . I passed the bodies of three Americans who had been killed by the Mexicans." The sight left him feeling vulnerable: "When in the distance I saw coming toward me a figure on a horse . . . I spurred my horse and he did likewise. We sped past each other, each being determined to escape death by the hand of a Mexican. But as we hurried past, each saw that the other was an American. We then turned, saluted, and continued on our journeys. . . . This country has been infested by numerous bands of Mexican guerillas, and life and property have been very insecure."[23]

The murder that triggered a major violent American response was that of a Mr. Miller from Reading, Pennsylvania, who owned and operated a roadside tavern and store with his wife. Seven Mexicans entered his store one night (some sources said there were six Mexicans and a white man), one of them engaging in friendly conversation while everyone enjoyed a few drinks at the bar. One of the Mexicans bought a sword. He thrust it at Mr. Miller, then laughed, as if it was in jest. Some while later, the swordsman lunged again when Miller's back was turned and pierced his heart. Some newspapers claimed Miller's wife was also killed. An overnight guest came out of the back room to see what the screaming was about and shot one Mexican dead, but on seeing how many there were, he turned and ran for help, night dark covering his escape route. The bandits, meanwhile, looted the store and mutilated Miller's corpse. (Although no names were assigned to the assailants in press reports, the deceptive murder method used was later mimicked by members of the Joaquín band.[24]) Miller's fate caused his friends to want to "issue an edict compelling every Mexican to leave the country," but Enos Christman thought such talk unjust.[25] Most Mexicans were hard-working and well-disposed. He did not want to see the innocent suffer with the guilty, but they did anyway.

When a Mexican and three Miwok Indians were discovered burning a tent with two corpses inside, they were arrested by four American miners and marched to Sonora town, where they were seized by a lynch mob and dragged to a hilltop tree. A noose was thrown around the Mexican's neck. Realizing he was about to die, "he fell upon his knees, kissed a cross he carried in his bosom, uttered a prayer in Spanish, and resigned himself to his fate," wrote Christman. Judge Tuttle "begged the people not to assume so great a responsibility but to let the law take its course and justice would be done." They did not listen. Perkins saw Judge Tuttle and Sheriff Work, with a couple of deputies, mount a charge on the lynch mob, firing over the heads of the would-be executioners and seizing their prisoners. The Mexican ran to save his life, as the other end of the noose was tied to the retreating sheriff's saddle pommel. He managed to stay on his feet and all four prisoners were placed in jail.[26]

The jail was closely guarded while a coroner went to examine the partially burnt corpses. He came back and said the two had been killed several days before they were set afire. The prisoners had told the truth; they had found the bodies by the stink they made and agreed to burn them in keeping with Miwok sepulture customs.

Meanwhile sixty heavily armed Americans came marching into Sonora town "to the sound of fife and drum, and bearing the American flag" as if marching to war. They were from Murphy's Camp, wrote Christman, and they came seeking the Mexicans who murdered Miller. "They halted opposite the court house, where Judge Tuttle addressed them . . . urging them to . . . respect the laws." While they were refreshing themselves at local saloons, a rumor spread to the effect that the Mexican and the three Indians in jail were members of "a band of guerrillas, headed by a notorious Mexican chief, in a camp some three or four miles distant, who plundered and murdered the people whenever an opportunity offered."[27] Harry Love would liken Joaquín Murrieta's confederates to bands of Mexican guerrillas in 1853. In 1852 Claudio Féliz would be depicted as the chieftain of a guerrilla band, and in 1857 Juan Flores and Pancho Daniel would be given the dubious honor. But in 1850 the guerrilla band leader had no name.[28]

Sheriff George Work tried to dispel the rumor of a Mexican guerrilla band but could not. Fearing what the men from Murphy's might do if he remained disengaged, he agreed to select twenty of their party and go investigate the suspected Mexican camp. The camp was full of peaceable family groups, but Work's overzealous posse insisted on treating them like enemies. To protect them, Work persuaded the Mexican men in camp to go with him to Sonora for questioning. He told them of the recent murder of Mr. Miller and said the men with him were looking for the murderers.[29] Seeing twenty mounted Anglo-Americans march over a hundred Mexican pedestrians to Sonora town attracted attention. Soon several hundred North Americans arrived in armed bands, all of them mobilized by rumors of Mexican guerrillas at war with American authorities.

The Mexican men were confined to a corral and questioned one at a time. A bilingual young man from among them offered to interpret. They all said the same thing: their caravan had only just arrived; they had set up camp yesterday; they did not learn about the murders until they were arrested; and they had no idea who the killers were. This caused mistrust of the interpreter, who was suspected of hiding the truth. He was taken to a tree and dangled by the neck several times but he consistently insisted he had nothing to hide. Finally allowed to go, the unlucky immigrants were again transformed into Mexican guerrillas by American rumors. "It was reported," wrote Christman, "that an armed Mexican force of over one hundred men had just passed within sight of the town, meditating an attack," but it turned out the Mexicans "with their pack animals . . . [were] on their way home, poor and dispirited. They had come here, many of them with their families, for the purpose of becoming good citizens and settling in this country. They thought, and very justly, too, that they should not have to suffer because a few bad men" were their countrymen.[30]

Among those "few bad men" were teenagers like Claudio and Reyes Féliz, Pancho and Bernardo Daniel, and Joaquíns Valenzuela and Murrieta. Murrieta was arrested on November 28, 1850, in Stockton, for stealing a pair of boots from Hyman Mitchell's store. When questioned, he said he had come from Camp Seco in Calaveras County, where he worked as a miner, that he was eighteen years old, and that he had been in Stockton for the past five months or so. As for the boots, those were given to him. The court record, however, did not record the prisoner's sentence. Given the content of Teodor Vásquez's confession, which historian James F. Varley discovered, Murrieta served a short jail sentence and suffered a flogging before being released.[31]

The Vigilante Response to Crime

Although the notorious Foreign Miners Tax Act was rescinded in the fall of 1850, murders continued to be reported and vigilantism became the popular response. (American merchants in Stockton and elsewhere were the ones who caused the state legislature to rescind the law: the sharp decline in the mining population left them with far fewer customers, and their businesses faced financial ruin if the unpopular law was not rescinded.) A frigid winter and the floods that followed interrupted crime at the mines for a time, then came reports of more murders and robberies. By 1851 the Claudio Féliz and Joaquín Murrieta band had been active from Yuba County to Mariposa County. In the spring of 1851 Perkins admitted it was "next to impossible to say who are the guilty parties" in murder cases, but in his opinion Mexicans were to blame. "The Mexicans . . . are actually *fond* of butchering the white men, . . . they show no mercy, but butcher with all the savage cruelty of wild beasts." He went on to echo what Christman had said a year earlier: "There are organized bands of Mexicans headed by white men; the former warring against the Americans for revenge, the latter for plunder." The white men were reportedly "bad characters" from Sydney, Australia. "A murder committed by a white man," wrote Perkins, "is done in the shortest and most simple manner and the body left where it falls." Only when the corpse was found "disfigured and mutilated" was it the work of Mexicans thirsty for revenge, in his opinion—an opinion influenced in part by actual events.[32]

Both William Perkins and Alfred Doten took part in vigilante trials and executions of Mexican aggressors in June 1851. For Perkins the case involved three Mexican miners who conspired to murder Captain George W. Snow, from whom they bought a claim on credit. When the captain came to collect payment, one of them attacked him with a knife. He struggled and shouted, "Murder! Murder!" Twisting out of his attacker's grasp, he ran for help to a camp about a quarter of a mile away, where he collapsed. Snow had been stabbed several times. He was carried to Sonora town and there died. Perkins saw him and was horrified. Captain Snow was in his fifties, and at the time of the attack he was unarmed. A search for the culprits resulted in the arrest of two Mexicans who were identified by Snow before he died. One broke down and confessed. The other only glowered. William Perkins served on the vigilance committee that tried, condemned, and hanged both of them.[33] He was confident that the hanging would deter other criminals, and for awhile it seemed to work.

Alfred Doten took part in a vigilante act in December 1851. Four days before Christmas, following a tranquil day of panning, he was writing in his journal when interrupted by the cry, "To arms! To arms!!! Get your rifles!" He dropped his pencil, picked up his revolver, and went out to see what was up. About twenty others did the same. They followed the sentinel to a Mexican camp just up the gulch that had only been there for two weeks. Their purpose was to find the Mexicans who attacked Alex McDonald and Jacob E. Chinn with swords.[34]

While on their way to the Mexican Camp, the sentinel explained how McDonald, Chinn, and several others—himself included—had gone to a bar at the Mexican camp, but found the place crowded. Alex McDonald and Jacob Chinn wanted to order drinks at the bar but could not get near enough to do so. Alex became impatient and nudged a Mexican aside, causing him to bump into his friend. Angered, the two left, the one who was pushed saying "espera un poco" (I'll be back). They returned armed with swords and attacked Alex and his friend, Jacob. Alex was unarmed and shouted at Jacob to shoot. Caught off guard, Chinn backed through a canvas wall while struggling to draw his revolver. Meanwhile Alex shielded himself with his arms and backed out the door. He fell over a log just as the Mexican coming at him lunged, the sword blade passing over him. The Mexican turned to go, but found his escape path blocked by James "Old Uncle Jimmy" Plydale. He struck Plydale on the head with the pommel of his sword "purely because he was a white man," wrote Doten, and made good his escape. An American helped Alex to his feet just as Jacob freed his pistol and fired. He missed his assailant, but Alex cried out that he'd been shot. Jacob fired again and hit his Mexican assailant in the hip, causing him to retreat quickly.[35]

Doten was personally acquainted with both Alex and Jacob, the latter being a fellow musician. He helped carry Alex to Perry's store and sat up with him all night. The doctor said he would likely die, as the sword wounds on his arms and hands were grave. Watching Alex McDonald suffer provoked Doten into summoning vigilantes the next morning and going in search of the culprits. Jacob Chinn led another party. They arrested a large Mexican, who was hiding under a bed, and also the one Chinn had wounded in the hip. Both Mexicans were taken to Perry's store where Doten worked part-time as a clerk and bartender and where the gravely wounded Alex McDonald lay dying.

Alex died before his friends and fellow Mexican war veterans from the mining town of Columbia arrived. Grief-stricken and bitterly angry, one of his friends wanted to shoot both prisoners but Doten and the others insisted on holding a trial. Alfred Doten served on the ad hoc jury. "We had not brought in more than half of our evidence, but as this was considered enough, the jury retired—about this time the rest of those friends of Alex who started from Columbia . . . arrived." The jury knew they had no choice but to condemn the Mexicans to death as they would most certainly be lynched or shot in revenge for Alex's death. "The wounded one hardly moved after he was run up and seemed to die easily," wrote Doten, but the other Mexican was a tall large-boned man, who, "being very heavy, . . . the rope broke and he dropped. . . . He got on his knees and cried 'pardón! pardón! Santiago!'" He was strung up again and "writhed about and seemed to die hard. . . . The howling and roaring of the wind through the tall pines and the warring elements rendering the scene awful and terrific in the extreme and one that will never be effaced from the memory."[36] There was thunder and lightning over nearby mountains. For Doten, who was from Plymouth, Massachusetts, the scene must have brought to mind stories he'd grown up with about the hanging of accused witches at Salem. The nightmarish experience was not one he cared to repeat. He never again answered a call to arms, even when living four miles outside Mokelumne Hill at the height of the Joaquín scare in the winter of 1853.

What Doten's and Perkins's experiences show is that when a violent act occurred, whether provoked or not, citizens often took it upon themselves to satisfy the requirements of the law to the best of their ability. Their efforts resulted in hastily carried-out executions in cases involving deadly assault of unarmed men. Perkins believed the immediate hanging of murderers was necessary in order to discourage others from plotting murder. Doten believed the death sentence was inevitable, given the extreme grief and lust for vengeance exhibited by Alex's friends. Doten and Perkins also reveal, through their diaries, the impact that vigilante justice could have on a man. Perkins was ready and willing to take part in such procedures again if necessary. And he came away with a much lower opinion of Mexicans as a people. He had already begun to see them as blood-thirsty, untrustworthy, and prejudiced against whites. Doten, on the other hand, recognized that prejudice was not unique to any single group and that hanging a man—however deserving—was horrific. A couple of days after the hanging, Doten saw a sulking and drunk Mexican come into Perry's store to buy some dry goods. Alex's friends were sharing drinks at the bar and saw the embittered Mexican glance at them and utter an insult aimed at Americans in general. One of Alex's friends swung around and belted him. Then he and his drinking buddies began pummeling the Mexican bloody with fist and boot. Doten and Perry intervened, risking their lives to stop the well-armed Americans from killing the man. Doten was so devoid of prejudice, he even went back to the Mexican camp where he had helped make arrests and sat down to play cards in one of the gambling tents.[37] He saw good and bad on an individual rather than a group basis. He made no mention anywhere in his diary of a Mexican guerrilla threat.

Clashes like the one that cost Alex his life were common in gold rush California. Sometimes it had to do with a perceived insult. More

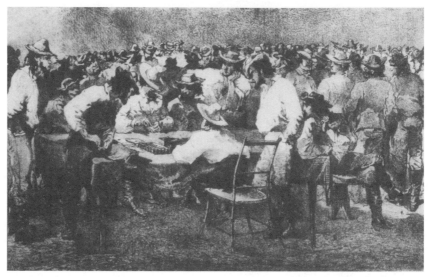

10. Monte at the mines. Lithograph by J. D. Borthwick, *Three Years in California* (1857).

often it had to do with women. Joaquín Murrieta was undoubtedly present when a fight broke out in a fandango tent at Melones (now under the Melones water reserve). William Perkins recorded what he heard of that event. On the night of June 13, 1851, two women, one with an American gambler, the other with a Mexican, started fighting. Their dance partners intervened. Then the Mexican drew a sword and made an ineffectual pass at the American. According to the *San Francisco Herald*, it was Captain William M. Acklin, of Alabama, who stepped forward to make peace and was wounded by the swordsman, even though a number of Mexicans, Joaquín Murrieta among them, shouted at their countryman not to kill the captain. Murrieta was probably the monte dealer who lost his bank—to the amount of twelve hundred dollars—during the melee that followed.[38]

Three Mexicans were killed and a dozen wounded during the melee. The Mexican swordsman ended up pinned to the floor with his own sword. In his last burst of fury he shouted, "Mata, mata a los carajos Yengis!" (Kill them, kill the damned Yankees!)[39] Perkins's opinion of Mexicans as a people had fallen so low by then that he was convinced they all were too cowardly to die fighting. He suspected the fallen swordsman was a Chilean but was called a "Mexican" because all Hispanics were Mexicans and "greasers" to ignorant Americans.

The melee at Melones occurred after a new tax law was passed requiring foreign miners to pay four dollars a month to work a claim. Bands of American thieves saw easy money and, pretending to be tax collectors, took advantage of ignorance and fear. Meanwhile the real tax collectors found large foreign mining companies well-armed and defiant.[40] They refused to pay the tax. These companies were depicted as threatening in newspapers, even as Mexican outlaw activities continued to arouse fears of an organized guerrilla band. The melee was cited as evidence of a secret confederacy of Mexicans. According to Perkins's sources, Acklin's American friends had reached for their guns when a sword was drawn against him, but the Mexicans, who outnumbered the Americans, disarmed them and turned their guns on them, forcing them to leave. After they left, the triumphant Mexicans fired into the air and celebrated with exuberant dancing and fanfare. They were caught off guard when the Americans returned with reinforcements at dawn.

Close Encounters with Members of the Band

Although there were newspaper articles about Mexican guerrilla bands and their chiefs during the summer of 1850, there was no mention of Joaquín Murrieta or Claudio Féliz until the confession of Teodor Vásquez was published in February 1852. Teodor said that during the summer of 1851 Claudio and Reyes Féliz, Joaquín Murrieta, Miguel Sasuelta, a Chilean, an American, and five other Mexicans, rode to San Jose, stole forty-five horses and mules from a Mr. Gee, herded them to Marysville and sold them. Then they rode to Camp Seco in Calaveras County and lost all their money playing monte.[41] The earliest mention of Joaquín and Claudio in private journals appeared in those of Alfred Doten and William Perkins.

Perkins and his Chilean business partner Ramón Navarro traveled to San Francisco during the first week of April 1852 to purchase supplies, their warehouse being empty after a long, harsh winter. On the way they stopped in Sacramento. While there, they heard about a recent highway murder and robbery that had been committed in broad daylight. They took the steamer to San Francisco, purchased goods, arranged to have them shipped to Sonora by riverboat, and, after enjoying some good entertainment, returned home by way of Stockton. Navarro continued on to Sonora, riding Perkins's horse, Perkins having decided to stay with their goods all the way to Knight's Ferry and take the stagecoach home from there. Knight's Ferry was then owned by the Dent brothers and called Dentsville.

Perkins arrived at Dentsville too late to catch the stagecoach. While there he heard an old teamster talk about how he had been driving toward Stockton alongside a young man who was also driving a wagon, and they had been followed by three Mexicans. He described them in detail. He said that he stopped to light his pipe less than a mile from Knight's Ferry, but the young man decided to continue on and soon disappeared behind a knoll. When he caught up with him, he found to his horror that the young man had been shot dead and was lying in his own blood, his pockets having been rifled.[42] It was April 8, 1852, when Perkins wrote the following entry:

> For sometime back there have been stories rife of a certain 'Joaquin' a valiant Mexican, who, for many injuries received from the Americans, has vowed a bloody revenge, and he has formed a band of brigands who scour the country and assassinate white men whenever they can do so with impunity. This Joaquin is already a celebrated character, and many stories, that would do honor to Dick Turpin, are told of him by the Spanish races, and some of them are marvelous enough. Whether they be true or false, the fact is that many people have mysteriously disappeared, and four murders committed on the Stockton Road within a couple of weeks.[43]

Perkins had to borrow a horse from the Dent brothers to get home. It was a fat, sturdy animal, but not particularly fast. He hoped the three Mexicans the old man had seen were no longer in the area, but they were.

> I had barely traveled a couple of miles, . . . when just in front of me I saw the very three men so accurately described by the old teamster, . . . I am not ashamed to say that my heart jumped to my throat. The men were coming toward me. . . . I drew the pummel of my revolver to the front, grasping it with my right hand and cocking it in its pouch; with my other hand I

pulled my horse out of the road and let him fall into a walk. . . . I put on as fierce and careless a look as possible, looking full at them as they passed me and turning well round in my saddle to keep them in view. They did not salute, as Mexicans almost invariably do on the road, if peaceably inclined. . . . As soon as I had got to a respectable distance, I dug the spurs into my fat horse's side and got him into a gallop, . . . but during my four hours ride that night, my imagination was continually suggesting the sudden apparition of the three Mexicans from the bushes and on either side of the road.[44]

The next day, still troubled by the experience, Perkins scribbled, "Whether the much talked of 'Joaquin' be a myth or a bona-fide personage, I cannot say, but that murders and robberies on the plains, on the roads and in the mountain fastnesses are becoming rife, is an indisputable certainty. There is no doubt at all that the ruffians of the country are systematizing their operations, forming bands, and acting under chiefs to form regular plans. . . . This state of things is a natural consequence of the laxity of the administration of the laws and the unpardonable carelessness of the government."[45] Two months later his business partner said he was going to sell his share in the business and return home to Chile. He invited Perkins to join him, adding he would be happy to introduce him to his sisters. Perkins joined him and ended up marrying into the Navarro family while making a new life for himself in Chile. It was a wise choice, for the warehouse they had sold burned down a month after they left.

Meanwhile Alfred Doten was still mining and working part time in Perry's store. He was robbed several times by Mexicans in 1851 and 1852. His life was even threatened once by a surly member of the Claudio Féliz band. However Doten never concluded that all Mexicans were thieves. He admired Mexican musicians and dancers as much as they admired his fiddle playing. In August 1852 he wrote, "Some Mexicans paid us a visit and we had quite a fandango as one of them played the violin well and another one danced very well indeed—rattles on his feet."[46]

Later that week he joined a fandango band of five Mexicans and two Chileans and thoroughly enjoyed himself. Then a drunk Mexican came

11. Alfred Doten, c. 1864. Pencil drawing by the author.

into Perry's store while Doten was working as clerk and bartender. He was loud and obnoxious. Doten ordered him to leave. He refused. "I drew my revolver," wrote Doten, "and told him to go or I would shoot him— He was very much frightened and started off, I followed close at his heels . . . for about a mile and then bade him good night and telling him that if he came back again I would shoot him—He stayed there about Don Juan's house, making a great noise and wanted a pistol so that he could come back to shoot me." No one gave him a pistol.[47]

On September 4, 1852, the same troublesome Mexican came back into Perry's Store, but this time he was quiet. He spent an hour or so browsing, then bought some bread and left. Doten's Mexican neighbors told him to be on guard as the young man was lurking about and making threats. Doten assured them he always kept his gun in good condition and within easy reach at night and that his dog—a stray he had adopted— would sound the alarm if anyone approached while he slept.

That night his dog barked on and off. The next morning the threatening Mexican showed up again, bought some crackers, and left. Two days later, Alfred Doten wrote, "My Mexican does not visit me!"—as if he missed the thrill of the threat. He then recorded what he'd learned about him: "He is one of a band of robbers, six of them in all, who are going about the country stealing what they can—They are headed by Cladne [sic] a noted desperado and a very brave fellow." He then recorded the adventure Caleb Dorsey participated in, during which Claudio and band rescued his brother, Reyes. "He [Claudio] had two colt revolvers and he fought them till he fell from his horse with many wounds and then fired away at them as he lay on the ground—They took him prisoner to Stockton [sic] where by some means or other he was acquitted and set free again and with a paper from the Governor, certifying to the goodness of his character. . . . As soon as he recovered from his wounds he organized his band again and is as bad as ever."[48] At the time Doten wrote about Claudio in his diary, newspaper stories were describing Claudio Féliz as the chief of the guerrilla band in Tuolumne County that had reportedly been "broken up" in July 1852. Dorsey believed that Claudio had reformed as he refrained from criminal activity for several months, but he apparently did so because of his wounds. Once healthy, he was back in the saddle.

Alfred Doten was clearly impressed by Claudio's courage, but unlike Enos Christman he saw no evidence of a well-organized band of Mexican guerrillas. And unlike William Perkins, Doten never saw Mexicans as inherently cowardly and vengeful by nature or as hating all white men. Although he did use the derogatory word "Greaser" when writing about Mexicans in his diary, he also scribbled observations about how Mexicans used the word "Yankee" as an insult. To him it was funny hearing someone snarl "Yankee!" He was proud of his Yankee roots and embraced the word.[49]

Christman, Doten, and Perkins recognized that prejudice was not unique to white Americans. Everybody in California seemed to think they and their countrymen and women were better than everyone else. They were unapologetic about their preferences but often proved capable of setting aside racial and cultural differences. Perkins did so when dealing with Chileans like Navarro and when admiring Mexican women;

Christman did so when expressing alarm at racist edicts forcing all Mexicans out of Sonora, thereby punishing the innocent and industrious while the guilty and dangerous hid in the hills; and Doten did so whenever sharing harmony and rhythm in moments of merriment and mingling. Even outlaws did so when they formed multi-racial bands.

Mexican Guerrillas in Post-war California

Talk of well-armed, well-organized Mexican guerrilla bands in California began in the summer of 1850 and continued for several years. Clashes like the one at Melones, in which Mexicans reportedly disarmed Americans, fed such rumors. Louise Smith Clappe wrote a letter describing how eight young Mexicans and one woman in men's clothing pledged to stand together against Anglo-Saxon assailants. One of them knifed an Irish-American to death for insulting the Mexicana in vaquero attire and then paraded about, waving the bloody murder weapon with pride until American vigilantes arrived. He escaped, but one of those he left behind was flogged, and all the others were exiled.[50]

Murrieta, Valenzuela, and the Féliz and Daniel brothers grew up in a country that frequently suffered from armed clashes and guerrilla warfare. Indian guerrillas rebelled violently against taxation and land confiscation beginning in the 1820s in Sonora, Mexico. They sacked and burned rural towns and isolated haciendas where they had worked as farm hands, cowboys, and miners—without being paid for their labor. Political factions also took up arms against each other, sometimes inciting Indian guerrilla bands against their opponents. Apaches raiders also swept in, pressing further and further south and forcing the seat of the government of Sonora to move from Arispe to Ures. Sonora was not a place where boys learned to be obedient and docile. To survive, they had to be quick, cunning, and suspicious of nearly everyone.

The idea that Mexican teenage boys had formed guerrilla bands in California did not come from Mexicans familiar with such bands. It came from Americans. Many North Americans felt threatened by Mexican outlaw bands and with good reason, but the solution to an outlaw problem was in upholding and enforcing the law as did Sheriff Work. However the solution to a guerrilla threat was war against Mexicans in California. There were calls for extermination, meaning forced exile from the state. Forced eviction happened frequently at the mines. The men who called for this kind of action were often supportive of filibuster invasions of Baja California and Sonora. They hoped to see the American border pushed south of the Gulf of California. They were caught up in a post-Mexican American War euphoria and coveted still more wealth and power. They came from New York and from the South, they were Yankees and future Confederates. Some of them ran for office and served in the state legislature in California. As legislators they urged the passing of laws that would, for example, deny constitutional rights to mestizo citizens based on how much American Indian blood ran in their veins.

The perception of the Joaquín band as a large and threatening Mexican presence in California that some vociferous Americans wanted to exterminate gave rise, many decades later, to the Mexican-American perception of the Joaquín band as a force fighting back in the face of racial persecution. There is no evidence that anyone in the band ever set out or even thought about setting out to fight persecution, but there is also no evidence supporting the claim that the band posed a Mexican guerrilla threat. North Americans who called for removal of Mexicans in the 1850s seem to have been caught in a war mentality. Ironically, the legendary Joaquín band, depicted as a large (hundreds strong), well-organized guerrilla band, has become an empowering image to Mexican-Americans retrospectively, even though that depiction of the band originated with white people whose aspirations were shaped by manifest destiny.

In reality, armed outlaws in the 1850s were dangerous in the same way armed criminals are today. It is only in legends that bandits become something other than what they really are. It will always be fun to read about being kidnapped by Caribbean pirates long ago but it is not fun actually being kidnapped by Somali pirates today. William Perkins had reason to be alert and tense when he crossed paths with three armed Mexicans soon after hearing about a robbery and murder committed in the vicinity by three armed Mexicans who matched their description. Real bandits are indiscriminate and often deadly.

3. The Perspective of the *Los Angeles Star* and *La Estrella*

Another point of view regarding bandits appeared in *La Estrella*, the Spanish section of the *Los Angeles Star*. *La Estrella* served descendants of Spanish colonial and Mexican pioneer settlers in southern California—the "Californios." The editor, Señor Manuel Clemente Rojo, was a Peruvian immigrant.[1] Joaquín Murrieta and band became newsworthy in his columns between November 1852 and September 1853, a period in which the band was featured in virtually every other newspaper in the state. But *La Estrella* offered Spanish readers a point of view not found in English language newspapers of the day.

Manuel Clemente Rojo had settled in Baja California in 1848. Two years later he made his way north to Los Angeles, crossing an uncharted border. He knew that a war between Mexico and the United States had ended with the signing of a treaty that ceded Alta California and other Mexican territory to the United States, and that Mexican citizens in California were invited to stay and become U.S. citizens. Rojo found that idea appealing. He admired the U.S. constitutional government and its comparative stability.

The Californios who read *La Estrella* had lived through some of Mexico's post-revolutionary turmoil. Mexico's original egalitarian constitution, as drafted by liberals who tried to copy the example set by the still young United States to the north, was popular with Californios, as were the liberal governors Mexico sent them in the 1820s. But in the 1830s conservatives forced the liberals out and revised the constitution to insure a hierarchical system. They replaced California's liberal governor with a series of narcissistic tyrants who provoked rebellions. In 1836 the Californios were finally permitted to be governed by one of their own, Juan Alvarado, but during his term in office, the more conservative southern Californios threatened to break away from their northern California liberal-minded state government. They appealed to Mexico's dictatorial president, Antonio López de Santa Anna.

Santa Anna sent them General Manuel Micheltorena, with an army of three hundred *cholos* (also can mean "soldiers") to govern California. Micheltorena did not have the means to pay his soldiers, and so they indulged in crime. He, too, was ousted, mostly because he made no attempt to discipline his soldiers. Don Pío Pico of Los Angeles became governor in 1845, although not without opposition from northern Californios. A year later North and South came together to fight the invading U.S. military, although not out of any sense of loyalty to Mexico. Pío Pico's brother, General Andrés Pico distinguished himself in battle before the Californios were forced to surrender.

The Californios who read Manuel Clemente Rojo's columns in *La Estrella* had employed cholos, Sonoran immigrants, and local Indians when fighting American soldiers in 1846. When they lost they signed a truce well before the war was over and began to look for ways of maintaining a voice in a new local and state government now run by North Americans. They watched U.S. politicians vie with each other for power and took sides based on what best matched their own political agendas. The Picos of Los Angeles sided with the Southern Democrats. Manuel Rojo, who shared a law office with Isaac Stockton Keith Ogier, Esq., a Democrat from Charleston, South Carolina, was influenced by Ogier and join the Democratic Party.[2] Rojo served at local Democratic Party conventions as interpreter. Criminally inclined cholos, meanwhile, finding no work as soldiers, reverted to stealing horses and robbing people. Many of them joined outlaw bands, like the one affiliated with Joaquín Murrieta, Claudio Féliz, and Pancho Daniel.

On November 6, 1852, Manuel C. Rojo wrote an editorial criticizing American politicians for courting Californio voters by declaring themselves "friends of peace" while accusing the opposition of being "enemy instigators" of the recent war with Mexico. Such superfluous animosity was a waste of ink and paper, he argued. American Democrats should instead point out the key differences between Whigs and

Democrats. Whigs were centralists. They favored sending a large percentage of California's wealth east, to the central government in Washington DC, while Democrats insisted California's gold ought to be spent on California interests. He favored the latter position, as did his fellow Hispanic Democrats.

Rojo's editorials were never translated and reprinted in English language newspapers, though he often translated and reprinted news from their columns, including news about Joaquín. His employers had connections with papers in the North. Indeed they had come to Los Angeles from San Francisco. They established a dual-language newspaper, not out of a sense of public duty or desire to serve the sizeable Spanish-speaking sector in southern California. They did it for money. Government funding was available to newspapers that published the new state constitution and laws in Spanish for the sake of Californio citizens. Manuel C. Rojo was perfect for the editorial job. He was bilingual and already serving as a courtroom translator and legal adviser, as well as being a lawyer and avid student of American law.

Los Angeles Star proprietor John A. Lewis had sent his partner, John McElroy, to Los Angeles in March 1851, but lack of paper caused printing delays. The first issue came out in May. It was printed in a room on the second floor of the Bella Union hotel and saloon, in downtown Los Angeles. When young Horace Bell stopped by there one evening he found Rojo working alone. Another local resident, Harris Newmark, remembered Rojo as "a clever, genial native of Peru" who "translated testimony well" and was "honest and conscientious."[3] In addition to printing a translation of the state constitution and recently enacted laws, Rojo published love songs, philosophical dialogues, news clips from Mexican and South American newspapers, and Catholic moral lessons contributed by the local parish priest, Fr. Anacleto Lestrades. Local news included horse races, weddings, funerals, dances, picnics, and, of course, crime stories.

In spite of fairly regular fights between gamblers and Indians over women and real or perceived insults, life in the sun-baked pueblo of Los Angeles was slow and a bit dull. The town was composed of adobe structures squatting back to back, with most local houses, stores, bars, and restaurants looking alike. Few buildings had windows, so doors were

12. Bella Union Hotel in Los Angeles, from an 1857 lithograph. Author's collection.

left open to let in light, with the result that horses and dogs wandered in, amid flies. Lumber was scarce, so floors were of hard packed, swept dirt. It was along Calle de los Negros, the only part of town boasting covered boardwalks, that people indulged in "drinking, smoking and gambling, and . . . dancing," Harris Newmark recalled. "Men and women alike were to be found . . . dealing monte and faro. . . . Those in charge of the banks were always provided with pistols, and were ready, if an emergency arose, to settle disputes on the spot."[4] Although American farmers, ranchers, public-office seekers, and gamblers were sprinkled throughout the county, Los Angeles looked and sounded Mexican. Even the black men in town spoke Spanish: they were Californios or emigrants from Baja California and the descendents of freed slaves.

Mexican emigrants from Sonora and Sinaloa, Mexico, and New Mexico Territory in the United States, built a neighborhood known as "Sonora Town" on the east side of the Los Angeles River (not to be confused with the Sonora town near Marysville or the one in Tuolumne County). The river's clay-colored waters roared violently after winter rains, then dropped to a quiet swirl of clear water in which children bathed and women washed clothes. The Sonoran side of town was the Los Angeles

Joaquín Murrieta visited, but he and Reyes Féliz, Juan Flores, and Pancho Daniel also visited mission towns and Indian villages or *rancherías* at San Gabriel, San Juan Capistrano, and Santa Ana. Not far from San Gabriel was El Monte, an American town built by wagon train families from Utah, Missouri, Arkansas, and Texas. A militia known as the "Monte boys" policed that neighborhood and occasionally fought Indians who stole horses and other goods. They were the kind of Americans Hispanic youths like Daniel and Murrieta admired for their rugged independence, and hated for their lynch law tendencies.

Other Hispanic youths, like fourteen-year-old Francisco P. Ramírez, admired Yankees like John McElroy, who loved the American free press and its power to influence public opinion. Ramírez worked as an apprentice for McElroy and Rojo, but both McElroy and Ramírez left in fall of 1851. Ramírez was sent by his parents to attend a Catholic college in Northern California, and McElroy went north after John Lewis and William H. Rand came to take over the *Star*. It was Lewis, Rand, and Rojo who covered the first vigilante trial held in Los Angeles. The crime was highway murder and theft. Murrieta and Reyes Féliz were in town, but they were not the perpetrators, though they were undoubtedly acquainted with those who were.

Harry Love and the Joaquíns Murrieta and Valenzuela

Joaquín Murrieta had slipped quietly into Los Angeles County in June 1852, just ahead of Harry Love and his partner. Love stopped by the *Star* office to inform the editors that he and his companion had been trailing a band of Sonoran robbers some three hundred miles and had captured one of them. They had come from Mariposa. In mid-April two Mexican miners at Agua Fría, near Mariposa, were murdered, the robbers having riddled their bodies with bullets and slit their throats. A fourteen-year-old Mexican boy was mortally knifed a few days later, but the murder that motivated Harry Love and partner to take action involved a U.S. citizen.[5]

On Monday, April 19, 1852, young Allen Ruddle was killed while driving a wagon from his family's ranch in the vicinity of the Merced River to Stockton, where he intended to purchase furniture for his mother. He was ambushed near Forbe's ranch on the Tuolumne River. Reportedly unarmed, he used his whip as a weapon, but was shot in the arms, then lassoed, dragged and shot through the torso and head. He was robbed of four hundred dollars. The Ruddle family offered a reward for the capture of Ruddle's killers, prompting several posses to go in pursuit.[6] Ruddle's sad fate was attributed to Joaquín Murrieta in legend.

Harry Love and partner were the most dogged pursuers. They stopped at Joaquín Valenzuela's house near the Merced River, suspecting he had something to do with the murder and robbery, or, if not, that he might know something. But Joaquín was not home. His wife was unsure of his whereabouts. Love asked her about the fair-haired, blue-eyed six-year-old white girl called Ann who was living there and spoke only Spanish. She said Ann had been entrusted to her and her husband at Marysville, two years ago. Suspecting illicit practices, Harry Love took the girl to Allen Ruddle's brother, Mariposa County Judge John Ruddle, who served as the child's guardian while advertising in Stockton newspapers for the parents. Her widowed mother claimed her about two years later, after moving to Stockton and seeing the ad.[7] Meanwhile Love and his partner learned that three Mexicans on fatigued horses had been seen crossing the Merced River on a ferry where it emptied into the San Joaquin River.

The outlaws traded in their horses for fresh ones at Rancho Orestimba, west of San Jose, then headed south with a small herd of stolen horses, mingling briefly with twenty or more horse thieves in a valley west of Mission San Juan Bautista and southwest of Pacheco Pass. Local Indians and various bands of thieves shared a corral that held up to a hundred horses. Most of the bandits were Mexicans or Indians, newspapers reported, but there were North American bandits, too.[8] Harry Love, an unnamed partner from Mariposa, Sebastian Nuñez, and Yrenero Corona of Rancho Orestimba tracked Joaquín Murrieta and band all the way to Tejon Indian country, where Chief Zapatero's men reported having captured the robbers.[9]

The Indians delivered up all the horses and tack that bore the mark of Rancho Orestimba to Nuñez and Corona, who then returned home. Harry Love, however, continued looking for Ruddle's murderers and finally arrested one of them on the road between San Buenaventura and Los Angeles. At Rabbit's Bend, "about eight miles this side of the river," Love told the *Star* editors, his prisoner "complained of thirst and pointed to a ravine near at hand." The *Star* reported that "Mr. Lull [*sic*] dismounted and proceeded with the man . . . when the prisoner darted forward" in an attempt to escape. Harry Love lunged after him and tried to knock him out with his pistol when it accidentally discharged and put a bullet through the young man's head. The name of the prisoner was not published, but before the year ended everyone in Los Angeles knew that his given name was Pedro and that he had been in company with Reyes Féliz and Joaquín Murrieta.[10]

Harry Love's report was printed only in the English section of the *Star*. Rojo had no space to spare, having filled his columns with news from Baja California and Sonora, territory that filibusters in California coveted. Rojo's law partner, Isaac Ogier, wholly supported filibuster "settlers" and the idea of pushing the U.S. border still further south. In fact, Rojo noted, the governor of Sonora had invited people in Alta California to come settle in northern Sonora and fight Apaches, an offer French miners in California accepted. Rojo himself considered accepting the offer. U.S. citizens were not welcome, but Peruvians were.

Harry Love and his companion left Los Angeles without making further arrests. Joaquín Murrieta and Reyes Féliz successfully avoided capture—for the time being. Sixteen-year-old Reyes had been mauled by a bear and spent a couple of months recovering. Twenty-year-old Joaquín, meanwhile, enjoyed the company of Ana Benites, played monte, and probably worked part-time training horses—perhaps the same horses he would steal later. While he and Reyes Féliz avoided trouble, a fellow Sonoran and a Californio fugitive committed murder using an ancient Yaqui Indian weapon: the club.

Zabaleta and Rivas Provoke Vigilante Action

In early July 1852 two livestock buyers identified as B. F. McCoy and a German named Ludwig were reported missing under suspicious circumstances. They had come from San Francisco aboard the *Robinson*. At San Pedro they purchased two saddle ponies and supplies, and then they set out for San Gabriel, buying beef cattle and horses along the way. They continued on toward San Juan Capistrano, where they intended to make more purchases, the plan being to drive the herd north to Sacramento and sell at inflated prices. A disastrous flood had wiped out livestock in the Sacramento Valley, making horses and cattle scarce. The two of them had about four hundred dollars on them when they vanished. The same day they were reported missing, Don Manuel Gárcias reported that one of his finest sorrel horses and best saddles had been stolen, an exhausted saddle pony having been left in its place. He suspected Doroteo Zabaleta, who had recently escaped from jail. He and Sheriff William Barton set out in pursuit with a couple of deputies, one of them Barton's good friend, Dr. William Osburn. (Both Barton and Osburn would play roles in later crime investigations involving the Joaquín band when Juan Flores and Pancho Daniel were the band leaders.)

The sheriff's posse tracked the horse thief north into Santa Barbara County. Meanwhile the sheriff of Santa Barbara, Valentine Hearne, had already been notified of a Los Angeles jail break. Hearne and his deputy, Jack Powers, found the fugitive, Doroteo Zabaleta, spending liberally in a local saloon. When arrested, Zabaleta gave an alibi and named two Sonoran youths, Francisco Carmello and Jesús Rivas, as witnesses.[11] Rivas and Carmello were also in Santa Barbara. When they were taken before County Judge Joaquín Carrillo and questioned, they said they did not know Zabaleta, destroying his alibi but resulting in their instant release. Deputy Jack Powers, however, suspected they lied and had Carmello and Rivas followed. (Powers had been a leading member of the San Francisco Tammany Hall–style gang known as the "Hounds" until it was disbanded by vigilantes in 1851. Personal experience with lawless men undoubtedly gave him some insight into certain behavior patterns.)

When the Los Angeles posse arrived, Powers pointed out Carmello to Manuel Gárcias, who instantly recognized the horse and saddle Carmello was using. Placed under arrest again, the frightened Carmello immediately confessed that Rivas had boasted to him of murder, that he had accepted the horse as a gift from Rivas before he learned of the murder, and that he knew nothing more. Rivas was then arrested, but he said nothing. All three prisoners were taken back to Los Angeles, along with stolen goods found in their possession. Joaquín Murrieta, Reyes Féliz, and Pancho Daniel were undoubtedly acquainted with Rivas and Carmello. The latter were never mentioned in the Joaquín band legend, but they have a place in the band's history in that their case reveals differences in news coverage given when Hispanic outlaws were the topic in Spanish and English sections of the *Los Angeles Star/La Estrella*.

Star editors Lewis and Rand were eager to follow the example set by friends and colleagues in San Francisco the previous year, when citizens of the Bay City had formed the first vigilance committee in California history. Newspaper editor William Walker, soon to become a filibuster leader, had led the vigilante battle cry up north as editor of the *San Francisco Herald*. The *San Francisco Alta California* also voiced strong support for the vigilantes.[12] The story made their newspapers famous. *Star* proprietors Lewis and Rand aimed for the same result in Los Angeles, and the Rivas and Zabaleta case seemed the perfect vehicle.

In July 1852 a public assembly in Los Angeles soon became a vigilante committee meeting, with John Lewis serving as secretary and Manuel C. Rojo as Spanish secretary and interpreter. The prisoners were cross-examined by Anglo-Americans, Rojo serving as translator. At first only Francisco Carmello confessed. He said he was with Rivas when they met Zabaleta in San Gabriel, about the first of July, but they parted company. Zabaleta and Rivas left together, Rivas saying they had a job and expected to be well paid. He thought they were referring to herding cattle for the American stock buyers. Rivas told him he would meet him in Santa Barbara afterward, so Carmello started the long walk north. He did not expect to see Rivas again so soon. When Rivas made a present of the horse and saddle and also gave him thirty dollars, he did not know everything had been stolen. Carmello's experience reveals one of the ways which outlaw leaders like Joaquín Murrieta and Pancho Daniel could and probably did use to win recruits.

After Carmello's confession was read aloud to Zabaleta, he, too, broke down and confessed, but he blamed the murder entirely on Rivas, probably in retaliation as Rivas had destroyed his alibi. Zabaleta depicted himself as an unwilling participant in crime. He had left with the livestock buyers, who had hired him to help with herding. Rivas joined them later, took Zabaleta aside, and told him that if he wanted their money, he should kill them and take it. Zabaleta claimed that he told Rivas he did not want to kill the men. That night Rivas took a club and struck heavy blows to their heads. Afterward Rivas took a knife from one of the dead men and slit their throats. Then he took their guns and gave them to Zabaleta. Rivas took their money, split it with Zabaleta, and told him to help him hide the bodies. Zabaleta offered to show the sheriff where the bodies lay.

Jesús Rivas scowled when he heard Zabaleta's confession read aloud. He had remained stoically silent, a characteristic he shared with many of Joaquín Murrieta's confederates. However, "after about twenty interrogatories had been put to him, he requested permission to retire with M. C. Rojo, Esq., promising to make a true declaration," wrote John Lewis. Two hours later Rojo, "in the presence of Rivas and with his approval, gave the purport of the conversation he had held with the prisoner."[13] The twenty-year-old Sonoran said Zabaleta planned the murder, they each clubbed a man to death, and Zabaleta threatened to kill him if he did not cooperate. Carmello, he said, had told the truth. He had no part in the murder and no prior knowledge of it.

John Lewis printed all three confessions in the *Star* on July 31, 1852, even as the San Francisco papers had done with their vigilante news in 1851. He also gave a detailed report of the committee procedures, listing the names of those who served in various capacities, half of them being Californios. He described the search for the bodies and the recovered stolen goods. Zabaleta was found to be in possession of most of the money. He and Rand gave a full account of the trial, verdict, and unanimous vote in favor of executing Zabaleta and Rivas. Like his San Francisco colleagues, he and Lewis trumpeted their success. Vigilante justice, they argued, was justice for the people and by the people, and in Los Angeles the Californio and North American people had worked in unity to see justice done. Los Angeles was a safer, more secure place now, thanks to the vigilantes.

A week later, a disheartened Lewis complained about how the Californios did not celebrate the triumph of justice as he thought they ought: "A gloom which the events of last week cast over our city . . . [is] remembered more as a painful dream than the thrilling reality which it was." He blamed it on the speeches Zabaleta and Rivas gave from the scaffold. The local Catholic priest "was particularly pained, and has since remarked that he regrets they were allowed to speak to the people."[14] Lewis and Rand did not publish the offending speeches, but Manuel Clemente Rojo did and also expressed indignation at their words. He defended the vigilante proceedings against rumors sympathetic to Doroteo Zabaleta, even though he knew it was sympathy for Doroteo's mother and brother that provoked the mournful discontent. Zabaleta had played the part of a martyr, asking forgiveness and then offering forgiveness for taking his life when he was innocent of murder, as he insisted. As he saw it, his crimes did not merit the death sentence.

Jesús Rivas had confessed and been absolved as had Zabaleta and was expected to admonish other youths to avoid his sad fate, but the Sonoran youth stood that moral lesson on its head: "¡Jóvenes! [Young people!] Look at me! See what I have come to? Never join those who call themselves friends if they are known to give advice of the sort that leads to the gallows, as it has for me. The truth is, I am guilty of the murders! So my advice to you is this: don't invite others to join you when you are about to commit such a crime."[15] Joaquín Murrieta and Pancho Daniel ignored his advice, both of them preferring to operate in company with two or more trusted companions. Unlike Rivas, they were able to inspire loyalty. However an outlaw named Benito Lopez would not only take Rivas's advice but copy his method. Then he made the mistake of boasting about it to Murrieta's lover, Ana Benites, as will be seen.

Manuel C. Rojo responded to Californios who blamed the Anglo-Saxons for passing sentence and then carrying it out so hastily. He pointed out that "the people of Los Angeles and inhabitants of the surrounding ranches and many from other places within the county" had participated in the trial and sentencing. In fact most of those present were Hispanics. He also argued that everything had been done in keeping with the law and that the Americans were not eager to hang innocent men. If they had been, they would not have agreed to a light sentence for Carmello. Zabaleta's family was innocent, true, but he was not. He had lied when he said he had an alibi, and he had lied when he said Rivas joined him later. Why should anyone believe he was innocent of murder? Even if Rivas committed the murders, Zabaleta had agreed to the plot and ended up with most of the loot. Justice had been the goal and justice had been achieved. In spite of these arguments, misgivings about American justice continued to be expressed.

In September the Star jokingly reported that Carmello had recently proved an ungrateful jail tenant, having dug up the floor and run off with his shackles! Francisco Carmello, to his credit, never made the news again in company with criminals, but another local youth did. Juanito Ramírez stole a pistol, then shot Pablo Lopez and fled to the hills. Ten months later he was seen with Joaquín Murrieta and band. By that time Joaquín's notoriety had spread statewide.[16]

Murrieta and the Death of General Joshua Bean

Joaquín Murrieta's name surfaced repeatedly in testimonies recorded during an investigation into the shooting death of General Joshua H. Bean, a murder that legend assigned to Murrieta. Mortally wounded at around midnight on Sunday, November 7, 1852, Bean died two days later. Fluent in Spanish, Joshua Bean sported ranchero attire and enjoyed attending Mexican dances and other amusements, including *las maromas*—Mexican rope acrobatic "circus" acts. Joaquín Murrieta and his fellow Sonorans enjoyed watching maromas acrobats, too.

Joshua Bean had traveled overland to California in 1849 and settled in San Diego. There he ran a trading post and saloon and served as alcalde and then as mayor. In 1851 he sold his business and moved to Los Angeles, where he opened another combination store and saloon. He had not been in Los Angeles long when Cupeño Indians began raiding local ranches, murdering vaqueros and stealing cattle and horses. A state militia was mustered, and Joshua H. Bean was appointed Major General. He found an ally in Cahuilla Chief Juan Antonio.

A year later General Bean pursued Tejon Indian horse rustlers, who fled into the brush-covered mountain canyons northeast of Los Angeles. Bean billed the state for his services, collected, and then used the money to buy the old convent at San Gabriel. There he opened yet another store and saloon. (The church sanctuary, cemetery, and parsonage remained in possession of the Roman Catholic Church by law.)[17] An old friend of his, Dr. H. L. Sturgis, who had been living in the mining town of Mokelumne Hill in northern California, was in San Gabriel at the time Bean was shot.

Sturgis wrote a letter to Judge Stakes at Mokelumne Hill, about the murder of General Joshua Bean. An excerpt of his letter was published in the *Stockton San Joaquin Republican* on December 4, 1852: "I have to perform the unpleasant task of informing you all of the death of General Joshua H. Bean, who was shot by an assassin unknown, on the night of the 7th inst., and expired at 20 minutes past 2 on the morning of the 9th. . . . He was sensible until about 30 minutes before he died. We have

13. Nineteenth-century print of Mission San Gabriel Arcangel. Courtesy of the California History Room, California State Library, Sacramento, California.

got, as yet, no direct clue to the assassin. . . . He had the evening before said that he had a great desire to see Judge Stakes, though he did not say for what."[18]

Judge Stakes, who brought the letter to the editor of the *Republican*, said that he suspected Joshua Bean wanted to see him about the "ten cutthroat villains" he and Bean had arrested in Roma, Texas, during the war with Mexico. The prisoners had frequently threatened bloody vengeance but were nonetheless released after the war. Some of them had since migrated to California and Baja California. Stakes suspected that one of them had carried out his threat and assassinated Bean, but he was guessing. The only information he had, after all, was in Sturgis's letter.

Every effort was made to discover the assassin, but suspects with alibis and suspects who had gone missing made it difficult for Los Angeles's second vigilance committee to repeat the success of the Zabeleta-Rivas case. Meanwhile the editors of the *Star* and *La Estrella* offered completely different coverage of the Bean assassination. On November 13, 1852, for example, Lewis and Rand made Bean's death front page news. "Assassination of Gen. Bean!" read the headline. The general "was shot in the right breast, the ball taking an upwardly direction, and passing entirely through him. . . . By whom the deed was committed appears to be shrouded in the deepest mystery and although the coroner's jury has

been unceasing in its endeavors to gain some clue to the murderer, success seems as distant as ever." The paper went on to say that Bean and
everyone else in San Gabriel had gone to the maromas that evening. "He
was returning to his lodgings in the Mission building when waylaid by
the assassin," reported the *Star*. "It seems probable from the nature of
the wound, that Gen. Bean must have approached within a very few feet
of the murderer, and that he was not aware of the presence of a foe until
after the death wound had been given. He then drew his pistol and fired
three times. . . . He then walked a short distance and fell. The report of
the pistol being distinctly heard in the neighborhood, several persons
immediately repaired to the spot." Joshua Bean, the *Star* eulogized, "possessed many noble qualities. He was a general favorite and could boast
many warm and devoted friends. His death has created a deep sensation
in this community." During the funeral the sheriff, who was in atten-
dance, received complaints from various residents of San Gabriel valley;
their horses and mules had been stolen the night before. Joaquín Murrieta and a small company of fellow horse thieves were at large.

The *Star* went on to say that Bean's friends in San Gabriel and Los Angeles were determined to find the killer. "Gen. Bean, in his last moments,
used the name of a native Californian in such a connection as led some
of his friends to suppose that he knew his murderer; but the person implicated delivered himself to the authorities and established a perfect alibi, as we are informed by several gentlemen who attended the examination." The unnamed man with a perfect alibi was undoubtedly Felipe Reid.
Reid was the son of Bartolomea "Victoria" Comicrabit, a Cahuilla Indian
woman of San Gabriel. Hugo Reid married Felipe's mother in 1837. (The
Reid home is now a historical site at the Pasadena Arboretum.)[19]

La Estrella echoed the story of horse thefts committed in the area the
night before the funeral, but with regard to Bean's death, M. C. Rojo ignored the coroner's inquest and focused instead on a religious scandal
that had thrown his Catholic readers into a state of turmoil and confusion: "It is with a heavy heart that we announce to our fellow citizens
the unfortunate and ill-fated death of General Joshua H. Bean. . . . He
died like a true Christian [meaning a true Catholic], but he was buried
like a protestant [meaning a heretic]. . . . The parish priest of this city, Fr.
Anacleto Lestrades, denied him sepulchre [burial] in the Roman Cath-

olic pantheon."[20] Don Antonio M. Coronel was one of several Californio gentlemen who had given Fr. Anecleto Lestrades their word of honor that they had seen the priest of San Gabriel go in and confess the dying Joshua Bean, and they were present when said priest gave him Extreme Unction in preparation for burial. Lestrades demanded further evidence, but the body had putrefied and the burial couldn't wait, so Bean's funeral was presided over by a Presbyterian minister.

On November 20, 1852, the *Star* reported that vigilantes had gathered in the courthouse after the funeral and had declared, "Gen. J. H. Bean came to his death by a shot received from some person or persons unknown to the Jury, that they suppose [Juan] Patricio Ontivera [Ontiveros] to have been in some way connected with the commission of the crime, either directly or indirectly. . . . Patricio Ontivera is now undergoing an examination before Justice [S. Thompson] Burrill. It appears that Gen. Bean, a few hours before his death, said that Ontivera and another person who has not yet been arrested, were together when he was shot and that Ontivera handed the pistol to the person who shot him."[21] In legend that person was Joaquín Murrieta.

La Estrella had no room in its few columns to report on the investigation because one full page featured the first installment of a two-part philosophical dialogue titled "Diálogo entre D[on] Severo Justícia y su page Timoteo Verdades" (Dialogue between Sir Justice and his page, Truth). In it Justice and Truth debate Fr. Anecleto Lestrades's refusal to bury General J. H. Bean.

The next issue of *La Estrella* featured part two of the dialogue between Justice and Truth, while the English section reported that half a dozen people were arrested and cross-examined. Patricio Ontiveros, a patriarch in good standing who was for that reason above suspicion among Californios, had named other suspects whom he saw at the scene of the crime shortly after General Bean was shot. There were Cipriano Sandoval, Juan Rico, Padre Eleuterio Estenaga (the Catholic priest at San Gabriel), José Alvizu, "y un tal Reyes y otro" (and one Reyes and another). A couple of women were also taken into custody and questioned. There were "other persons . . . suspected" as well, reported the *Star*, "and strong efforts are being made to have them arrested. We are requested not to give further particulars till something more definite is ascertained as to their whereabouts." One of them was Cristóbal Duarte. Another was Joaquín Murrieta.

Meanwhile a Mr. White, a Mr. Courtney, and several immigrants who had but recently arrived at San Gabriel reported that they were missing some horses and mules. "At first the robbery was supposed to have been committed by Indians," reported the Star, "but from present indications it seems more probable that the same band of outlaws . . . a part of whom . . . are now in the hands of the people, are the guilty ones. . . . Four or five men have started on their track, prepared to follow them even to the mines," which is to say, the horse thieves were herding their stolen animals in a northeastern direction. The Star editors went on to assert that if the vigilance committee proceedings "lead to the detection of Solomón Pico and any of his party, our citizens shall be well repaid for their exertions, though no atonement can be made for the many travelers who have been the victims of these desperadoes. . . . It is hoped . . . that passion will not get the better of justice and judgement."[22] The focus continued to be on Solomón Pico and band throughout the investigation, even though it was Murrieta's name that surfaced most often. (Decades later both Pico and Murrieta would be named as the original inspirations for the fictional character Zorro.)

Manuel Clemente Rojo had been appointed Spanish secretary and interpreter for the vigilance committee, but he did not write about the proceedings until December. Unfortunately what he wrote has been lost to posterity, for no December 1852 issues of the Star/La Estrella have been preserved. However some of what the English section of the Star published that month was reprinted in the San Francisco Alta.

The interrogations went on for two weeks. Rojo was present through it all, forming opinions and reaching conclusions that would shape the way he would interpret later news from the North about Joaquín and band. Among the testimonies he heard (which were condensed and presented to the jury in a form similar to the one that appeared in the Alta) were those of Ana Benites, Benito Lopez, and Reyes Féliz. Ana Benites and another woman—probably La Molinera—were entrusted to William Osburn, who kept them in custody in his house and used various methods to get them to talk. One of them incriminated Reyes Féliz early on. Féliz was told what had been said about him and responded to questions in a disjointed, contradictory way. After he had been interrogated over and over again, his testimony was finally whittled down to what he repeated most consistently and what was supported by the talkative women.

Reyes said he was born in Real de Bayareca, Sonora, and that he was fifteen or sixteen years old. Asked if he was acquainted with General Joshua Bean, he said no. Nor did he know who killed him. Asked again he asserted, "I heard some gentlemen, whose names I do not know, say that Murieta's woman had said that Joaquin Murieta had killed him." The posse that went after Joaquín Murrieta returned with some horses but no prisoners.

Féliz was implicated in several murders about which he was asked. He responded, "I . . . own but one murder; the man I killed was called Anselmo Marias. I killed him with a shot at the camp of Sonora; it is a year since I committed this crime. . . . I had a dispute with Anselmo. He was going to kill an American . . . who was a 'padrino' of mine." He hoped that by saying he killed a Mexican who threatened an American he would win sympathy, but it didn't work. Fatalistically he went on to admit, "I belong to the company of Joaquin Murieta and the late Pedro, who was killed by Americans in the 'cuesta del conejo' [rabbit's bend]. I was not then with Pedro; I was then ill in the Tulares of the effects from bites of a bear. We robbed, Joaquin Murieta, the late Pedro, and myself. In Avisimba [Orestimba], in 'orilla de la Sierra' [at the foot of the mountains], in front of the pueblo of San Jose, we robbed twenty horses which we brought to the Tejon. There the Indians took some of them from us; others, the owner took, who went in pursuit of us. I don't know his name; he was a Mexican." Reyes Féliz's confession was written into legend, as was his fate.[23]

Reyes Féliz was found guilty of the crimes to which he confessed and of being party to the assassination of Gen. Bean in that he admitted belonging to Joaquín Murrieta's "company." This company was seen as part of "the notorious band of robbers and murderers who for a long time have infested this portion of the country and at the head of which is the villain Solomón Pico."[24] Pico had gained local notoriety for having attempted to assassinate Judge Benjamin Hayes in Los Angeles in 1851. The assassination attempt was provoked by the role Judge Hayes had played in arresting and jailing Pico's cousins Francisco and Benito

Lugo, when they were accused of murder by a man considered to be of ill repute. Hayes dodged the bullet and Pico was hotly pursued. Although wounded by his pursuers, he managed to escape into Baja California, where he soon joined the national guards at San Tomás and rose to captain. The American press in Alta California, however, continued to call him a bandit chief. His soldiers were depicted as threatening Mexican guerrillas and outlaws.[25]

Reyes Féliz was condemned on a stormy Friday night. Fr. Lestrades confessed and absolved him the following morning. He was hung at noon on November 27, 1852. "Just before he was launched into eternity," reported the *Star*, "he addressed a few words to the assembly, saying that his punishment was justly merited and advised others never to put faith in a woman."[26]

Ana Benites not only implicated Reyes Féliz in various crimes, she also got Benito Lopez into trouble. Lopez was arrested after the talkative Benites said he told her that he once served as a messenger and carrier of provisions for Solomón Pico. She also said he came to her house in Los Angeles once, bringing with him "a roan mare, a black mule and a rifle, all of which he told her he had taken from two Americans" up at the mines. And she said he had "stolen some handkerchiefs in town a week or two ago, for which he was severely flogged." Lopez was young, like Jesús Rivas, whose murder method he used, but he did not kill any North Americans up at the mines. He stole the horse, mule, and rifle from a Comanche and his woman, who was a black runaway slave. He met them on a road between San Buenaventura and Los Angeles and camped with them. They said they had killed two Americans at Coloma in a dispute. Lopez murdered the sleeping couple with a club and took the things they had taken from the two Americans, then boasted to Benites of his deed, perhaps hoping to impress Joaquín Murrieta as well. Lopez offered to show the sheriff where he hid the bodies of his victims.

Confined in the same room with other male suspects, all of them innocent and fearful, Lopez decided to take the fall for them. He said he killed General Bean. Cipriano Sandoval and the others were released, but then Lopez, "upon a more rigid examination, made several contradictory statements." His interrogators began to doubt his assertion, especially after Ana Benites failed to support his claim. That failure caused her interrogators to suspect she knew who killed Bean. In desperation she finally named Sandoval. Lopez, on seeing he was not believed, admitted, "I told Sandoval [and the others] that they might let them go, that I would be responsible for them." He wondered why his interrogators trusted a woman like Ana Benites. "She belonged to the gang," he said. "She herself told me that she was the woman of Joaquin." To him Joaquín Murrieta was noteworthy among outlaws. Benites, he said, had told him that Joaquin "had gone to the Tulares to sell about thirty horses that he had stolen." Benites admitted this was true and said Murrieta would be back in about twenty days. However he did not come back until June 1853. By then he was no longer a suspect in the murder of Joshua Bean, thanks to Benites.[27] He was, however, a wanted man.

Manuel Clemente Rojo was present when Ana Benites was interrogated, serving as translator for the Americans. She was born in Santa Fe, New Mexico, and was twenty-two years old. Asked about Féliz's statement to the effect that she was Murrieta's woman, she readily admitted it, perhaps with some pride. When told what Reyes Féliz had said regarding several gentlemen who believed that Joaquín Murrieta shot General Bean, she replied that those men were mistaken. She had not said Murrieta killed Bean. Murrieta was with her that night. They had gone to the maromas together and then retired together to the ramadita (a small thatch-roofed outdoor kitchen area) at Juan Avila Rico's home:

> Myself, Joaquin Murieta, Juanito Rico and a young lad who I do not know slept on the Rama dita. After I laid down and before I went to sleep, . . . I heard some shots, and during the three shots, heard voices; could not however distinguish whether they were Americans or Mexicans. A short moment afterward I heard some more shots, the voice of Gen. Bean, who arrived, crying, "Rico! Rico! Rico!" I then sat up and saw Bean, who was dragging a cloak. Señora Jesús [Rico] opened the door. . . . Juanito Rico was already holding him in his arms and said, "Mother, it is General Bean." . . . I told Joaquin Murieta to go in search of a doctor, but in the first place an alcalde, in order that they might see what had taken place.[28]

But if Murrieta was with her, who shot Bean? She said she asked the same question: "I asked Bean who had killed him, whether it was an

American? He answered No. Sonorian? No. [Joaquín was Sonoran.] Californian? Yes, sir-in English, in the affirmative manner." Then she said that Sra. Jesús Rico "took me by the shoulders and said to me, You meddle in things that you have not to care about. There is also Christoval [Cristóbal Duarte], wounded, asking for a confessor."[29] Cristóbal, however, was missing. Benites was pressed to name another suspect and chose Cipriano Sandoval, a poor man without influential allies:

> Cipriano . . . told me that he had killed him [Gen. Bean].
> . . . I saw him when I came from San Gabriel to Los Angeles,
> where he overtook me and Joaquin Murieta, which was the
> time when he told me that he had killed Bean. . . . Murieta
> and myself came to Los Angeles and after having passed the
> little ditches close to the mission, Cipriano overtook us and
> spoke to Murieta. He said: "Hombre, I confide or charge you
> with the secret . . . and charge your woman to act the same as
> yourself, in order that among the Americans they may not get
> anything out of her against us." Cipriano came very much ex-
> cited—wore a serape on his shoulders and a six-shooter in his
> waistband. Then I asked Joaquin: "Is that the one that killed
> Bean?" "Yes," he said. "And why?" "Because the general was
> very much intoxicated, dragging the Indian woman [a ser-
> vant] of the sister of Christoval."[30]

In the end Ana Benites's "statement regarding Cipriano Sandoval is believed to be true," reported the *Star*. In spite of inconsistencies, she was said to have "uniformly told the same story" or at least a more consistent story than Benito Lopez and Reyes Féliz had told. And because she had exposed the crimes of Lopez and Féliz and did not deny what they said of her—that she was Joaquín Murrieta's woman—she was deemed believable. Nonetheless there were still doubters, among them Manuel C. Rojo. Why hadn't she confessed all this about Sandoval to begin with? he asked. Because Murrieta had threatened her, she said. "If by chance they should call on you as a witness, say that you do not know," he had told her. "They shall not get anything out of you; neither shall they harm you. Moreover, if I learn that you say the least thing, I shall be your worst knue. If you should ever put yourself into the guts of the Yankees, I shall take you out. They shall not take from you what I shall do to you."[31] The word *knue* was one Rojo could not translate as it is not Spanish; it is a New Mexican Indian word similar to the Navajo word *kqnooyee*, meaning "firebrand used to punish." Joaquín would punish her fearfully if she talked, she said. And yet she talked.

Manuel C. Rojo probably supported the death sentences given to Lopez and Féliz for crimes not related to the one being investigated. After all, they had confessed to murder, but Cipriano Sandoval's case must have been disconcerting. Arrested again and informed of what Benites had said, the silent cobbler broke down and told Rojo the truth. He had heard the gun shots that night and went to see what happened when Felipe Reid, running in the opposite direction, ran directly into him and knocked him to the ground. When he got up, Reid gave him five dollars and told him not to say anything about their encounter that night. Being very poor, he took the money and said nothing—until now.

Felipe Reid was a handsome, well-educated Cahuilla Indian who had been adopted by his stepfather, Señor Don Hugo Reid, one of those who helped write the California state constitution. Felipe was also a trustworthy employee of dry goods merchant Abel Stearns. He was fond of showy attire and horse racing and protective of fellow Cahuilla Indians. On being informed of what Sandoval had said, he delivered himself up and flatly denied he was the man Cipriano ran into that night. Reid was released and Cipriano Sandoval's statement was interpreted as an attempt to save his own neck.[32]

Manuel C. Rojo was there when Sandoval was condemned to death. He learned that when he confessed to Fr. Lestrades, he did not list murder as one of his sins. Indeed he really wasn't much of a sinner. From the scaffold the impoverished shoemaker insisted he was innocent of any crime, unless it was a crime to accept silence money when desperately poor. Rojo was not convinced of Sandoval's guilt or of Ana Benites's honesty. In an editorial he wrote ten months later (during yet another vigilance committee meeting) he referred to the Sandoval case. The Anglos were, at that time, accusing local Californios of washing their hands of Sandoval's innocent blood and blaming his execution entirely on them. Rojo said this was not true. Those who had stayed away from the meeting condemned Sandoval by their silence, and those who attended voted in favor of his execution. Very few had protested. Rojo and Fr. Lestrades were likely among those who did question the death sentence in Sandoval's case. Given what he later wrote of Murrieta, Rojo seems to have concluded that Joaquín was the likeliest suspect, as Reyes Féliz had said.[33] John Rollin Ridge would reach the same conclusion when penning the legend of Joaquín and band, although for a completely different reason. Ridge was telling a story, not judging a case based on evidence.

Cipriano Sandoval and Benito Lopez were hanged together with Juan "Barumas" Moran, a Sonoran who had stabbed José Dolores, a Cahuilla chieftain, in the back after they had argued over a woman. Dolores died and Barumas fled, but the culprit was soon captured by Cahuilla scouts and handed over to the authorities. Two months later he had yet to be tried. The Cahuilla sent a delegation to the vigilance committee asking that justice be done in the Barumas case, and the request was honored. Barumas was found guilty by his own admission.[34]

News from the North about Joaquín and Band

Manuel Clemente Rojo learned a lot about Joaquín Murrieta during the investigation into Joshua Bean's death. From Reyes he learned that Murrieta was one of those Harry Love had been looking for in connection with murders and robberies in Mariposa County, that he was the leader, that Ana Benites was his woman, and that some gentlemen had heard her say Murrieta shot Bean. That seemed entirely possible to Reyes Féliz, who knew Murrieta well and who said a lot more about his own and Murrieta's activities in his various conflicting stories which the newspapers did not print. Rojo also knew that Joaquín had recruited followers and started stealing horses the day after Bean was shot and that the Joaquín band left the area with a posse "prepared to follow them even to the mines." That was the direction the horse thieves were headed, according to the posse, which returned from Tejon with some horses and no prisoners. Murrieta and band had probably left some recovered horses at Tejon to appease the Indians or else to make it look as though the Indians had stolen the horses.

Given what he had learned of Joaquín and band, M. C. Rojo was not surprised when news came from the North that a band led by Joaquín was stirring up excitement in Calaveras County about six weeks after

Murrieta had headed in that general direction. However it was not until mid-February that the *Los Angeles Star/La Estrella* published clips on the subject. By then there was a price on the head of Joaquín Carrillo and a detailed profile in circulation that did not match Murrieta's description. Lewis and Rand reprinted the profile in the English section, confident that this Joaquín Carrillo was connected to Solomón Pico's band. Joaquín Murrieta was of less interest to them, even though he, too, was believed to be part of Pico's band, which was said to have its headquarters in Baja California.

The profile that Lewis and Rand reprinted had originally been published in the *San Francisco Daily Whig*, the writer claiming his account "may be relied upon; . . . [as] the facts are furnished by an intelligent Mexican who knew him in Mexico." But this nameless "intelligent Mexican" did not know his geography:

> Joaquin was born in the Villa de Catorce, in the department of Jalisco [San Luis Potosí], is aged about 35 years, and has ranked among the most crafty and daring guerrillas in Mexico. He is chief of a notorious band of robbers now infesting the vicinity of the city of Mexico, and though living in California, has a regular chain of communication with his associates in his own country. He . . . has been arrested several times but through the expertness and influence he wielded among the soldiers, he has been discharged. He is about 6 feet in height and of immense muscular power, is well versed in the use of arms and in disposition is cruel and sanguinary. He has a dark sallow complexion, and during the Mexican war, was known to wear a coat of armor. He has committed numberless murders, burned many ranchos, and . . . has frequently obtained information of Mexicans leaving California with money, who have been dogged and robbed by detached portions of his band. In some instances they have been robbed on their arrival in Mexico—the news of their departure and sums of money they had about them, having been forwarded by means of the associates living along the road. Joaquin belonged to the band of guerrillas commanded by

the famous Padre Jurata [Fr. Celedonio Jarauta], who was captured and shot during the Mexican war. The Mexicans look
upon him as a brave man and he is considered a person of
some education.[35]

The author of this profile may well have been William Walker. He was
at that time plotting a filibuster invasion of Sonora and Baja California,
Mexico. Exploiting fears of a guerrilla chief named Joaquín was one way
to rally support. The war veteran, guerrilla chief described as a terror to
the Mexican people north and south of the border was just the kind of
tyrant American filibusters boasted they would overthrow, allegedly for
the benefit of the Mexican people. John Lewis was a friend of Walker's. He
trusted Walker and wished him well in his filibustering endeavors.[36]

Manuel C. Rojo ignored the profile (as did most northern California
newspapers). He had never heard of this Joaquín Carrillo, but he knew
about Joaquín Murrieta. Rojo chose to translate a clip he found in the
San Francisco Alta instead, which, however, he edited to fit his own idea
of who Murrieta was and how he and his band operated:

> The Sacramento papers are full of news about the robberies
> and recent murders committed by the famous Joaquín. One of
> them says: "On Saturday the 11th of this month, some people
> from Jacksonville found the dead body of Mr. Lake who had
> been murdered, and that of a Chinese man who also died of a
> bullet wound. It is not known who committed the murders.
>
> On Saturday, three Chinese were killed between Sutter's
> and Jackson, within four miles of each other.
>
> The driver of a stagecoach that was on the way to Stock-
> ton, and two passengers, were murdered on the same day
> by Joaquín and two companions, said to be Mexicans. These
> three had been shot dead and the horses stolen from the coach.
> On the same day, the same gang headed for a Chinese camp
> where they robbed fifty Chinese of all they had, and [illegi-
> ble section].
>
> On Thursday, Joaquín rode through the middle of San An-
> dreas at a gallop and fired his pistol at three Americans who
> were walking down the street and killed them. Joaquín is a

young man of 19 years of age and is one of the best pistol-
firing sharpshooters that can be found in this or any other
country, as all three Americans at whom he discharged his
weapon died slowly and painfully.

All the bands together number sixty persons, the majority being Mexicans. The people have been greatly alarmed
and many think they should get together a large number of
all those [illegible section], which will leave in pursuit of the
murderers.[37]

The Joaquín in this article has two companions; so did Murrieta when
he arrived in Los Angeles in June 1852. He looked about nineteen years old,
as did Joaquín Murrieta. He shot people with a pistol, the same weapon
used to kill Bean, and they died slowly and painfully, as did Bean. The
original version in the *Alta* did not say that the Americans who were fired
upon at San Andreas died slowly and painfully, only that two of them
were hit in the neck. Presumably they didn't die. The *Alta* also said that the
young Mexican on a galloping horse *may* have been Joaquín. The original
also said, "The whole band . . . consists of about sixty men, all of whom
are thought to be Mexicans." But Rojo did not believe that there was one
large band, nor that it was composed solely of Mexicans. He edited the
story to fit his own conclusions based on what he had learned during the
interrogations of Ana Benites, Reyes Féliz, Benito Lopez, and others.

The Joaquín of Calaveras continued to be a popular subject in northern California newspapers for some time, but in Los Angeles nothing
more was printed about him until June 4, 1853, when Lewis and Rand
reprinted a flippant clip from the *San Francisco Alta*: "The Legislature, at
its last session, passed a law empowering Capt. Henry S. Love to raise
a company of twenty men for the purpose of capturing 'the five Joa-
quins-Joaquin Muriati, Joaquin Ocomorenia, Joaquin Valenzuela, Joaquin Botiller, Joaquin Carrillo- . . . and their banded associates.' It is
barely possible that THE Joaquin is included in the above enumeration,
but if so, his identity is destroyed. . . . A dangerous name is 'Joaquin'. . . .
The legal proprietors . . . of the respectable names outlawed by the Legislature should petition for a re-baptism."[38] It was an election year, and
Lewis and Rand favored the Whig candidates. Like other political adver-

saries of the ruling Democrats, Lewis and Rand made fun of the ranger bill and the Joaquín whose profile they had printed. Perhaps even when they printed the profile they suspected it was invented.

M. C. Rojo ignored the flippant remarks and reported simply: "In one of the last sessions of the state senate, the governor of the state authorized the formation of a company of 20 men, with a monthly salary of $150 each, to apprehend the famous Joaquín." He had no doubts at all as to the identity of "the famous Joaquín."[39]

Who is Joaquín?

A week later two short articles in the English section of the *Los Angeles Star/La Estrella* mentioned Joaquín, but nothing appeared in the Spanish section. The first story poked fun at an outlandish rumor: "The report . . . that our esteemed fellow citizen, Dr. Gaylord, had been shot, stabbed, hung, drawn and quartered, and decapitated . . . turns out to be pure fabrication. Consequently, that ubiquitous scoundrel, Joaquin, has one less crime to answer for." The second said, "There seems to be an opinion prevailing . . . that Joaquin the robber and murderer is prowling about in this vicinity. . . . A native Californian boy, who was searching for horses a few days ago, was shot through the thigh by a Sonoreño. . . . The boy was fortunately mounted on a fleet horse and escaped although hotly pursued."[40] Was it Joaquín Murrieta and band, or was it just a rumor?

By June 18 there was no longer any doubt. Rojo reported, "There are varied and contradictory reports circulating with respect to Joaquín, but we dare not affirm anything from anyone except that with which all are in agreement and that is that this celebrated bandit has been seen within the vicinity of this town." Although he did not expressly say "Joaquín Murrieta," his American colleagues did: "Many men of veracity assert positively that Joaquin Murieta and his band are now somewhere between San Juan Capistrano and San Diego. . . . That Joaquin passed through this city is just as certain as anything else; and it is equally certain that no one was frightened."[41] Though famous enough to warrant mention on the list of Joaquíns that the state legislature had paid the rangers to capture, Murrieta could be so unobtrusive or beguiling as to stir more rumors than alarm in Los Angeles. Meanwhile both sections of the local newspaper reported that Pedro Sánchez, who was well known in the area, had been killed in a fight with a Spaniard at mining camp Martinez in Tuolumne County. Lewis and Rand labeled Sánchez "a ringleader of Joaquin's band," while Rojo called him "uno de los amigos de [one of the friends of]" Joaquín.[42]

The *Star* also published an excerpt from a private letter sent to John Lewis from "W. A. W." He wrote from San Pedro, about 26 miles south of Los Angeles: "Joaquin, with about eight men, was seen today in the vicinity of [rancho] Machado. . . . Machado's vaquero reports that . . . today he was seized by three men, two of whom, Juanito Ramírez and Rafael Mazuca, wanted to kill him, but the veritable Joaquin interfered and saved his life upon the ground that he was of no account. The supposition is that they are waiting an opportunity to rob the stage. Our vigilant mayor [of San Pedro] has been practicing rifle shooting this afternoon. . . . If Joaquin does attack this city, he will be welcomed to a bloody time."[43] Joaquín robbed no stagecoaches while in Los Angeles County, nor did he attack or rob anyone in San Pedro. He undoubtedly paid Ana Benites a visit and learned of Reyes Féliz's fate. He had passed through Monterey and San Luis Obispo counties on his way south, and so would have learned of Claudio Féliz's fate as well. Meanwhile the *Star* reprinted news from up north about Captain Love and his rangers that Manuel C. Rojo ignored. Instead he offered his readers the following thought-provoking editorial:

WHO IS JOAQUIN? This is the question everyone is asking, and although it appears easy to answer, not many can answer it categorically.

We live in the age of spirits and so far, science has only been able to make them, by means of magnetism, depart from the realm of the dead long enough to communicate with mankind. Now we know there are good and evil spirits, and many, in answering the above question, assure us that Joaquín can be none other than one of the damned, as he indulges in practicing evil. This is based on the way his spirit has made him invisible to people, for nobody sees Joaquín and yet he appears in three or four places at the same time, and always as the scourge of humanity.

Some of those who have reasoned in this way are so certain that Joaquín is a spirit, they have bought a round table in order to conduct experiments, and when they do not achieve good results, it has been because they lacked a medium and two more participants who share the same belief. In spite of this, they remain convinced his spirit can be summoned.

Others believe Joaquín is a demon who dines on the flesh of his victims and satisfies his insatiable thirst by wringing the blood from their hearts.

Many more think that Joaquín does not exist, in body or in spirit. He is nothing more than a name that is valued in some regions by highwaymen, because then they can attribute to him the crimes they have committed. In this way they manage to redirect all the search parties after one who does not exist, enabling them, thereby, to commit crimes with greater impunity.

There are others (and these are the silliest) for whom he represents a hero, an avenger of various personal grievances that we have received from the Americans. Yes, it is hard to have to confess it, but it is necessary; there are people who are entertaining antipathy against the Americans, who have made it their duty to protect a beast they would normally chase away. Poor souls! They don't see that a man accustomed to crime, whose conscience is blunted, does not distinguish between nations. The only thing he wants is silver, in order to maintain prestige among the men he commands, and horses, in order to make good his escape; and with the goal of securing these two prizes so necessary to his way of life, he would sacrifice even his own father. The most diplomacy he has shown is to make believe he respects the lives of the Spanish races, which he tells to all those who protect him in his life of adventure.

Joaquín, to our understanding, is nothing more than an astute and daring highwayman: astute because he knows how to create prestige for himself by telling stories to the credulous, and daring in the way he has taken chances; exceedingly

dangerous, he is fully aware of his own desperate standing.
He knows that there is no alternative for him in the end but
to hang, and yet this same finale he must disdain, whatever
the danger, as long as he can.[44]

Written with humor and honesty in his usual unornamented style,
Rojo's editorial exposed the widely variant views circulating among Spanish-speakers in southern California. Joaquín Murrieta, so recently seen
in Los Angeles, had excited rumors and arguments about the identity of
the famous Joaquín. He was the one who would inspire a lasting legend,
but there were other Joaquíns and outlaws who used that name as an alias
and who were known to the Spanish-speaking community in Los Angeles County. Different people had reached different conclusions based on
their beliefs and experiences. Manuel C. Rojo argued that many of the
conclusions others had reached were without foundation. Rojo did not
consider rumors newsworthy, as a rule, but he decided that their popularity merited a commentary.

He had encountered people who talked of Joaquín as if he was a demon or spirit and others who said there was no Joaquín—it was just a
name bandits hid behind. Then there were those who knew who Joaquín
Murrieta was, and among these were those who thought of him as an
avenger of his people. Manuel Clemente Rojo saw a moral lesson being
lost in all the blind arguments he heard that attempted to answer the
question: who is Joaquín? He set out to correct that by undermining ignorant arguments.

The spiritualists, for example, reached their conclusions based on the
paranormal science of the day as influenced by Catholic teaching and
local Indian myths. The necromancers knew Joaquín indulged in vice.
That meant he was damned to wander the earth as a ghost, a lost soul, a
dangerous demonic spirit that, by means of magnetism, could be summoned by a medium, but only when that medium was strengthened by
the presence of believers who joined their thoughts to his. This Joaquín
could answer questions by rapping on the table: once meant yes, and twice
meant no. The spiritualists, Americans among them, cited inconsistent
northern California newspaper reports as evidence. Joaquín was reportedly able to disappear (which was actually due to the fact that most peo-

ple did not know him and therefore did not know what he looked like). He was also reportedly in several different locations at the same time, something only a spirit or ghost could do.[45] And San Gabriel did have a ghost, that of "the famous marauder" Joaquín.

The San Gabriel Joaquín had been born and baptized at the mission in Spanish colonial days, the son of Cahuilla Indians. Raised more or less as a slave, he was branded on the lip and had his ears cropped for rebelling against an abusive Spanish foreman. He fled to the mountains in the 1830s and became a notorious brigand chief and marauder, the terror of the rancheros, a threat to travelers. In 1846, on what is now Mount Wilson, Don Benito Wilson met with him in hopes of persuading him to surrender before the Mexican military arrived. Wilson recorded the adventure in his diary, saying Joaquín was friendly and open until he saw the soldiers coming. As soon as he saw them he leapt to his feet, called Wilson a traitor, and "whipped an arrow from his quiver and strung it on his bow" so fast, wrote Wilson, "I had no chance to raise the gun to my shoulder and had to shoot it from my hand," which is to say, at hip level. They fired simultaneously. "His shot took effect in my right shoulder and mine in his heart."[46] Wilson had to retreat at a run to the nearest river and wash his wound because the arrow tip had been poisoned. The gunshot knocked Joaquín down, but did not kill him instantly. His small retinue initially fled but then, in response to his roar, turned and fought to the death, while their chief "lay on the ground uttering curses and abuse against the Spanish race and people" until those he cursed finished him off. This is a valiant Joaquín, a guerrilla rebel chief in his day, a Cahuilla who wanted to rid his country of the abusive, treacherous, and hated whites of Spanish and other descent. In many ways his history matches the myth that arose around Joaquín Murrieta and band.

Already the subject of local folklore, the Cahuilla Joaquín undoubtedly inspired rumors of a bloodthirsty spirit, for in life he had been as ruthless as a demon, and some demons, in Southwestern Indian mythology, wrung blood from human hearts and drank it while yet warm. Even in Roman Catholic tradition, demons in Church art that was used to teach the Indians about damnation and salvation, were depicted as dwelling in a flaming hell tearing fallen souls apart and dining on their limbs. Gory Joaquín folklore like this bled into the news in rumors like the one that had falsely reported a gruesome end to the life of one Dr. Gaylord. This depiction of Joaquín would be transferred, in legend, to Three-Fingered Jack, who is described by John Rollin Ridge as delighting in gore, especially when the victims were Chinese miners.

Manuel Clemente Rojo contrasted believers in a demonic Joaquín with those skeptics who did not acknowledge the existence of a bandit leader named Joaquín who merited the kind of fear and wrath the North Americans expressed in California newspapers. Pointing to the same evidence the spiritualists cited—that he was seen everywhere simultaneously and yet no one knew where he was—the rationalists said this was because Joaquín was just a sham, a name other bandits used to direct attention away from themselves so that they could carry on their depredations with greater impunity. Rojo acknowledged that there were bandits who did just that. Had he written his essay a year later, he might have cited Luis Burgos, who "often declared himself to be the veritable and terrible Joaquin."[47] But what inspired Burgos to take that name and not another? The fact that it belonged to a famous bandit, argued Rojo: Joaquín Murrieta.

Murrieta was not only famous, he was a very real danger to anyone he deemed an enemy. His seemingly simultaneous appearances in different places were due merely to false, confused, and questionable newspaper reports, and to the fact that other bands than his were active at the same time he was, his actions often inspiring theirs. Even as General Joshua Bean's old friend Judge Stakes could only guess who shot Bean, so too, correspondents and reporters often had to guess at the validity of incongruous crime reports. Rojo was instinctively skeptical of any sources that did not match his own experiences and did not come from sources he trusted. Joaquín Murrieta was someone he knew about, so when he read news and heard reports about a famous outlaw named Joaquín, he selectively published only those accounts which matched the profile he already had of Ana Benites's lover and Reyes Féliz's company leader.

Joaquín Murrieta was famous, he explained, because he had a remarkable talent for losing his pursuers, because he could manage horses with uncommon skill, and because he was utterly indifferent to the fate he knew awaited him. He was also a dangerous pistolero. And he had a way with people, including American Anglos. He could win people over when it suited his purposes. Californio rancheros hosted him, youths admired him, and many of the Americans who met him dismissed him as harmless. He did not look intimidating to them.

Among those who met him and liked him were Californios and Sonorans who saw him as a *vengador* (avenger). They embraced the stories Joaquín told them of having suffered injustice and of having turned against the Anglo-Americans. Murrieta, argued Rojo, *wanted* to be seen as the "avenger of . . . personal grievances we have received at the hands of the Americans." He found that by winning sympathizers he could impose on hosts to provide him with provisions, horses, and recruits. He knew Hispanic listeners could empathize if he spoke of being abused and cheated because he had heard them, too, complain of injustices suffered at the hands of unscrupulous Anglo-Americans. Even those Californio rancheros and farmers who had initially greeted the post-war government as the hope of the future had suffered losses at the hands of unscrupulous North American lawyers and squatters. The Berreyesa family, for example, lacked the political acumen or education to maneuver through the legal loopholes that American courts manipulated and they lost everything, even the family home. Such a climate made it easy for Joaquín Murrieta, Pancho Daniel, and other bandits to find recruits and to encourage sympathy in *paisanos* (countrymen) born and raised in what had been part of Mexico.

M. C. Rojo understood why his readers mistrusted Anglo-Saxons, but he warned against putting their faith in a bandit. Those to whom an outlaw offered "the diplomacy of one that respects the lives of those of Spanish race" should not be so gullible. Trusting a man "whose conscience is blunted" was dangerous. His countrymen had been among his band's victims and those who hosted bandits were not immune to theft or murder at the hands of such guests. Rancho Orestimba had been robbed. The man Reyes Féliz killed was not an Anglo-American. Race-based diplomacy, argued Rojo, when offered by a bandit was but a clever ruse. Joaquín was not an avenger. Rojo refused to be gullible. He admitted that Murrieta had become famous because he was, after all, an artful storyteller and a reckless daredevil, an adventurer who spurred his horse down the lawless slope toward destruction, knowing full well that his foolhardy and immoral conduct would cost him his life and perhaps even his soul. The sooner Joaquín and his kind met their inevitable fates the better, for as long as they kept singing their own praises so convincingly, the more often they would corrupt vulnerable young men of good family into emulating ruthless lawlessness.

Don Andrés Pico and Joaquín Murrieta

In July Lewis and Rand sold the *Los Angeles Star/La Estrella* to James McMeans, who decorated the first column of the front page with a Democratic Party banner and announced that the *Star/La Estrella*, which had been politically independent, was now a Democratic Party vassal. That suited Democrat Manuel Rojo.

Perhaps Rojo's editorial about Joaquín had an effect on readers, and Murrieta found fewer willing hosts in the South. He and his band reportedly stole horses and mules in the vicinity of Santa Ana and were ambushed. Forced to leave the stolen herd behind, the band turned north again, but did not round up any animals in the vicinity of San Juan Capistrano, San Pedro, or San Gabriel, probably due to the vigilance of local vaqueros. Finally while crossing the wide San Fernando Valley the band of seven stole fifty horses and herded them toward the Santa Barbara Mountains. Last seen near Rancho San Francisco (present day Newhall), a vaquero there recognized the brand on the horses as that of General Andrés Pico.

Pico was captain of the California Lancers—an Hispanic volunteer militia that helped fight marauding Indians and hunt down outlaw bands. The vaquero told Murrieta that robbing Pico was not a good idea. Murrieta handed over forty-three animals, saying he and his men had need of the horses on which they were mounted. The well-mounted band then headed for the Santa Barbara mountains, stealing a few more horses en route to the mountains behind Santa Inez. From there they turned east along trails leading to the Tulare Valley, about forty miles south of Panoche Pass. They stopped to rest at a watering hole near the dry bed of Cantua Creek, on July 24, 1853.[48] On August 6 James McMeans quoted a *San Francisco Alta* story of July 30, 1853, describing how Joaquín was killed in the vicinity of Panoche Pass. *La Estrella* offered its own rendition of that news:

From a postal dispatch from Capt. Love that arrived in Stockton on the 29th last month: . . . news was received that . . . a party of volunteers under Capt. Love and commanded by Capt. Burns [Byrnes] met a party of seven commanded by Joaquín. The instant they met both parties shot at each other, the result being the death of Joaquín, and of a Californian known to the Americans by the nickname 'Three-Fingered Jack.' They succeeded in taking two prisoners, . . . the three remaining, . . . undertook to escape. Capt. Love has cut off the head of Joaquín and preserved it in a jar of spirits. It was sent to San Francisco so that his identity could be verified there. These are the only particulars that have been received about the tragic and deserved fate of the unfortunate Joaquín. If only this example might serve as a warning to others!"[49]

The only reporter to call Joaquín's death tragic and unfortunate, M. C. Rojo nonetheless believed Murrieta deserved his fate, but he added the didactic hope that Murrieta's fate would serve as a moral lesson and discourage other youths from following his nefarious example. Had Murrieta come from a Californio family in good standing, as did Solomón Pico, Rojo would not have been able to support the Anglo-American opinion that his fate at the hands of the rangers was deserved. As has been seen with Doroteo Zabaleta, Cristóbal Ontiveros, and Felipe Reid, family mattered. Indeed, it mattered enough to cause most young men to avoid lawlessness, lest they bring shame on their families. Had the Anglo-Americans been content to send Zabaleta to prison rather than hang him, many more Californios in Los Angeles would have been convinced that U.S. laws and those who enforced them were just. As for Rivas, who like Murrieta had come from Sonora, everyone in Los Angeles agreed he had deserved his fate. Wayward Sonoran immigrants were seen in much the same light as the cholos that plagued the state during the Mexican era. Nonetheless the deaths of Jesús Rivas, Reyes Féliz, and Joaquín Murrieta were tragic because they were so young.

The news of Joaquín's death at the hands of rangers whom the state legislature had employed with the Democratic governor's support prompted a politically motivated debate among newspaper editors in the North. James McMeans entered the debate on August 20, 1853: "The Northern papers publish a very circumstantial account of the capture and killing of Joaquin. But some of them believe the whole thing to be a fabrication. . . . They allow that some poor devil has lost his head, but they say it was not enough to take a shaggy head from somebody and to get plenty of men to swear it to be that of the terrible Joaquin. From the information we have and the fact that Joaquin is known to have been in the neighborhood of Panoche Pass, about the time of his reported capture, we strongly believe that his head was put up in whiskey."

In *La Estrella* Rojo also had to respond to doubts expressed by Spanish speakers. "With respects to Joaquín's tragic end, only one doubt remains . . . [T]o which of the bandits by that name does the head . . . belong? The published documents proving his identity, and the confessions of his own men who were taken prisoners during the skirmish, leave us no room to further entertain the least doubt that it was Joaquín Murrieta, so well known in our county and that lived for some time at Mission San Gabriel." Rojo then followed up with a translated excerpt from the August 13, 1853, issue of the *San Francisco Sun*: "The last words he exclaimed as his horse fell were 'shoot no more; I'm dead' and he expired instantly." Rojo also reported that two of Joaquín's companions were arrested at Cantua: "Antonio Lopez, a man of athletic stature and about thirty years of age and Salvador Méndez, age twenty-three. This last gave his name as José Ochovo, but he was recognized by some of his countrymen who gave his real name."[50]

James McMeans also reported, "Joaquín's head is in San Francisco and . . . has been recognized by many persons, among them Andrés Pico and Hon. [John] J. Warner, as the head of Joaquin Murieta." He then reprinted the *San Francisco Herald*'s description of the head, the details providing enough information to confirm to anyone who had known Joaquín Murrieta in life that the head was once his. "It is that of a man . . . between twenty and twenty-five years old. The forehead is high and . . . the cheek bones elevated and prominent, and the mouth indicative of sensuality and . . . firmness. The hair, of a beautiful light brown with a gold tint . . . is long and flowing; the nose high and straight, and the eyebrows, which meet in the middle—dark and heavy. The eyes, now closed in death, are said to have been dark blue. . . . The face tapers off to the chin, upon which, and on the upper lip, there is a thin beard like

14. "Joaquín Murrieta, after the head preserved in alcohol." Pen and ink sketch by Pierre Boeringer. (The eyes were closed in death; Boeringer drew them open.) Courtesy of the California History Room, California State Library, Sacramento, California.

that of a young man who had never shaved. Under his right eye there is a small scar."[51] This is one of the sources that fed folklore and oral tradition about Joaquín Murrieta's appearance, as Walter Noble Burns discovered. It is a source John Rollin Ridge chose to ignore, preferring to depict his Mexican hero as having black hair and dark eyes as he himself had and as did most of the Mexicans he met in California.

Spanish speakers in the 1850s did not find descriptions of a dead man convincing evidence of his identity. The word of an honorable man, however, carried weight. Manuel C. Rojo wrote, "One of those who has recognized [the head] and assures us that it is that of Joaquín Murrieta, is Don Andrés Pico." Andrés Pico was popular in Los Angeles. A self-effacing, jovial, generous, and frank cavalry officer, during the Mexican-American War Pico had distinguished himself in a brilliant maneuver by which he defeated a much larger U.S. force in Los Angeles. And when the Californios had lost, he was the only one who courageously stepped forward and opened negotiations with the Americans for a peaceful transfer of power.

Andrés Pico undoubtedly attended the maroma performance in San Gabriel in November 1852 and very likely met Joaquín Murrieta on other occasions as well. An honest and reliable man, when he saw the head the rangers were exhibiting, he recognized it at once as that of Joaquín Murrieta. "For this reason," wrote Rojo, "we believe there should not be the least doubt about the identity of the individual to whom it belonged." Andrés Pico had seen the head when he went north to collect the horses the rangers had taken from Murrieta's band, the rangers having posted announcements in newspapers inviting claimants to step forward.[52]

The One the Americans Called "Three-Fingered Jack"

The outlaw shot and killed with Joaquín Murrieta was identified as Emanuel "Three-Fingered Jack" Garcia. In September *La Estrella* offered an abridged translation of a correspondence from Monterey that was published in the *Stockton San Joaquin Republican*. Rojo translated the Anglo-Saxon nickname as "Juan de tres dedos" because there was no Spanish equivalent of that nickname in the 1850s. "Three-Fingered Jack" was a popular and oft-used nickname among English speakers, for they traditionally derived such nicknames from physical traits, often in combination with foreshortened proper names like "Bill" for William or endearing nicknames like "Jack" for John. Spanish nicknames might also be short versions of a proper name, such as "Pancho" for Francisco, but descriptive nicknames in the nineteenth century denoted a personality trait or occupation, not a physical feature. For example, a prosperous and hardworking San Gabriel resident called Richard "Handsome Dick" Laughlin in English-speaking circles, was known among Hispanic women as "Buenmozo," which means "good catch."[53]

The depiction of Three-Fingered Jack written by Benjamin Kooser, a U.S. soldier stationed at Monterey, was translated by Manuel Clemente Rojo as follows:

At the battle of Salinas he distinguished himself as a bold enemy of the Americans and afterward . . . won the admiration of the Californios. . . . He commanded the party that reeked [sic] havoc on Capt. Borrough's company. . . . Juan de tres dedos was the one who killed Capt. Burroughs and took possession of his horse and saddle. This horse was the famous "Sacramento," a sorrel bay that some time ago had been a gift to Col. Fremont from Capt. Sutter. The horse, unbeknownst to its new master, soon returned to the American encampment.

Eighteen months later, I [Benjamin Kooser] met Jack when he was in Monterey. . . . He appeared to be about 28 years old and his features were most disagreeable and repugnant. I learned that he had just returned from Mexico where he had been employed as a vaquero by a certain general [in Baja California]. . . .

During his stay in Monterey, where he was reunited with an old comrade named Frederico de la Montaña, he learned that the famous horse, Sacramento, had joined a band of mustangs and was enjoying sweet liberty on the open prairie. . . . So he left town, in company with others, swearing he would not return until he had caught the noble animal; he has faith fully fulfilled his promise, for he was never seen in Monterey again and the horse still runs free on the prairie![54]

James McMeans shared the same story about Three-Fingered Jack on September 17, 1853. Unlike Joaquín the identity of Emanuel García was never questioned. Spanish and English readers alike did not doubt that the rangers killed him, even though the only evidence they offered was a three-fingered hand. He was better known among Californios than among Anglos for his battlefield prowess in 1846. He had been famous in his own right several years before Joaquín Murrieta set foot in California. No one even asked why he was with the Joaquín band of horse thieves, suggesting he was a cholo, an unpaid soldier who committed theft out of desperation. Like so many other cholos, he took to stealing as a livelihood when there was no work for him as a soldier. (The U.S. military employed only Anglo-American soldiers to garrison forts in California.)

The differences in news coverage of outlaw and vigilante activity in the English vs. the Spanish sections of the *Los Angeles Star/La Estrella* reflected different cultural perspectives that shaped how judicial and vigilante experiences were viewed. Most of the prisoners in Los Angeles were Mexicans, Californios, and local Indians. Comparatively few Anglo-Saxons who were arrested in Los Angeles for murder were hanged. This fact encouraged an already-existing mistrust, a belief that the Anglo-American vigilantes were too eager to hang men like Zabaleta and Sandoval. To Hispanic-Americans, the Anglo-Americans acted as if Hispanics were unable to judge a prisoner justly. They also concluded that Anglo-Americans were unwilling to judge justly. In a few years, this racial mistrust would grow. Meanwhile in northern California, differences in news coverage having to do with outlaws, posses, and vigilantes were shaped not only by racial tensions but also by political rivalry and filibuster plots.

4. Northern Newspapers and the Politics of Bandit Hunting

Joaquín and band made the news in northern California newspapers far more frequently than in the South, but content was much less consistent. Unlike Manuel Clemente Rojo, editors of northern California newspapers never interrogated members of the band, so they had no single point of reference. John White of the *Stockton San Joaquin Republican* (referred to hereafter as the *Republican*) and Edward C. Kemble of the *San Francisco Alta California* (hereafter the *Alta*) are good examples of editors who selectively published news and views of Joaquín and his band as influenced by reader interest, geographical proximity, and differing political perspectives.

Reader interest was a given. Horse thieves and highly mobile highwaymen posed a threat to ranchers, travelers, small mining companies, and roadside businesses. As for geographical proximity, Stockton, where John White lived, was between fifty and sixty miles west of Sonora town, Martinez, Columbia, Angel's Camp, San Andreas, Mokelumne Hill, and Jackson—all gold-mining towns at the foot of the Sierra Mountains in Tuolumne and Calaveras counties. Murrieta, his friend Pedro Sánchez, and the Féliz brothers, Claudio and Reyes, made frequent visits to the area in the early 1850s. And all of them passed through Stockton at times, as did Joaquín Valenzuela and Pancho Daniel. The clapboard city surrounded with tent dwellings squatted beside the San Joaquin River between the Mother Lode and the San Benito coast range of mountains. It was a popular stopping point for west- and east-bound travelers, those heading west being on their way to San Jose, Monterey, or San Francisco.

In contrast the hastily built clapboard and brick port city of San Francisco, where Edward Kemble worked on the *Alta*, was the door through which thousands of foreign immigrants and American migrants came to or departed from California almost daily. San Francisco is located on a wide and calm bay that is blanketed with fog every morning. California's business owners purchased most of their supplies from San Francisco importers. Even newspaper editors shopping for printing equipment found it in San Francisco, Edward Kemble having imported paper and presses from New York City to sell. Miners went to the city to turn their gold dust into cash at banks and to send and, hopefully, fetch mail. They also attended balls and concerts while in town. Though plagued with pickpockets, thugs, and arsonists, and full of gamblers and prostitutes who worked in luxurious saloons, the city also had numerous churches, a synagogue, several schools, and a hospital. There were even a bull-fighting ring and theaters.

In addition to the influence that geographical location had on the news that various papers featured, political perspective shaped content. Politics, as well as prejudice and even pranks, affected the way the Joaquín band was covered by editors like John White and Edward Kemble. Good political commentaries and editorials were what sold papers. Both White and Kemble wrote editorials about Joaquín as Manuel Clemente Rojo did, but their remarks were motivated by their prejudices, political and otherwise, as well as by what people were saying. Their differing political perspectives were shaped in part by who they were and where they came from.

Edward C. Kemble, for example, was a Yankee from Troy, New York, who moved to New York City when sixteen years old and was hired by Samuel Brennan to set print for a Mormon weekly. He sailed to California with Brennan in 1846, prior to the war with Mexico, arriving after the war started. At eighteen, Kemble signed up to serve under his boyhood hero, John Frémont, but became disillusioned, quit, and returned to Monterey. There he began working for Brennan on the *California Star* in January 1847. He went gold-seeking in the spring of 1848 and returned to San Francisco with enough gold to buy Brennan's print shop and presses. He then persuaded his good friend Edward Gilbert to be chief editor of the *Alta* and opened shop in January 1849.[1] By 1853 Kemble was twenty-

15. Edward C. Kemble, cropped from an 1850 daguerreotype of Edward Gilbert and Edward Kemble. Author's collection.

five years old and well-known in California newspaper circles, as nearly everyone in the business had bought their presses from him. Kemble was described by an acquaintance as possessing the character of "a gentleman of strict integrity and moral worth," and his editorials were "always couched in elegant phraseology and high moral tone."[2] Because he chose to remain politically independent, Kemble could criticize politicians of both parties. However he tended to be less critical of Whigs than of Democrats.

Democrats, in Kemble's experience, were either U.S. Southerners who wanted California to be a slave state (and he favored abolition of slavery), or else they were European immigrants like those who continually flooded into New York City. The latter he saw as unwanted "rabble" who kept corrupt city bosses in power by trading votes for favors. Kemble accused the Democratic governor of California and his administration of pocketing public funds for private use and leaving a gold-rich state with a deficit.

Unlike Kemble, John White viewed Democrats as generous and loyal, and Whigs as stingy and aloof. Whigs reminded him of the aristocrats and the rich bourgeois elite in Great Britain. Born in Abergavenny, Wales, in 1825, he grew up among underpaid Welsh miners and factory workers. He moved to New York City in the early 1840s and to California in 1849. In California opportunities abounded, but so did temptations, and White had a weakness for liquor and poker. He also made a game of taunting self-righteous Whigs who, as he saw it, sought to confine the American spirit of independence by means of strong central government policies heavily influenced by big city banks in the North. Democrats, on the other hand, stood by the oppressed immigrants in the United States, people who, like White himself, had fled European homelands hoping to throw off the hierarchic social barriers that kept land and positions of power in the hands of the few. John White and fellow countryman H. H. Radcliffe opened a store in Stockton and in the back room started printing the independent *Stockton Times* in 1850. They sold the *Times* to the Democratic Party in 1852, and the Party rechristened it the *San Joaquin Republican*. John White was retained as editor.[3] (John White also started the *Sonora Herald* and hired Enos Christman to set type for it.)

Although Kemble and White became political adversaries in their newspaper columns, their racial prejudices were similar. Both of them viewed mestizos as inferior to Anglo-Saxons. Kemble's prejudice was based largely on traditional Yankee notions of racial and moral superiority, but it was limited by his Abolitionist views and his love of fair play. John White's opinion of Hispanics—that they were cowardly and sanguinary—was shaped by a history handed down to all British subjects. While Texans in California remembered the Alamo every time they saw a Mexican (Davy Crockett and other Americans died defending the Alamo against General Santa Ana's Mexican troops), British-Americans remembered the Spanish Armada (Spain's sixteenth-century attempt to invade Great Britain) whenever they heard Spanish spoken. And while Americans viewed their recent wartime victory over Mexico and subsequent annexation of Mexican territory as God's manifested destiny for them, the

British viewed their defeat of the Spanish Armada as divinely ordained.[4] Thus history with its inherited prejudices inevitably influenced what was said of Joaquín and band in Northern California newspapers.

Of Bandits and Mexican "Guerrilla" Bands

Northern California newspapers reported at length on the impact of the Foreign Miners Tax in 1850 and the subsequent rash of crimes blamed on Mexican guerrillas, initially said to be led by a white man. They also reported in detail the first vigilante movement in San Francisco in 1851, and the shooting of Sheriff Buchanan of Marysville. They published the confessions of Teodor Vásquez in February 1852, of Zabaleta and Rivas in July and August, and of Reyes Féliz, Benito Lopez, and Ana Benites in December. Four of the six named Joaquín Murrieta as a horse thief, gambler, and outlaw leader.

As mentioned in earlier chapters, it was in April of 1852 that James Clark was shot while attempting to arrest Mexican horse thieves at Willow Springs. On the same day Claudio Féliz rescued Reyes sixty miles to the south. (Three days later William Perkins heard about the murder and robbery of a young teamster and suspected the three Mexicans he encountered near Knight's Ferry.) Two weeks after that Allen Ruddle was killed twenty miles southwest of Knights Ferry. That same week a Mexican named Joaquín who was suspected of shooting Clark was arrested at Jackson and taken to Willow Springs to be identified and, it was supposed, hanged. (News snippets of this sort shaped the legend as written by John Rollin Ridge.)

The prevalence of crime reports in newspapers was one of the reasons most Americans went about armed. Three times as many people died of cholera, dysentery, smallpox, influenza, exposure, and infected wounds caused by mining accidents as died at the hands of murderous thieves, yet there was something sinister about the thief and murderer that made them a more worrisome reality. Hasty vigilante trials and executions were carried out by men like William Perkins and Alfred Doten when sentiment was excited by a murder and culprits were caught. Crimes were committed and punishment dealt to all kinds of people, including Anglo-Saxons, but only those who were seen as being affiliated with what became known as the Joaquín band excited talk of a Mexican guerrilla threat.

To the press, vigilante activities and crimes committed by a Mexican guerrilla band not only made sensational news, it was politically relevant in California. Anglo-Americans who formed and served on the vigilance committee in San Francisco in 1851 were angry at the Democrats in office. Officers and justices were accused of failing to protect people and their property both from hoodlums who had come to California from Tammany Square, New York, and from the "Sydney Ducks"— believed to be former penal colonists from Sydney, Australia. The Los Angeles vigilantes had also attempted to blame the Democrats for the same kinds of failures, suggesting, for example, that the jail guard allowed Zabaleta to escape after receiving a bribe from the family. But the charge proved false, and the vigilante effort there included office holders. Office holders also participated in the vigilante movement in Sonora town where William Perkins served on the jury investigating the murder of George Snow. In the end it did not matter who participated—vigilante movements were popular with the people and with most newspaper editors throughout the 1850s.

The politically ambitious throughout the southern mining districts agreed with what Thomas Butler King had written in 1850: the presence of too many Mexicans posed a threat to the state's economic welfare. Even though the first Foreign Miners Tax had gravely disrupted the local economy by scaring away the customers on whom local merchants depended. The sudden increase in crime that followed, largely carried out by Mexican bandits, led to the circulation of fears that a Mexican guerrilla band was at war with the United States in California. Indeed that fear was exploited by politicians and echoed in newspapers.

Not mentioned in legend but relevant to its history was news printed in June 1852 while Murrieta was in Los Angeles County. Southern Democrats from Texas, who styled themselves "Regulators," expelled foreigners from the mines in and around Quartzburg, Mariposa County, and confiscated their property. The foreigners, most of whom were Sonoran, complained to the county judge in the town of Mariposa. The judge said he could do nothing. However when the Regulators called for an edict evicting all foreigners from the entire county, the majority of Americans voted it down. The judge told the Regulators he could not pass the requested edict as it lacked popular support. Even so, companies of foreign miners and businessmen who felt unwelcome and feared more abuse packed up and left for other parts. The Regulators successfully exploited a political atmosphere to their own advantage, even though they did not have the kind of support they thought they would from their countrymen.[5]

Among those who left Mariposa County because of the Regulators was Don José de Llaguno, who was nearly lynched because he presumed to protest the confiscation of his costly and recently purchased mining equipment. A formerly wealthy businessman, he arrived in Stockton destitute. "The consequences of this renewal of distinctive laws for foreigners . . . is [sic] easily foreseen," reported the *Stockton Journal*, which favored the Whig Party. "The most immediate will be *revenge.*—These poor creatures, relying on American justice, . . . came to California to labor in the mines. They are driven out, persecuted, and compelled either to starve or rob.—Many of them will unite to attack innocent . . . travelers."[6] Indeed it appears that the actions of the Regulators may have provoked Claudio Féliz to break his promise to Caleb Dorsey and lead a band of eager new recruits from Mariposa County through Tuolumne County and on into Calaveras County. So it was that in the same month the *Alta* reprinted news from Los Angeles about the arrest of Zabaleta and Rivas, Kemble also covered news of the Regulators clashing with foreigners. He also wrote of Americans near Saw Mill Flat (also called Shaw's Flat), Tuolumne County, responding to rumored threats from a band of Mexican guerrillas.[7]

The Democratic *Republican* reported on July 14, 1852, that a band of Mexican horse thieves camped near Martinez had instigated the "Battle of Sawmills Flat." After one of their party was arrested, they supposedly poisoned the wells at Saw Mill Flat in retaliation, making several people sick. The businessmen in the area all received warnings that these Mexicans were plotting "a descent upon the whites." One of the Americans sent to Columbia for assistance, and it came, small artillery and all. The Mexicans fled to the mountains. The *Alta* version of this affair came from two sources, both of them letters to the editor. Neither mentioned poisoned well-water.

T. Robinson Bours wrote to L'Echo de Pacifique on July 11, 1852, his French letter being translated and reprinted in the Alta. Bours said that a letter in Spanish sent to him by his Spanish neighbor and business associate warned him that two hundred heavily armed Americans had convened at the Columbia Hotel and passed a resolution expelling foreigners from Shaw's Flat. Bours' neighbor owned and operated a large mine and employed a good many Mexicans. He said he had decided to resist and urged Bours to do likewise. Bours agreed, then learned that the Americans had arrived in an orderly fashion that night, but nothing happened. Next morning the Americans began ordering his neighbor's Mexican employees to stop working. Their employer rode to Sonora town and complained to the county judge and the justice of the peace. "I do not pretend to deny that there are many bad Mexicans in the country," wrote Bours, "but I assert boldly, from actual proofs, there is a majority of good people among them, who are as ready to punish crime among their own countrymen as the most zealous Americans . . . ; and as long as they conduct themselves properly, they have a right in common with all our citizens to the protection guaranteed to them by treaty."[8]

William Stacey, of Shaw's Flat, read Bours' letter in the Alta and felt compelled to make corrections, as he saw it. Stacey said that a Mexican woman living with an Italian man had received a letter from a friend, warning her that the proprietors of a store in that neighborhood had been marked for a revenge killing because of their role in the arrest of Reyes Féliz some months ago. "The letter came from a guerrilla band that infest the county," wrote Stacey, "and range between Mariposa and Mokelumne Hill, having their haunts and spies along the whole line."[9] The Italian was afraid and so sent to Columbia for help.

Help came, but never with the intention of dispossessing foreigners of their property or driving all the Mexicans out, Stacey insisted. However they did order the Mexicans dwelling in two tents to leave because they were known to have harbored members of the guerrilla band. As for the two hundred armed Americans from Columbia—there were only twenty volunteer militiamen. Stacey said they came and asked for his hospitality, but he sent them elsewhere. (Caleb Dorsey recalled that the militiamen passed the night at Ira McRae's store and that they "gave a good example of their destructive powers by charging upon the eatables and

16. Romaggi Inn and Store at Albany Flat, now a California historical site. Photograph by the author.

drinkables, completely cleaning out the small supply of both."[10]) Stacey added that he felt Bours had slandered the American character: "I, for one, cannot sit down quietly and allow ourselves to be branded villains, vagabonds, and robbers."[11] Among foreigners like Bours (and sympathetic Americans) it was the behavior of the armed Americans and their antiforeigner laws that threatened the peace, but to Stacey, he and his countrymen were above reproach. The only real threat came from a band of Mexicans who had their headquarters in Martinez, the Claudio Féliz band that would soon become known as the Joaquín band. Shaw's Flat did not suffer any trouble from Mexican outlaws, but Albany Flat did, and so did Chinese Diggings in Calaveras County.

On September 4, 1852, the *Republican* announced, "There is no doubt of the existence of a formidable band of guerrillas in the mountains around Sonora. We have received several communications from which we learn that the party is guided by one 'Cloudy' [sic] a noted Mexican guerrillo [sic] chief." The nineteen-year-old was said to lead a band "some 40 strong" that preyed on Chinese and Mexican miners, most recently on an isolated business owner at Sullivan's Creek and others at Chinese Diggings. The *Alta* reported on the same day that a gentleman who lived at Yorktown Gulch in Tuolumne County said, "A ruthless band of fifty Mexicans have left for the lower county on a plundering expedition. They have stolen about eighty animals . . . , committed several robberies and two or three murders, and are now on their way to Los Angeles to join a party that is waiting for them at that place. They are headed by a Mexican named Cloudy, who was in jail in Sonora last winter. . . . He has a brother named Reyas now in jail in Monterey, and it is said that . . . his party have it in view to release him by force." To this the *Stockton Journal* added, on September 7, 1852, that one of the bandits was shot while trying to escape Sonora town's marshal James McFarlane. The well-dressed young Mexican had been mounted on an exhausted and foaming horse. He refused to surrender and threw away a purse containing five hundred dollars while in flight. Gravely wounded, he was cross-examined and, like Reyes Féliz, told contradictory and incongruous stories, but some of what he said matched recent news reports: "It is understood that they have a 'correl' some fifty miles from here, in one of the most secluded spots in the [San Benito] mountains, where there are some hundred and fifty of the best Spanish and American horses." This was the same corral Harry Love came across while tracking Allen Ruddle's killers. In legend this was Joaquín Murrieta's hideout, a place where members of the band congregated and stored loot.

About two weeks after Claudio Féliz was proclaimed chief of a guerrilla band, he and three members of his band were killed at Salinas, in Monterey County.[12] A few newspapers announced his death and the breaking up of his band, but that was not the last of the Mexican guerrilla band. In October 1852 the *Alta* reported that two Americans named Biddle and Smith were assaulted and nearly killed by two Mexicans at Bear Valley, Mariposa County: "The Mexicans were part of the guerrilla band recently broken up near Sonora [where McFarlane shot a member of the band] and it is supposed their only object was plunder, as they took about $250."[13] Even though they were called a "guerrilla band," it was admitted that they behaved like common criminals. Still, Whig, Democratic, and independent newspapers reported stories of a Mexican guerrilla band threat. The company of armed Americans from Columbia, who had brought a small canon with them to do battle with Mexican guerrillas at Saw Mill Flat had marched as if to war. They were only

17. Gun store advertisement in the *San Joaquin Republican* (1853).

twenty strong but were full of confidence. No one was calling for military or government action—yet.

Joaquín of Calaveras

Joaquín Murrieta and his Los Angeles recruits herded stolen horses under sunny skies at first, but there followed cold wind and heavy rains that forced pursuers to give up the chase. The horse thieves probably sold stolen horses while en route to Calaveras County. That was where a band of Mexican horse thieves attracted suspicion the week before Christmas, but no arrests were made.

On Christmas Day 1852 a violent hailstorm pelted the county. That night thieves robbed the Levinsky, Levi and Company store in Jackson of three hundred dollars, five Colt revolvers, and sundry provisions while the proprietors slept off the effects of liquored celebrations. A couple of days later Edward Cameron "was fired upon by two Mexicans, and wounded so badly in the abdomen that he died shortly afterward," reported the Stockton Journal. The assailants tried to rob him but fled when they saw Americans coming. Cameron was shot on the road between San Andreas and Angel's Camp, about twenty miles south of Jackson. That stretch of road would soon be revisited by Mexican highwaymen armed with revolvers, but not until after the snow melted.[14]

Bad weather forced travelers and highwaymen alike to seek shelter. On January 6, 1853, the Alta printed a letter from a miner who complained, "We have had nothing but rain and snow for the last three weeks . . . snow is two feet deep." The second week of January saw warmer weather, but as snow melted under heavy rain, creeks and rivers flash-flooded. Cabins, mills, bridges, and mining equipment were washed away in rock-tumbling, clay-tinted waters. Muddy roads patched with slush and ice and creased with rain gutters were impassable. In Sonora, Tuolumne County, provisions ran out. People began to starve. Mining camp merchants in Tuolumne complained that they ran out of provisions because they could not buy sufficient amounts when they went to restock their shelves. Bay City merchants held out for the highest price, limiting the amount that mining camp merchants could purchase. The state government called on San Francisco merchants to send relief, which they did once the floods had subsided enough to use waterways for transport.

However winter never lasts long in California's foothills. On January 15 the Alta reported, "Our latest intelligence from the southern mines represents a great improvement in the weather. [The] Calaveras route is represented to us as being very good from Mokelumne Hill." From Stockton came even better news: miners were finding lots of gold. Gold placer knocked free of quartz deposits by flash floods lay near the surface, plentiful and easily gathered from where the waters had receded. This news attracted thieves. Not all thieves were Mexican, but those who attracted the most attention were, and their behavior excited so much alarm that newspaper correspondents would, for the first time, call for state government intervention.

First came reports from Angel's Camp that two Chinese miners were robbed by three Mexicans armed with pistols and knives. They carried off two bags of gold dust worth one hundred sixty dollars total. The same trio then entered another tent near Cherokee Creek and robbed two more Chinese miners of one hundred fifty dollars in gold dust. A third miner named Akop resisted and was run through with a knife. His body was found about seven miles north of Angel's Camp near Yaqui Camp on the Calaveritas River, just a few miles south of San Andreas. John White of the *Republican* also reported news that came via Brown's Express carrier service: "The band of thieves who have recently infested Calaveras county have at length been discovered. Their place of encampment is in a lonely gulch between Double Springs and Angel's."[15] Double Springs lay twenty miles northwest of Angel's Camp, with the Calaveras River gulch in between. The horse thieves had a rendezvous in the Hogback Mountains overlooking the river gulch and within view of San Andreas. A Mexican named Reis Juarez was arrested for killing Akop and taken to Angel's Camp, where he was either jailed or lynched. News that three unidentified Americans had been killed and robbed provoked still greater alarm.[16]

According to the *Calaveras Chronicle*, as reprinted in the *Republican* on February 2, 1853, it all started when a well-mounted young Mexican stopped by Bay State Ranch, owned by John Hall: "Mr. Hall having a suspicion that the horse was stolen" placed the Mexican youth under arrest. Along came a Mr. Davis, who owned a river ferry nearby. While he and Hall were conversing about what to do next, the dexterous prisoner slipped off his boots and with them the bonds that fettered his feet. The Americans glimpsed him running downstream and ran after him, but, said Hall and Davis, "we were stopped on the road by three mounted Mexicans who drew their revolvers, one of them taking up the prisoner behind him, and all dashed off in the opposite direction. They left the road and took up a gulch, which heads about the Calaveritas," which is to say, in the direction of Yaqui Camp, a mining camp founded by Yaqui Indians from Sonora and Chihuahua, Mexico.

Davis and Hall fetched their horses and weapons and sent word to Sheriff Charles Ellis of San Andreas of the escaped prisoner. The sheriff and two deputies soon joined them in pursuing the Mexican horse thieves.

The outlaw trail headed southeast through Yaqui Camp and Foreman's Ranch, then turned west and crossed the road between San Andreas and Angel's Camp. They continued on in a northwesterly direction, zigzagging up the Hogback Mountains. The posse spotted the band "resting their horses on the highest peak of a hill [today called Joaquin Peak], from which they had watched the movements of the Americans, and ascertained their number." The band appeared to have at least a dozen horses now and perhaps as many men. (John Rollin Ridge's legendary account of the Joaquín band includes the adventures of Davis, Hall, and "Capt. Charles Ellas" [sic].)[17]

Sheriff Ellis decided to advance under cover of trees to within rifle range, one of the deputies having brought a rifle. The deputy aimed and fired. "One of the Mexicans was seen to leave the ranks, and retire from the front of the hill. The Mexicans then . . . came dashing down and as they swept by, discharged their revolvers at the Americans, who . . . returned fire; a good many shots were exchanged, which resulted in three Mexicans being wounded," reported the Calaveras Chronicle. The discouraged posse returned to San Andreas without any prisoners. While they rearmed and regrouped, news came that a young American named John Carter had been shot that night and killed either at Yaqui Camp, according to one report, or else at Foreman's Ranch, according to another. A well-armed posse of twenty men followed the sheriff to Yaqui Camp next morning. There they arrested a Mexican called "Big Bill" who had boasted of killing Americans. He was lynched. (In legend, he was a Mexican gambler who had a dispute with Americans and started a fight, but Joaquín Murrieta did not take part, saying it was not his fight.) The sheriff's posse also learned that during the night the outlaws had broken into Phoenix Quartz Mill, which was only a half mile away. Two American night watchmen had heard them break and enter. The watchmen fired shotguns and wounded one. The thieves fired back and killed both watchmen.[18]

Calaveras Chronicle editor Henry Hamilton (who would later become editor of the Los Angeles Star), reported that a blood trail was found and the posse followed it due west toward Cherokee Flat. As they approached the Flat, two Mexicans suddenly dashed out of a tent shooting. One was gunned down. The other surrendered and was hanged from a tree nearby.

His shoulder was full of buckshot, a wound he had suffered at Phoenix Quartz Mill. The sheriff returned to San Andreas frustrated, for although his posse had caught up with some of the thieves, the leader was still at large.

Throughout the remainder of the week, bands of well-armed volunteer Anglo-American militiamen guarded Calaveras River and Stanislaus River crossings, marched around interrogating and imposing upon foreigners. Some of them robbed traveling Mexicans of arms and horses. Ignatius Moretto was arrested and brought to San Andreas, where he would have been lynched by an angry mob had not Italian-American Judge Theophilus W. Taliaferro intervened and dissuaded them, with the support of Sheriff Ellis.[19]

In spite of all of these efforts the bandits must have crossed the north fork of the Calaveras River, for on Friday night, January 21, a Chinese opium den in Jackson was robbed of two thousand four hundred dollars in gold dust. That same night Hall's & Co. butcher shop was robbed of two revolvers and some provisions, and at Jackson Gate a mile away a German-owned bakery and house were robbed of over a thousand dollars in gold dust and coins, all while the residents slept.[20] As no one was killed, John White concluded that the Jackson burglaries were the handiwork of Anglo-Saxon safe-crackers, but he hinted that they were affiliated in some way with the Mexican horse thieves Sheriff Ellis had been chasing.

Not long after the Jackson robberies, horses were stolen from Double Springs. On Wednesday, January 26, 1853, angry American officials in Double Springs passed a resolution exiling all foreigners. Double Springs was but a few miles from the Camp Seco near Turnersville, the same Camp Seco in which Teodor Vásquez said Joaquín Murrieta and others had lost all their money playing monte after selling stolen horses in Marysville in 1851.

While French, Italian, Mexican, and other foreigners packed up and moved out of Double Springs, a party of forty or so Americans from San Andreas descended on Yaqui Camp and ordered the people to quit the county. Then they sacked and burned the camp. Alfred Doten, who had moved to a ranch four miles southwest of Mokelumne Hill and eight miles north of San Andreas, wrote about it in his diary on January 26, 1853:

> Lately the Mexicans on the upper part of the Calaveres have taken to robbing, murdering, stealing horses, &c—. . .—A large number of horses have been stolen in this part of the country within a few days, and yesterday and the day before, a large mounted and armed party of Americans went up in the mountains above San Andreas. . . .—They came across several of the missing horses, and the Mexicans who had them, they killed—They found two of the murderers of the two Americans, and hung them at Yankeeville [sic]—They then started the Mexicans out, and ordered them away . . . and set fire to all their houses—. . . [T]oday I saw several of them on the road for Stockton with their women, children, and what they could pack on their backs.[21]

As Doten had not heard that Claudio Féliz had been killed, he was sure Claudio was a leader "among the cut-throat rascals." However the name that surfaced in newspapers was Joaquín.

This was the beginning of what became a California legend. It started with a series of robberies and murders and continued with a series of chases in the first quarter of 1853—an election year. The notoriety of the Joaquín band would soon become a political tool in newspaper columns and later in the state legislature. As to where the name Joaquín came from, this had to have come about when the band members were hung. They were dangled repeatedly in order to extract confessions, and one or more of them mentioned Joaquín.[22]

On January 27, 1853, as exiles from Double Springs and Yaqui Camp began pouring into Stockton with their varying accounts of events, John White published an "Extra" and sent copies to other newspapers by express riders. The *Alta* reprinted an abbreviated version.

> Great Excitement at Calaveras!—General Expulsion of the Mexicans from the County-Execution of the Robbers. Todd's Express brought us an *extra* from the office of the *Stockton Republican* dated [Jan.] 27th . . . giving the particulars and origins of a terrible affair. . . . It is well known that during the winter months a band of Mexican marauders infested Calaveras county, and weekly we receive the details of dreadful

murders and outrages committed in the lonely gulches and solitary outposts of that region. The farmers lost their cattle and horses, the trader's tent was pillaged, and the life of every traveler was insecure. Success had recently emboldened this band of villains to commence a system of outrage more daring still. . . .

The band is led by a robber named Joaquin, a very desperate man, who was concerned in the murder of four Americans some time ago at Turnersville. He levied his "black mail" generally upon the Chinese population. . . . With his band, he would frequently enter their tents, and compel them to furnish him with money and cook for him and his accomplices whatever food they required. . . .

We publish this horrible and terrible news just as we received it. A portion was supplied by Mr. Stevens, of Brown's Express, who arrived yesterday from Murphy's, and a portion from a French Canadian, who was afraid to remain in the county. He says the utmost consternation prevails amongst all the foreign population.[23]

The "Extra" employed explosive language like "outrage" and sweeping statements like "the trader's tent was pillaged" and "the life of every traveler was insecure," language that resonated with alarm and excused the American reaction against Mexicans and foreigners in the area. The alarmist tone mimics that of August 1850 reports about the murder of Mr. Miller, the innkeeper who was stabbed in the back with a sword. Such was the alarm that armed Anglo-American bands began patrolling Calaveras County. One company marched to the sound of fife and drum as if going to war, as they had in 1850 when foreign miners protested the onerous mining tax. However in 1853 the American response was limited and the perceived threat viewed as containable. The Joaquín band had yet to be described as a guerrilla band. That soon changed.

Some of the Mexicans sent into exile crossed the Stanislaus River into Tuolumne County, where they no doubt had family and friends at Martinez and Sonora. Their arrival caused a few American correspondents in Tuolumne County to express fears that the Joaquín band was among

18. Brown's Express advertisement in the *San Joaquin Republican* (1853).

the exiles. The *Alta* quoted the *Columbia Gazette & Southern Mines Advertiser* as saying, "Several desperadoes of Joaquin's Calaveras gang, have found their way into Columbia. It is said that an Englishman, formerly of Stevenson's regiment, is connected with the band of villains."[24] Horses were being stolen in the vicinity.

Edward Kemble's good friend, the deceased Edward Gilbert, had served as a lieutenant with Stevenson's volunteer Regiment Company H of the U.S. Army during the war with Mexico. Through him Kemble learned that some of Stevenson's regiments included men from Tammany Hall,

New York City, among them, John "Jack" Powers. Powers managed to appear to be law-abiding while living in Santa Barbara on land he had seized illegally. His ranch became an outlaw haven familiar to Joaquín Valenzuela and others. Although Powers had assisted in the arrest of Zabaleta and Rivas, he also pitied Zabaleta enough to buy him a fine suit to wear on the day of his execution, that he might die with dignity.[25] In Edward Kemble's experience, it was not surprising that men like Jack Powers were connected with the Mexican bandits in Calaveras.

For editor John White of the *Republican*, there did not appear to be any hint of Anglo-Saxon outlaw involvement. The Joaquín band was too bloody. They left murder victims behind. That was how Sheriff Ellis had tracked them. That was why the whole county was up in arms. He published a correspondence on January 29, 1853, from Mokelumne Hill and signed "W. M." "It was while pursuing the gang that the murdered men were found." He mentioned that one Mexican was caught and hung in San Andreas. He also mentioned more arrests had been made. "On Sunday [January 16] a Mexican was lodged in jail at this place . . . on the charge of murdering two Indians at Camp Seco on Saturday last. Two more from the same camp were also committed . . . today for robbing a Chinamen's tent." Camp Seco's justice of the peace, E. T. Beatty, made the arrests. The prisoners were Juan Nevie, Cruz Ramos, and Joaquín Madina, but Beatty knew Madina was not the band leader.[26] He continued to be alert to news of the movements of the Joaquín band for another month.

In another correspondence, W. M. joked about a militia leader dubbed "Capt. Cady"—a name borrowed from the character in a popular folksong about Captain Jack Cade (pronounced Kay-dee), leader of a peasant's revolt in London in 1381. (The name also surfaces in William Shakespeare's plays, which were popular entertainment at California's gold rush theaters.) The Calaveras Captain Cady led a band of thirty armed men accompanied by fife and drums into a Spanish camp called Jesús María, on Sunday, January 23, 1853, and proclaimed martial law. "He stationed sentinels at the different places of access to the town," wrote W. M., "with peremptory orders to let no one pass . . . [and] appropriated to his own use and that of his men such articles of provisions and bedding as they choose . . . [saying] that it was in accordance with the usage of war."[27] They left after exhausting supplies they did not pay for (like the men from Columbia who had marched into Shaw's Flat four months earlier). Indeed, the Captain Cady episode has about it the same kind of inflated folly that resulted in the so-called "Battle of Saw Mill Flat." Some groups of Anglo-Saxons knew how to exploit public alarm to their own immediate advantage.

Bandit News Spiced with Political Jargon

While the Joaquín band was being pursued all over Calaveras County, Edward Kemble printed a "Letter From the Mountains" written by John Judson Ames. Ames (who often used the penname "Peregrine Pilgrim") was a Southern Democrat, one of those who envisioned pushing the border with Mexico still further south. He had left his friend George H. Derby in charge of his newspaper, the San Diego Herald, and traveled to Tuolumne County on invitation from Governor John Bigler, who asked him to organize a miners' convention there. Tuolumne County businessmen leaned toward the Whig Party, but it was an election year, and with Ames's help, the Democratic Party hoped to punch a few holes in Whig support in Tuolumne County.

John Judson Ames was also friends with William Walker, who was then preparing for a filibuster campaign to Sonora. Edward Kemble was also on good terms with William Walker, as it was Walker who moved the people of San Francisco to take the law into their own hands and convene a vigilance committee in 1851. His editorials in the Herald had denounced as corrupt various local officials, especially Judge Levi Parson, who responded by having Walker arrested. The people rallied to Walker's support. When released, he was a local hero. Kemble admired Walker's bold editorials and courage, but he was more ambivalent about Walker's filibuster efforts, which involved a violation of the treaty with Mexico.

Walker presented his filibuster plot in guarded language, insisting he was responding to an invitation to resettle northern Sonora and fight Apache Indians. (Northern Sonora was under-populated, the vast majority of the inhabitants having left because of a prolonged drought and persistent, ruthless Apache attacks.) Indeed the governor of Sonora had published an invitation, in Spanish, offering land and mining rights as compensation. Two companies of French settlers had taken advantage of the offer and then behaved like filibusters. They were sent back to California. American citizens were not welcomed at all, but Walker chose to ignore that fact.[28] He found enthusiastic support in much of California while seeking recruits and investors. J. J. Ames undoubtedly helped his cause while in Tuolumne County. Henry Crabb, a Democrat who was running for office in the state assembly, also supported Walker's plot. (He would later hatch his own filibuster plot.)

Edward Kemble printed Ames's letter on the front page of his paper, even though he had a low opinion of Democratic Governor John Bigler and his supporters. Ames's letter was front-page worthy because it was about a miner's convention at which complaints would be made about San Francisco's merchants, whom mining town merchants had accused of price-gouging during the food shortage in early January. Demands made by miners at a convention could undermine San Francisco's political clout in state government. San Francisco and the mining districts had been locked in a power struggle over the state's rapidly growing economy since the state's founding, with the Bay City tending to favor Whig candidates and miners tending to favor Democrats.

John Judson Ames not only wrote about the convention, he also took Joaquín-related news and used it to argue in favor of sending all the foreigners in California back to where they came from. "I was told of a circumstance yesterday that beautifully illustrates the system of taxing foreigners —A gang of villains well armed, in the vicinity of Angel's Camp, made a descent on a lot of Chinamen, and representing themselves to be tax-collectors, compelled them to pay over $380. . . . If Chinamen are allowed here they should be taxed. If they are taxed they will be robbed, so let us not have them."[29] This kind of manipulation of news items to make political points would occur more and more frequently as the weeks passed.

Joaquín and Band Pursued all over Calaveras County

On the first of February 1953 a Mexican youth arrested at Angel's Camp was dangled several times in an attempt to get a confession and then hanged until dead. He was said to have confessed to being a scout for the outlaw band. Someone in the lynch mob claimed he recognized him as being at Yaqui Camp and Phoenix Mill. The youth was identified as

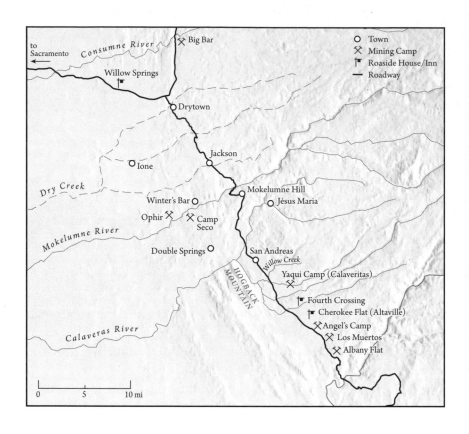

1. Calaveras County in 1853, with roads to Sacramento

Joaquín's brother by a Brown's express rider, but no name was ever assigned to him in press releases.[30]

About a week later Sheriff Ellis followed a tip and found a wounded Mexican youth in a tent at Los Muertos, a mile south of Angel's Camp. He managed to get his prisoner to the San Andreas jail without losing him to a lynch mob. Meanwhile a couple of men looking for two horses stolen from Angel's Camp tracked them all the way to Camp Seco, where they reported the theft to Justice Beatty. Beatty took over the search on Friday, February 4, 1853, and soon learned that three armed Mexicans had been robbing local Chinese miners. While he was tracking the thieves, local Chinese miners told him there were not three but five Mexican robbers, all well-dressed, well-armed, and well-mounted. He decided to go for help, but first he "ordered the proprietors of the ferry at Winter's Bar to let no one pass during the night."[31] However when five armed Mexicans demanded service that night on pain of death, the proprietors had no choice but to carry them across.

Justice Beatty and his posse crossed, too, and spent several days tracking the outlaws to Ione, and from there to an inn on the Jackson-Sacramento Road. There they learned that a band of Mexicans had robbed several businesses in a Chinese settlement at Big Bar on the Consumne River of six thousand dollars in gold and coins. From Big Bar they went to Spanish Town, where they were told that one of the outlaws had dealt monte all night on February 8, 1853.

From Spanish Town Beatty and posse rode along Dry Creek to Drytown and near there found the two stolen horses from Angel's Camp. The animals were exhausted and had been abandoned. Between Jackson Gate and Willow Springs, they found "the Stockton stage" without horses or driver, a source farther down the road saying there had been two passengers. Another source said the passengers were women. The stage had been en route from Sacramento to Mokelumne Hill via Jackson. It was feared the passengers and driver were killed, although no bodies or blood were evident. A German pedestrian who was walking to Sacramento along the same road said he was stopped by two Mexicans who threatened to shoot him if he didn't give them his money. They robbed him of six hundred dollars, then struck him a blow to the head and left him unconscious.[32] Beatty and party headed home with the recovered

19. Engraving of Chinese miners boarding a river ferry, from *Sam Ward in the Gold Rush* (1861). Author's collection.

horses, reaching Camp Seco on February 11, the same day a posse out of Jackson took up the chase.[33]

Throughout February Mokelumne Hill newspaper correspondent W. M. became the favorite source for confirmation of news about the Joaquín band. He wrote to the editor of the *Republican* on Sunday, February 13, "I hasten to give you the news . . . three Chinamen were murdered this afternoon, near Jackson, and robbed . . . supposed to have been done by Joaquin and his party." The story was confirmed late that night as he added: "The notorious outlaw, Joaquin, has been in the vicinity of Jackson, within five miles of Mokelumne Hill, . . . His band murdered five Chinamen and one American. . . . A party left Jackson in pursuit—overtook the gang and fired on them—wounding one . . . who, however, made his escape. A deputation from Jackson came to the Hill for the purpose of organizing volunteers to go in pursuit. . . . The . . . citizens appear determined to exterminate the banditti."[34] In a postscript he added that the American who was killed was a butcher and a resident of Jackson named Joseph Lake.

The next day, in another correspondence, he described waking up in the morning to the sound of bells, gongs, and drums as yet another posse leader issued a call to arms. People, moved by the sight of the dying Joseph Lake, heeded the call. Lake had been robbed and the horses from his wagon stolen. That same day, express rider Volney Smith rode into town at a gallop. A few hours later young John Horsley did the same. Both of them reported that armed Mexicans had tried to stop them on the road between Jackson Gate and Volcano, but they had been saved by the fleetness of their horses.[35]

Still more reports came in bits and pieces, forming a confusing web of mismatched details. For example the number of Chinese killed varied, as did the order of events and of the days on which they occurred. This kind of confusion would be exploited later, in the context of the election. Edward Kemble had limited space in his columns, so he abridged all news from Mokelumne Hill, editing out inconsistencies, even those that appeared in W. M.'s letters. One news account said that a lone Mexican youth—supposed to be Joaquín—had raced through San Andreas at a gallop, firing a revolver as he went, hitting three Americans in the neck. "Several reports are in circulation," complained W. M., "to the effect that Joaquin has been seen and shot at by Indians, Mexicans and Americans; also that his horse has been shot out from under him, but they are not sufficiently authenticated to report them for truth."[36] Though the outlaws seemed to move as fast as the rumors they excited, W. M. and the newspaper editors who printed his correspondences were confident Joaquín and his band would face justice soon.

The Jackson posse found two dead Chinese miners and one gravely wounded one, whom they carried back to Jackson to be tended by a doctor. They also came upon four Mexicans camping near Ranchería (a Miwok Indian village) and fired at them. One was wounded, but all escaped into the chaparral, leaving their equipment and three horses behind. The posse collected these goods and continued north through Dry Town to Fiddletown, from where one of the horses had been stolen. It was at Fiddletown that they heard Joaquín had had his horse shot out from under him as he was endeavoring to escape, but he was rescued by his confederates. The next day a posse from Mokelumne Hill stopped in Jackson to gather the latest

EXECUTION OF RAFAEL ESCOBAR.

The above engraving, from a Daguereotype taken by D. A. PLECKER, represents the execution of Rafael Escobar, in the town of Jackson, Amador County, California, for being implicated in the murder committed in the village of Rancheria, of the said county.

On the night of the 6th of August, a party of Mexicans, with one or two Americans, (called so *by name*,) entered the Rancheria Hotel, in the village of Rancheria, and commenced shooting down the inmates indiscriminately, without regard to age or sex, and succeeded in killing five men, the Landlady, one Indian, and wounding two other Americans, one of which was the Landlord, who saved his life by escaping from the house, the other saved his by falling down and feigning to be dead. After rifling the pockets of the dead and dying, they proceeded to break open a safe, out of which it is supposed they got $10,000 in coin. The excitement throughout the county ran almost to an alarming extent; the citizens armed themselves and turned out almost to a man, expecting to have a regular pitched battle at the village of Sutter, but when the undaunted Americans arrived near the field of Battle, the Mexicans (or Greasers, as they are more generally known,) fled like so many quails before a swift pinioned hawk; but being unable to elude their vigilance, a large number of them were captured, out of which three were found guilty and suffered the penalty of death on a tree near the village where the atrocious deed was committed, the following day, under the sentence of Judge Lynch. But the most lamentable part of

this bloody catastrophe is yet untold; a few days after its perpetration the brave and much esteemed Sheriff of the said County, Mr. Phoenix, and his deputies, with Sheriff Clarke of Calaveras County, and others, went in pursuit of a party of these desperadoes, overhauling them at Salvada, a small Greaser village near Chinese Camp, in Tuolumne County, and there, while sitting in a house, were surprised by the Greaser party riding up; both parties mutually recognized each other, and a fight immediately ensued, in which the much lamented Phoenix fell a corpse, in the exercise of his duty, by the discharge of a pistol in the hands of a Mexican who then fled; several shots were fired after him, but it is not known whether they had their desired effect. Another took refuge in a house, which being set on fire he rushed out with a six shooter in each hand and commenced firing at random in direction of the enemy until his shots were all discharged; in the meantime several holes were shot through him by the american party, but did not fall until he was cut down with an axe. The one hanging on the tree in the engraving, was captured in the town of Columbia, Tuolumne County, while asleep, and brought to this place by officer Durham of Amador, for trial; but on his arrival with the prisoner, he was taken charge of by the people, and in less than one hour's time placed in the position you now see him, making the tenth execution on the same tree.

Execution took place Aug. 10, 1855.

20. The hanging of Rafael Escobar at Jackson in 1855 was like that of Antonio Valencia, same location, in 1853. This item is reproduced by permission of The Huntington Library, San Marino, California.

intelligence, then picked up the trail from where the Jackson posse had left off. The Mokelumne Hill posse found no fresh corpses or camps and returned home for the night. But at a pre-dawn hour the next day, they followed up on a tip provided by a Mexican traveler and rode out to a mining camp called Ophir, twelve miles southwest of town. A Mexican woman revealed where a wounded Antonio Valencia, an unwanted and threatening guest, was hiding in her house. He was arrested and carried to Jackson, where he was identified by the Chinese survivor. Valencia confessed he was with the party that attacked and robbed the Chinese, but he killed no one; he only took the money." He was tried, convicted, and hanged, the body being left dangling for two days as a warning to other would be outlaws.[37]

Nine Mexicans had been arrested, four hanged, and one shot dead, yet their leader, Joaquín, remained at large, and that was unacceptable. A collection was taken up, wrote W. M. on February 17, 1853, "of nearly four hundred dollars, for the purpose of sending out six picked men, under the direction of [Charles] A. Clark, deputy sheriff of this county, to pursue the band of desperadoes." Clark was captain of the Calaveras Guards. He had served with distinction during the war with Mexico and had led the posse that captured Valencia. Everyone funding his posse expected he would succeed, but the financially pinched business community also began to look for other ways to compensate the guards. W. M. explained, "A petition is in circulation praying the Governor to offer a reward for the capture of Joaquin or any of his party." Undoubtedly a member of the business community himself, W. M. allowed his normally frank tone to become animated at this point:

> How long must the present deplorable state of things continue? How long must it be that we have to record the robbery and murder of men at their own doors and by the way-side, or while in the pursuit of their honest employment? Although the arena of their dark deeds is at present in this county, yet is it not a matter that interests and affects the whole community? How long before the cruel and wanton band may raise their murderous hands against other sections of the State? Can the public look so coolly on and leave the difficult work

of extermination to the enterprise of a few private citizens? May we not reasonably expect that prompt and effective measures will be taken on the part of the State in this serious and important matter?[38]

It was, after all, a gubernatorial and state assembly election year. If the governor wanted their votes, he needed to respond to their need for assistance in breaking up the Joaquín band, which was proving to be an expensive endeavor. Edward Kemble cut W. M.'s tirade, then added, "It appears . . . that Joaquin has neither been wounded nor surrounded, as rumored but is still at large."[39] Editors of independent newspapers like Kemble began to ponder how that was possible even while they predicted Joaquín's inescapable fate. Meanwhile Democratic Party papers like the *Republican* echoed W. M.'s call for government assistance. The Joaquín band was becoming a subject of political interest during an election year.

The Governor's Reward

When the petition reached Governor John Bigler's desk, he wasted no time honoring it, even though the petitioners failed to provide him with an adequate description. A proclamation was issued on Monday, February 21, 1853, and published in Stockton newspapers two days later.

> ONE THOUSAND DOLLARS REWARD.
> Whereas, it appears to me, that one JOAQUIN CARILLO [sic] is leader of a band of robbers and murderers in Calaveras and the adjoining counties, and has perpetrated a number of henious [sic] offences against the lives and property of the people of that portion of the State, and that the said Joaquin Carillo is now at large:
> Now, THEREFORE, I, JOHN BIGLER, Governor of the State of California, by virtue of the power in me vested by the laws and constitution of the said State, do hereby offer a reward of one thousand dollars for the apprehension and safe delivery of the said Joaquin Carillo in the custody of the sheriff of Calaveras county, to be dealt with according to the law.

WITNESS my hand and the seal of the State, at the city of
Benicia, this twenty-first day of February, A. D., 1853.

Attest—JOHN BIGLER, Governor.
J. W. DENVER, Secretary of State.

―――――――――――

DESCRIPTION: Said Joaquin Carillo is a Mexican by birth, 5
feet 10 inches in height, black hair, black eyes, and of good
address.[40]

This was the first time a surname had been assigned to the Joaquín
whose band had been plaguing Calaveras County. There could have been
only two possible sources: a sheriff or justice of the peace had heard the
name from an informant or robbery victim, or, what is more likely, one
of those arrested, perhaps Ignatius Moretto or Antonio Valencia, had
assigned the name to Joaquín, possibly merely nodding after someone
suggested it.

The same day John White published the governor's proclamation in
the *Republican*, he reprinted everything he had on hand about Joaquín,
filling several columns with the previous week's and even the previous
month's reports on the subject. He also inserted his own thoughts about
the bandit leader in an introduction and afterword to an abridged reprint
of the *San Francisco Whig & Daily Advertiser*'s filibuster-flavored profile of
Joaquín, the guerrilla chief from Jalisco, Mexico. Even though the profile's description of Joaquín did not quite match the somewhat vague one
on the governor's warrant, it did not contradict it either. (In legend the
San Francisco Whig description of Joaquín matches John Rollin Ridge's
description of Claudio.) The outlandish *Whig* account even claimed that
Joaquín wore chain mail under his shirt like a bullet-proof vest. This was
offered as an explanation for why all the well-armed North American
pursuers had failed to kill him or even seriously wound him. The *Whig*
description also claimed that Joaquín was a master of disguise, a depiction that John Rollin Ridge had fun exploiting in legend.

John White had initially ignored the *Whig* profile as if it was of doubtful
source, but now he used it to point out that "for some time past, a Mexican, named Joaquin, with a gang of bandits, and, it is supposed, some

white men, have committed numerous atrocities."[41] They had been pursued at great expense, and so the governor, in his benevolence, as Democrats saw it, had issued a warrant for Joaquín's capture, dead or alive. He was responding to a grave situation, out of consideration for the people of Calaveras County, who had been in a state of constant alarm for weeks. If some people had reasons to doubt that the Joaquín in the *Whig* profile existed, they would have to admit that the Joaquín of Calaveras— now identified as Joaquín Carrillo—was quite real.

Another description of Joaquín published in the *San Francisco Golden Era* weekly appeared in a letter from R. M. Ditson of Jackson. He insisted that the description he had read in newspapers of the Joaquín from Jalisco was erroneous. The author had clearly never met Joaquín. He knew someone who had; Joaquín was really rather ordinary looking, about twenty-two years old, five feet, six inches tall or perhaps taller with boots on, and he had a scar on his right cheek which he often covered with the chin-ribbon of his hat. He had belonged to Claudio's band.[42] This description is consistent with the one Caleb Dorsey gave of Joaquín Murrieta. It is also consistent with what the youth whom M. C. Rojo of *La Estrella* had in mind when he wrote of the outlaw, Murrieta.

Joaquín and Band Chased out of Calaveras County

The last posse to pursue the Joaquín band in Calaveras County was led by Charles A. Clark of the Calaveras Guards. It received immediate government support. The governor "caused to be transmitted to the Calaveras Guards a supply of ammunition,"[43] John White reported. The seven guards left Mokelumne Hill at noon on Friday, February 18, full of confidence. While on the trail they were joined by a posse of seven from Murphy's Camp who were looking for the murderers of three miners whose bodies had been discovered in a hole near French Camp, a few miles east of Phoenix Quartz Mill. The combined posse of fourteen started north along side trails, spending the night at Sutter's Creek, then continuing along more side trails to Ranchería and Drytown, from thence up alongside Big Indian Creek to the Consumne River. They questioned several Chinese miners en route. From there they turned south, stopping for the night at Willow Springs and proceeding next morning to Ophir, then on to Winter's Bar in the face of heavy rain and fierce winds. At the Bar they learned that a boat had been stolen the night before by four Mexicans traveling on foot.

On the other side of the Mokelumne River, they picked up tips that led to Camp Seco, where they learned that four saddles had been stolen the night before. They spent the night at Camp Seco. The next morning they headed to Chinese Camp and Double Springs, then they followed tips from Chinese robbery victims and the sound of gunfire. They discovered four dead and five wounded Chinese miners along the way. The outlaw trail then led across the Calaveras River to where Yaqui Camp had been and from there to Foreman's Ranch. While the posse slept at the ranch, the outlaws attempted to steal their horses, but Chinese night watchmen sounded the alarm and the outlaws fled. The guards went in pursuit immediately, though it was one o'clock in the morning and only the moon lit their way. With the help of a Chinese spy, they came upon the outlaw campsite, but before Clark's men had surrounded the camp, an overly eager posse member shot at the bandit look-out, only wounding him in the hand. The band scattered into the dark. They had kept their horses saddled and ready and were soon gone.[44]

The posse camped at the abandoned campsite until first light of day. Then they pushed hard and fast toward Cherokee Creek and thence to the Stanislaus River and Reynold's Ferry. John White of the *Republican* published Clark's full report, together with a comment from a friend of his who had ridden with Clark. He said that on February 23, 1853, they finally caught up with the outlaws again. "About five in the evening when we arrived on the summit of a hill, [we] saw them about three-quarters of a mile distant, robbing some Chinamen. They turned and saw us advancing, but they stirred not an inch until we were half a mile [away] . . . then they mounted their horses and rode off. . . . There were five well dressed Mexicans, well armed, and mounted on beautiful animals. We attempted pursuit, but our horses were worn out."[45] So were the riders. No one blamed them for their failure, not in light of what the recently executed prisoner from Los Muertos had confessed:

> IMPORTANT INFORMATION.—The Mexican who was hanged
> at San Andreas on Sunday last, made a confession, which dis-
> covered a plan of a well organized banditti throughout the

State. He was of Joaquin's party, but not a conspicuous or leading member. His obligations confined him to a certain district, out of which he dared not travel. He was compelled to
be in readiness at all times, and to . . . notice passing events,
and to apprise the company of fare. He was bound to shelter
and protect any of the brethren who were in danger, to procure
horses and assist them in their escape. . . . Such a combination
as this cannot easily be broken up, and it shows a skillful gen-
eralship in the leaders greater than they had been given credit
for. From this statement we can easily understand how Joaquin obtains his splendid animals. These agents know where
the best horses are kept . . . and on the arrival of the band are
required to procure them forthwith. Thus they have always
fresh horses and generally the best in the country. The leaders of the band . . . Joaquin, Claudio, and Reiz [sic] . . . were
the party that killed the Sheriff of Yuba [Robert Buchanan],
Claudio having fired the first shot. He was at Monterey when
last heard from . . . Reiz is still with Joaquin."[46]

The San Andreas prisoner was also credited with acknowledging what
McFarlane had said in the fall of 1852 with regard to Claudio and Reyes
Féliz. Joaquín Murrieta probably did not yet know the fates of either of
the Féliz brothers. Newspaper editors were better informed but none
of them reiterated reports of the recent deaths of Claudio and Reyes
in the context of the above confession, which was reprinted in numerous papers. Instead editors pondered how Mexican war veteran Charles
Clark's recent failure—the latest in a string of failed attempts to capture
Joaquín—made the Joaquín band seem more threatening than anyone
(except perhaps McFarlane) had thought possible. Edward Kemble edi-
torialized on the subject:

When we consider the numerous opportunities and facilities
afforded in the wild and thinly inhabited districts . . . , of the
systematic plundering and deliberate butchery of individuals or parties having treasure, . . . wonder ceases at the existing state of affairs. . . . JOAQUIN is the first chief of banditti
having under his command a regular confederation of cut-

throats, . . . that we have yet had in the State. . . . It is indeed remarkable that from the scape gallows hordes which have infested the State, there has not until now sprung up an active, open organization to prey upon the isolated camps and straggling "prospecters". . . . It is reserved for this Mexican guerrilla chief to set the example. . . . Other scoundrels will now, doubtless, follow . . . though this depends much upon the "length of tether" which the Fates allow JOAQUIN. Should his head suddenly pay the forfeit of his crimes the aspirations of many [a] Luigi Vamp [Luigi Vampa was a bandit from Dumas' novel The Count of Monte Cristo] in embryo may be effectually crushed.[47]

With complex sentences and elaborate vocabulary, Kemble, who had been hesitant to make much of the Joaquín scare, given that crime was widespread, now expressed open amazement that a band of mestizo Mexicans were the first to do what the "scape gallows hordes" of Anglo-Saxon thugs and thieves in California had overlooked. Joaquín and his band were gathering loot where city hoodlums had not ventured to go, and they did so with unmatched reckless, ruthless, and tireless rapidity. Of all the robbers plaguing the state it was left to this "Mexican guerrilla chief" to excite more alarm than the Sydney Ducks had in San Francisco two years earlier.[48] That the Fates had not yet shortened Joaquín's tether was startling to Kemble. Something had to be done lest other bandits follow his horrid example. In effect the independent journalist was acknowledging that the governor's reward was not unmerited, even though he had a low opinion of Governor John Bigler.

John White's opinion on the subject was colored by his familiarity with bandit and pirate lore. "Neither in the pages of romance nor in the authentic annals of history," he wrote, "have we found a robber whose career has been marked with atrocities half so dreadful as that of Joaquin Carrillo, who now ranges the mountains within sixty miles of this city." The guerrilla chief was still at large and too close for comfort. Although it was "the fashion of the historian and the novelist to trace in the characters of their bandit heroes some redeeming traits, . . . this blood-thirsty villain . . . [had] no qualms, no mercy or reproach. He rides through the settlements slaughtering the weak and unprotected. . . . So daring and reckless is he, that he marches in the day time through thickly peopled settlements and actually correls [sic] the Chinese by the score, and so accurate is his knowledge of the wild region, that he baffles his pursuers."[49] He was a "blood-thirsty villain" because he was Mexican, and Mexicans, to John White, were a mix of two morally deficient races: part cruel Spanish conquistador and part barbaric, heathen Indian.

White closed by quoting a friend who rode with Charles Clark's posse: "We had a right lively time of it after the greasers; . . . while we were on their trail, they killed and wounded 15 Chinamen and stole seven or eight thousand dollars. We got one or two chances at them, but they were so well mounted that they beat us running all to——."[50] To John White this Joaquín was a natural choice for scribblers of yellow-covered adventure novels, but his sordid tale would have to be shelved among those featuring the bloodiest and cruelest of bandits and pirates, for who could sympathize with a Mexican who had no sympathy for his victims? There could be but one explanation for his repeated escapes from justice: he had an extensive network of sentinels and relay horses at his beck and call. Though half a dozen Mexicans had been captured and hung or shot in the effort to break up his band and capture the leader, dozens more were still at large, including their chief. Vigilantes had cleaned out Yaqui Camp and expelled all the Mexicans from Double Springs, expecting that that would end their troubles, but it did not. Even W. M. wondered, "How long before the cruel and wanton band may raise their murderous hands against other sections of the State?"[51] Not long, as it turned out.

Betting High at Hornitos

A quiet but tense and watchful last week of February passed with armed volunteers policing town streets throughout Calaveras County. Chinese miners were more vigilant, too. No one knew for sure where the Joaquín band had gone or when they would strike again, but in time Calaveras County residents relaxed again, as it became apparent the band was no longer in their neighborhood. On Wednesday, March 2, John White reported from Stockton, "A friend upon whose judgment we place great reliance says that a Mexican informed him that two Sonoranians whom he recognized as dangerous characters, having known them in the state of

Sonora, were prowling in the vicinity of this city on Monday evening. He thinks it is probable that they belong to Joaquín's band." The Sonorans were said to be on their way to San Jose. Three days later, a gentleman from Mokelumne Hill came galloping into Stockton with a full money belt and said he was pursued and shot at by four Mexicans, but he was saved by his horse. Yet no one had seen the band leader, until word came that he'd been playing monte again, southeast of Stockton.

On Sunday, March 6, 1853, *Republican* correspondent A. J. Laseter wrote from Agua Fria, Mariposa County, about how, a few days earlier, a party from Quartzburg had come through town looking for Joaquín and band.[52] Quartzburg was about twenty miles west of Agua Fria and just a couple of miles from Hornitos. The party looking for the Joaquín band had come from a fandango house on the road between Hornitos and Quartzburg. "It *does* seem almost impossible to capture the robber Joaquín," complained Laseter. "It was but a short time since Joaquín was recognised betting at monte in Ornitos, against an American dealer: he got to drinking and betting very high." Betting high always attracted an audience, for the higher the bet the more intense the moment of revelation. American observers often remarked at how uncannily calm Hispanic gamblers were during big wins and losses. Murrieta, however, was not calm in an unsmiling stoical way. He drank and talked "and would in all probability have exposed himself to the dealer" had three confederates not interrupted and forcefully persuaded him to leave.[53]

He must have lost a good portion of his ill-gotten gains gambling, because he and his band took to stealing horses again. On March 3, 1853, Willis Prescott discovered that several of his horses were missing. He tracked them and in the evening saw them corralled outside a canvas fandango house a mile from Hornitos. It looked as though there were five or six Mexicans inside, so he went for help, returning late at night with seven armed Anglo-Americans from Quartzburg. Prescott entered the tent with a lamp; a young man named Henry Crowell volunteered to go in with him. Crowell "seized one of the supposed robbers when a party from outside fired in at the door, hitting Prescott in the side and Crowell in the hip. . . . Their wounds are not considered mortal," Laseter reported. "It is said that a Mr. Levining [Leroy Vining] burst two caps at one of [the Mexicans] while near enough for the powder to have burnt him; but neither barrel went off."[54] Various other versions claimed that five Mexicans suspected of being affiliated with the band were arrested the next day, that five Frenchmen were killed while sleeping in their tent, and that several Americans were in a melee at the fandango house after one of them—perhaps Crowell—recognized Joaquín and shouted his name. All accounts said that Joaquín and his band escaped.

Perhaps Harry Love joined the posse that stopped at Agua Fria looking for clues and refreshments. "It is to be hoped their labors will be crowned with success," wrote Laseter, "for the citizens are in danger" as long as the Joaquín band remained at large.[55] The posse continued north to Sonora, Tuolumne County. From there John J. Ames wrote to the *Alta* on March 5, 1853: "As yet I have heard of no enormous crimes in the vicinity . . . [but] a gang of suspicious characters has been lurking about in the valley between the Stanislaus and Montezuma [rivers], and people who say they know Joaquin well, positively declare that they have seen him." (Caleb Dorsey may have been among them.) Ames went on to suggest that Joaquín's guerrilla band posed a threat to the safety of California citizens and the security of their property on both sides of the Mexican border. "It is a source of great complaint about here," he wrote, "that the authorities do not take more active measures to break up this gang of banditti. . . . The Governor has already gone to the limit of his power in offering $1000 for the capture of the leader, . . . [but] there is a large gang of desperadoes . . . and if that amount were offered for each of them severally then it would be an object for a strong company to . . . exterminate the gang, nor can it be done without a long hunt."[56] William Walker was busy recruiting "a strong company" that could achieve the desired end if assisted by a company of rangers modeled on the Texas Rangers, who often pursued Mexican bandits on both sides of the border.

Ames believed that Solomón Pico was a bandit chief and had his headquarters in Baja California. He had reported, when in San Diego, that Mexican bandits made life insecure in the border region. He would soon link Joaquín to Pico, as had already been done in Los Angeles during the investigation into Joshua Bean's death. Indeed, it was widely believed among Americans in California that Mexican miners were carrying their gold back to Mexico and that this amounted to a kind of theft. In this atmosphere the filibuster version of Joaquín, the guerrilla chief who had

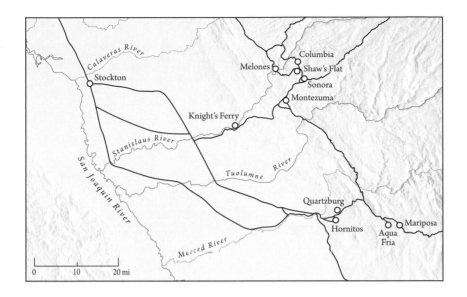

2. The Southern Mines and roads to Stockton

a chain of sentries and horse-stealing companies stretching from Mexico City to San Francisco, was not far-fetched.

When John Judson Ames called for a strong company that must be engaged for "a long hunt" he was echoing what W. M. wrote ten days earlier when he complained that the reward offered by the Governor was "entirely inadequate to the importance and expense of capturing Joaquín."[57] A.J. Laseter of Agua Fria and an anonymous Mariposa correspondent rang the same bell. "Will not Governor Bigler offer . . . a sufficient sum to pay a party of men to seek [Joaquín] out, and take him dead or alive?" asked Laseter. "We hope he will for the sake of his constituency." During an election year, listening to one's constituency was critical to success. The anonymous Mariposan was even more forceful: "The reward of one thousand dollars, offered by the Governor, would not pay the travel expenses of a party sufficiently strong to pursue him [Joaquín] with any prospect of success—accompanied as he is said to be, by a gang of forty or fifty desperadoes like himself."[58] Soon petitions were circulating in Mariposa County calling on the state legislature to act. Undoubtedly former Regulators signed the petition.

Legislators Debate the Joaquín bill while Murrieta Stops in Monterey

Later reports of Joaquín and band seem to draw a rapidly traveled northward loop up through eastern Tuolumne and Calaveras counties, hugging the mountains all the way. The *Alta* reported that Joaquín had been seen at Upper Ranchería in Calaveras County and that Mr. Pomeroy was sure it was him because he recognized the scar on his cheek.[59] Meanwhile the *San Diego Herald* published an outlandish claim by satirist George Horatio Derby to the effect that Joaquín Carrillo had come down "on a flying visit" to see Solomón Pico, who lay ill in Santo Tomás, Baja California. But who could believe Derby? Edward Kemble reprinted the "Interesting Intelligence from San Diego," adding that it could "scarcely be true, as it was only a few days since we had intelligence of his being in Calaveras County."[60]

John White refused to speculate as to the accuracy of any news about Joaquín. He knew that filibuster plans were incubating in Stockton and elsewhere, that it would benefit Governor Bigler during an election year

PROCLAMATION!

ONE THOUSAND DOLLARS REWARD

WHEREAS, it appears to me, that one Joaquin Carillo is the leader of a band of robbers and murderers in Calaveras and the adjoining counties, and has perpetrated a number of henious offences against the lives and property of the people of that portion of the State, and that the said Joaquin Carillo is now at large :—

Now, THEREFORE, I, JOHN BIGLER, Governor of the State of California, by virtue of the power in me vested by the laws and constitution of said State, do hereby offer a reward of one thousand dollars for the apprehension and safe delivery of the said Joaquin Carillo into the custody of the sheriff of Calaveras county, to be dealt with according to law.

WITNESS my hand and the seal of State, at the city of Benicia, this twenty-first day of February, A. D., 1853.

Attest—   JOHN BIGLER,
  J. W. DENVER,   Governor.
Secretary of State.

DESCRIPTION :—Said Joaquin Carillo is a Mexican by birth, 5 feet 10 inches in height, black hair, black eyes, and of good address.

Columbia *Gazette*, Calaveras *Chronicle* and Sonora *Herald* will publish four times.
feb23-4t1

21. Governor Bigler's reward bill for Joaquin Carrillo, *San Joaquin Republican*, February 23, 1853.

if Joaquín was caught, and that Democrats in Mariposa County were busy collecting signatures on a petition requesting funding for an excursion against Joaquín and his guerilla band. He reported that Joaquín was seen forty miles west of Upper Ranchería, at Forty Mile House in Clarksville, where he was recognized by a Spaniard while selling a stolen horse. He departed in haste. Later that day Mr. Lusk of Rhodes & Lusk's and Mr. Tracy of Adams & Company Express reported seeing six Mexicans, each carrying twenty-four rounds, pass through Colusa on the road to Marysville, which is seventy-five miles west of Clarksville. The band had avoided the cholera-stricken city of Sacramento and followed the north bank of the Sacramento River to Colusa, then continued on toward Marysville.[61]

A few days later Mr. Morse of Baxter & Company's stage line saw the same band. This time they were heading south through Colusa. One of them, "with a scar upon his cheek," Morse said, "and in other respects answering to the description of Joaquin, remarked to some persons that they might not know him then, but that they would hear from him in a short time."[62] Meanwhile residents of Mariposa County complained that various companies of the Joaquín band was still troubling their neighborhood and stealing horses. An Agua Fria correspondent to the *Republican* asked, "Can you inform us what the Legislature is doing? We scarcely ever receive any documents [or news] from the capital of the State and consequently we are kept in the dark as to what is doing."[63] He wanted to know what became of the petition after it was carried to the capital.

Democratic State Assemblyman Philomen T. Herbert of Mariposa presented the petition (which A. J. Laseter and Willis Prescott had signed) to the State Assembly on March 26, 1853, and then introduced a joint resolution urging his fellow legislators to require the comptroller to issue a warrant of a five-thousand-dollar reward for the capture, dead or alive, of "Joaquin Carillo" and his banded associates. Senator James Wade of Mariposa presented the Assembly with another petition asking the state legislature to authorize this reward. The resolution was referred to the Committee on Military Affairs. On March 30 Don José María Covarrubias, chairman of the committee, reported back saying they unanimously supported the act and urged that it be passed, but with amendments and changes. The Assembly invited Covarrubias to redraft the "Joaquin Act" and present it before the legislature for a final vote in two weeks.

While Covarrubias was redrafting the bill, a prank occurred in San Francisco that permanently changed the way Edward Kemble covered news about Joaquín. On April 9, 1853, he published in the *Alta* "a communication from a writer, who wishes his name concealed, stating that the renown [sic] Joaquin Carillo is now in this city. The writer says he knows him well, and describes his dress and person. He assures us that he is under strict surveillance and cannot escape."[64] The very next day, a humiliated Kemble admitted he had been duped:

> In our Saturday issue we published a paragraph . . . [from "a writer"]. Yesterday a rumor was circulated to the effect that the celebrated murderer and highway robber, Joaquin Carillo, had been captured and was confined in the city prison. Several hundred people waited to see the prisoner, and the open spaces in the City Hall were for a time literally crammed with the eager inquisitives. The prisoner was a poor mad Italian, [taken off a ship on which he had stowed away and] . . . carried up to the prison in a handcart, followed by an immense crowd, who entertained the belief that [he] . . . was the renown Joaquin endeavoring to escape from the country. . . . In connection with this subject we would say that there are several Joaquin Carillos in this State, gentlemen of acknowledged worth, and highly esteemed by all who know them, but the Joaquin Carillo of whom we speak is quite another person.[65]

Kemble's closing remark suggests that the unfortunate Italian had discovered his name to be a liability, Joachim Carillo being a fairly common name in southern Italy.

Humiliated, the Alta editor backed away from Joaquín entirely, ever afterward instinctively suspecting deceit or hyperbole when the subject came up. After all, more than a month had passed since the Calaveras Guards had chased the robber and his band, a month in which Joaquín and band had gambled at Hornitos, stolen some horses near Quartzburg, and then disappeared. The band no longer left a trail of dead bodies and empty pockets, not even among the Chinese. The threat Joaquín had posed seemed to have evaporated. To Edward Kemble and his staff at the *Alta*, Joaquín the guerrilla chief and his band of forty robbers was beginning to look like a spook conjured up by Democratic politicians seeking votes in an election year, a phantom invented by filibusters looking for funding and recruits to go fight Mexican guerrillas south of the border, and an excuse exploited by corrupt politicians in order to dip into state funds. For two months the *Alta* did not print another word about Joaquín, but Kemble did cover news from the state capital, where Don José María Covarrubias addressed the assembly on April 14, 1853.

Covarrubias said his committee had initially been in favor of the Joaquín bill, out of "a desire to prevent the perpetration of outrages and crimes and to ensure the safety of our people in remote and unprotected portions of the State from . . . the atrocities ascribed to this individual" and his band. He acknowledged "the failure of all attempts hitherto to capture him." But the committee members had changed their minds. A five-thousand-dollar reward was "not justifiable," nor was the proposed method "a safe and effectual mode of remedying the evil."[66]

He outlined several reasons. First, it was wrong to put such a high price on the head of an individual who had not been convicted under due process of law. Second, the committee "does not think that floating rumor and mere statements of newspapers should be taken as conclusive evidence . . . of the commission of crime or the guilt of one accused. On the contrary, they are confident that the accounts given are somewhat erroneous. Unless the said Joaquin be endowed with supernatural qualities he could not have been at the same time in several places widely separate from each other." Third, such a large reward would "stimulate cupidity to magnify fancied resemblance, and dozens of heads similar in some manner to that of Joaquin might be presented for identification," as had happened recently in San Francisco. The committee did not want to "tempt unscrupulous and unprincipled men to palm off, by purchased evidence, the head of another for that of Joaquin and thus defraud the State Treasury." Finally, there was "the danger of mistaking the identity."[67]

The legislature had just heard Thomas Berdue ask "that he might be indemnified for costs incurred in a prosecution wherein he was convicted of an infamous crime, which was afterward proved to have been committed by another . . . who resembled him in personal appearance." It was the vigilantes in San Francisco who, in 1851, mistook Berdue for Sydney Duck gangster James Stuart. Had Stuart not been arrested before Berdue was hanged, the outlaw would have remained free and an innocent man would have died. Coverrubias feared that in Joaquín Carrillo's case, it was the name that might prove a liability. It would be tragic if good citizens, "descendants of ancient and honorable families, who bear the name of Joaquín Carrillo . . . [among them] a very respectable citizen of the county of Sonoma and . . . the District Judge of the 2nd judicial district" in Santa Barbara, were put at risk while the outlaw used a pseudonym.[68] What was more, Joaquín did not appear to be a threat anymore. The committee therefore urged the state assembly to indefinitely postpone proceeding on the Joaquín bill.

The majority voted in favor of postponement. Had the government's role ended there, the legend of Joaquín Murrieta might never have been written. But Philomen Herbert and James Wade refused to give up. Wade went back to Mariposa to collect signatures on a more specific petition. This one asked for funding for a company of twenty state rangers modeled after the Texas Rangers and headed by Captain Harry Love, who would receive wages for the pursuit and capture of Joaquín and band.

Meanwhile Covarrubias's report became political ammunition to independent editors like Edward Kemble and his colleague John Nugent of the *San Francisco Herald*. Their newspapers were the megaphone and bullhorn of the business community in San Francisco. Though not totally convinced Whig candidate William Waldo would be a good governor, both said it was time to get rid of Governor Bigler and his regime, time to stop the nepotism and gross mishandling of state funds by Democrats who had left the state with a huge deficit. However John Nugent was less allergic to news about the outlaw Joaquín Murrieta. On April 18, 1853, he published a lengthy essay written by an erudite colleague who probably worked for the *New York Evening Post* before moving to Monterey, California.[69] His anonymous correspondence includes an oft-quoted "interview" with Joaquín Murrieta that would become the skeleton on which John Rollin Ridge hung his legend.

Written in poetic prose full of looping, complex sentences and coined words, the writer clearly had an intimate knowledge of the works of William Shakespeare and others, several of whom he quoted. He used Joaquín to illustrate the moral and political turmoil that accompanied the United States's sudden embrace of California. Joaquín was a symptom, like ink spilled on a page in history that if scraped away would leave a hole, a marked absence of truth.

The writer's sources spoke Spanish, so he himself must have had some fluency in that language. He began by pointing out that Joaquín Murrieta had been seen in and around the Monterey and San Jose areas "a few days before his visit to a ranch in the Salinas valley." On Wednesday, April 13, Joaquín, "with two of his band, surprised the inmates of a California house, on the Salinas Plains, one night last week, by knocking on the door and demanding entrance. After much hesitation, they were admitted, when they civilly asked for some refreshment." The ranchero was Don Francisco Pacheco. His late-night caller claimed he and his companions were lost and that they were on the way south to purchase cattle. Pacheco, seeing they were "armed to the teeth," was afraid to refuse them his hospitality. His family agreed to prepare a meal for the visitors knowing their business was of another nature than the one professed, but hoping they would not victimize their hosts. While food was being prepared Pacheco engaged the spokesman in conversation. "He was a tall handsome man about 21 years old, with a long beard and apparently false mustache," wrote the essayist in what could easily be a misinterpretation. He carried four revolvers and a large knife.[70]

After they had talked for awhile, the ranchero got up the courage to ask his guest if he'd heard anything about the Joaquín for whom a reward was offered. His guest "placed his hand to his heart and with grave politeness and a penetrating glance, replied, 'Sir, I am that Joaquin, and no man takes me alive, or comes within one hundred yards of me with these good weapons.'" Upon seeing his host's alarm at this boast, "the robber went on to relate the reasons for his conduct in his late career—he had been oppressed, robbed and persecuted by the Americans in the placers—had lost $40,000"—probably at monte tables, the author hinted.

Joaquín appealed to the ranchero's sympathy, knowing that he, too, had been a victim of American abuses in the form of tax collectors, land hungry lawyers, squatters, and Anglo-American outlaw bands. The desire to get even was natural, and Joaquín said he was determined to do so. The essayist quoted him as giving the following speech:

> I was once a great admirer of the Americans, and thought them
> the most generous, noble and liberal people in the world, from
> having seen them in my own country and here, . . . men of
> the most generous and honorable principles, to whom tyrany
> and injustice were as hateful as the rule of the Gachupians
> [Spanish immigrant settlers] to the Mexicans [like himself].
> I hated the insecurity and revolutions in Mexico and came

here thinking to end my days in California in peace, as a citizen of the United States. With an American friend, I took up a piece of land not far from Stockton, and was getting a fine little farm underway, when I was annoyed, insulted, and injured to such a degree, by my neighbors, that I could not live in peace. I then went in the [gold] placers and was getting on very well, when I was driven from my hole by some of my lawless neighbors. I was in trade and business there and was wronged and cheated by everyone I trusted. At every turn I took, I lost or was swindled and robbed, and that, too, by the very men for whom I had had the greatest friendship and admiration. I saw them daily commit acts of the most outrageous and lawless injustice, or of cunning and mean duplicity, hateful to every honorable mind. I then said to myself: I will revenge my wrongs, and take the law into my own hands; those who have injured me I'll slay, and those who have not I will rob—my track shall have a trail of blood, and he that seeks me shall bite the dust, or I will die in the struggle, I will get my money back some way or . . . at least will not submit, unrevenging, to outrage.[71]

After supper Murrieta paid his fare and left with his men at around one o'clock in the morning. The ranchero said he went south, and the Monterey writer concluded that Joaquín was on his way to Baja California. The people south of the border had "contracted a most bitter and acrimonious feeling against the Americans from the bad treatment some of them have received . . . [and] are disposed to visit their hate and revenge on innocent men, many of whom in vain cautioned them in kindness to keep out of company of rowdies and from the monte bank: but it is as much use talking to a stone wall as attempting to convince most Mexicans of the evils of gambling." Indeed too many Americans saw the bad habit as a means of easy profit. In San Francisco Mexicans saw "fine saloons filled with well dressed Americans, men and women, in open day, with all the accompaniments of music, and a splendid bar stocked with all kinds of liquors and nice things." Why listen to do-gooders when gamblers seemed to have all the fun?

Not only did Mexicans like Joaquín fall prey to these temptations, wrote the essayist, but "many of our countrymen have lost themselves in the same way; . . . their lives given over to pleasure and brawls."[72] The sad lack of morals exhibited daily in America's youngest state was threatening more than the lives of those Joaquín and his band assaulted. Americans had become a threat to one another, their behavior an insult to the image of their young nation in the presence of so many foreigners. Daily they poisoned international relations, and that was a tragedy. Those nations had once admired Americans and their democracy.

"I have told the story as I have heard it from several sources," wrote the Monterey correspondent, and he did not doubt but that the main incidents were true. But as for the vindication Joaquín gave for his crimes, that could not sway any "sensible and humane man," even if Joaquín's encounters with lawless Americans led to his fall. Indeed the writer did not doubt Joaquín's claim that he suffered wrongfully at the hand of rude Anglo-Americans, for it was but one more "indication of the fever which rages in the social and political system of California, which some say is tearing her very vitals out; and others that such things must be until things get better." If American poet William Cullen Bryant (1794–1878), editor of the New York Evening Post, "could live a day of California life and see the struggle of races and nations," if he could see "the world's future government" take root where the American people "experience every month . . . some strange crisis in their morals, legislation, commerce, or social feelings," it would doubtless bring to mind the words of one of his earlier poems: "Dost thou wail for the age, of which the poets tell, ere yet the winds grew keen with frost, or fire fell with the rains . . . ?"[73]

The rain of fire referred to in the poem was one of the most spectacular meteor showers in recorded history. In 1833 people in almost every town and city in the United States looked up at night and saw Leonid meteors dart and dash in such alarming numbers they outshone the moon, causing preachers and politicians to speculate on the significance of the omen. Some saw it as a sign from heaven that God had blessed America and that her people had a manifested destiny to spread the gospel of democracy. But how unholy the manner in which they were spreading that message in California! Indeed some of them were even plotting to spread their freebooter version of it in Mexico. It was like William Shakespeare said, wrote the Monterey correspondent: "What then shall cleanse your bosom, gentle Earth, from all its painful memories . . .—that so at last the horrid tale of perjury and strife, which men call history, may seem a fable, like the inventions told by the poets of the gods of Greece.'"[74] In other words, fables, legends, myths, and folklore are easier to live with than the truth, the essayist argued.

In ancient times mythology took the place of history. In California, the correspondent observed, where bandits like Joaquín depicted themselves as gay robbers so that the people might pardon their crimes, mythology was married to history. Joaquín, like Robin Hood, was "of good family" and had received "an excellent education" in Mexico. He had been "formerly of quiet, modest and honorable character, of which . . . there are thousands in our . . . sister Republic of Mexico," wrote the essayist. True, the Mexican people, like those of every nation, had vices, but they also had virtues. "Great have been their sacrifices for liberty and democracy; great . . . has been their liberality to thousands . . . in California and Texas. Let this not be forgotten."[75] Let the calls for expulsion and extermination stop, for such hardness of heart made good Mexicans desperate. That hardness of heart was why Joaquín Murrieta could convincingly portray himself as a victim turned avenger, excusing his malicious greed as justice and his bloody deeds as retaliation.

Joaquín's account of his own adventures, the author pointed out, was sprinkled with boasts that had about them an impish love of glory. He had told his host, for example, that when he was in Stockton he saw a bill posted offering one thousand dollars for his arrest and wrote on it, "I offer $10,000—Joaquín." Perhaps the young outlaw had "filled his memory . . . with those legendary songs and stories of Spanish robbers, with which the literature of Spain and Mexico are full." Perhaps he pictured himself as one of them, with "their dashing triumphs and their heroic end, meeting death without fear and immortalized in robber annals and popular glosses." If so it was a boyish fantasy he shared with Anglo-Saxon youths who also grew up reading adventure stories and dreaming of heroics, as did William Walker.

The Monterey writer closed his long epistle with a quote from a legendary conversation that gave a good example of the wrong-headed thinking to which young men in California were so vulnerable. "'What joys,

what cheers, what exultation, what crowds!—the people must love you; I
would give my life for such a moment, such a day,' said a green courtier to
Oliver [Cromwell] as he was entering Whitehall [in London] to be made
Lord Protector. 'Yes,' said he coldly, 'and there would be much more than
this, if I were going to be hung.'"[76] In other words, famous outlaws were
more popular than famous guardians of the law. In California, where the
law was so often enforced in an arbitrary way, no one better illustrated
where this moral tragedy led than did Joaquín Murrieta.

Whereas M. C. Rojo, in his editorial "¿Quién es Joaquín?" had sought
to dispel myths about the famous outlaw which were popular in Spanish-speaking circles, the Monterey writer dissected them from a North
American perspective. To him, "the horrid tale of perjury and strife which
men call history" was often romanticized into a more palpable myth,
and Joaquín was a part of that reality. Joaquín depicted himself as a just
avenger, and even to American ears, that was fitting in the context of
myth-making. Americans often painted themselves as above reproach,
but in California the reproach of foreign immigrants like Joaquín was
not unmerited. It was U.S. democracy and the spirit of independence
that Joaquín and others from abroad had admired, but in lawless California, they saw too much of a cruder version of independence: every
man for himself. The result was that instead of exporting democratic
ideals, North Americans in California were feeding a myth which made
the United States look tyrannical. For the erudite essayist in Monterey,
that fact was a source of grief. His country was so young and already so
tarnished.

The Monterey article was reprinted on May 4, 1853, in the *Republican*, along with another correspondence dated April 24 and signed "Don
K"—the nom-de-plume of Benjamin Park Kooser, a young army gunner
stationed at the Presidio fort in Monterey. Kooser wrote in a postscript,
"Joaquin is about, on the Salinas; so says report, but people are too busy
turning the sod to look after him." John White sent Kooser a note of inquiry and a few days later reported to his readers:

> Our Monterey correspondent has conversed with the author
> of Joaquin's confession. . . . He says: 'There is no doubt that
> Joaquin passed south, through Monterey county, and prob-

ably took the road for Loretto, in Lower California. The real name of the bandit is Joaquin Muliati [*sic*]. He speaks English fluently, and . . . was heard to say that he would never kill a Spaniard. About ten days ago, he was seen in San Luis Obispo.' Another gentleman, who is likely to be acquainted with the facts, says: 'Joaquin is now on his way to Lower California, and will keep . . . to the missions . . . through a barren, mountainous country. The conversation reported in the *Herald* between Joaquin and the ranchero is confirmed. He however, said much more than was reported.'"[77]

While John White was verifying the news from Monterey, the *Sacramento Union Steamer Edition* decided to paste a face on "Joaquin the Mountain Robber." On April 22, 1853, an engraving by Thomas Armstrong was published on the front page. *Union* editor Lauren Upson praised the work: "Every feature of the bold mountain robber is prominent . . . and his character as truly represented through the medium of his countenance." Armstrong gave the bandit a scar on the right cheek and nostril, no beard, a young mustache, thick, shoulder-length, wavy black hair, and a sallow complexion. It would be the prototype on which many a later artistic rendering would be based.

The Ranger Bill

Futile attempts to seize Joaquín and band were reportedly made in San Luis Obispo, Santa Barbara, and Los Angeles. In June the band rode as far south as mission San Luis Rey in San Diego County, stealing horses along the way. A San Diego posse claimed they caught the band off guard and scattered their herd, after which Joaquín turned north again. Meanwhile Philemon Herbert and James Wade succeeded in reviving the Joaquín bill surreptitiously. On May 10, 1853, Herbert "introduced a bill providing that Captain Harry Love be authorized to raise a company of mounted rangers for the capture and extermination of Joaquin and his band."[78] It lost in the house, but the next day, when there were many absences, it passed: ayes 30, noes 19. On Friday the 13th, in May 1853, "Mr. Wade . . . reported favorably on the bill [before the senate] and after a 2 hour discussion" it passed there, too.[79]

22. "Joaquin, the Mountain Robber." An engraving by Thomas Armstrong featured in the Sacramento *Union Steamer Edition*, April 22, 1853. Courtesy of the California History Room, California State Library, Sacramento, California.

The two-hour senate discussion was initiated by Senator Antonio María de la Guerra of Santa Barbara, who insisted something more definite be said regarding the identity of Joaquín. The resulting bill that passed the Senate gave the rangers three months to locate five Joaquíns: Murrieta, Ocomorenia, Valenzuela, Botiller, and Carrillo, together with their banded associates. *Alta* editor Edward Kemble commented sarcastically that the state legislature was supporting a war on Joaquín north and south of the border:

> In the Senate, the bill was passed authorizing the raising of a company for the capture of Joaquin and his men. This, we suppose, is for the purpose of keeping good the number of war claims on the Treasury. By the act, twenty men are to be raised who are to draw $150 per month each for three months. . . . This will allow a fine opportunity for organizing for any hostile . . . foray on the neighboring State of Mexico; and if the company confine themselves strictly to hunting after robbers, yet nothing can prevent others from joining them at their own expense, . . . to strike off for any filibustering purpose that may promise pay or plunder. We would be in favor of rewarding as liberally as any one, whoever might capture this famous robber, but we fear that this authority from the State will be greatly abused, and that . . . a great number of relief bills will be brought in . . . for service in the 'Joaquin war.'"[80]

The "filibustering purposes" Kemble alluded to were, of course, those of William Walker and friends. Walker enjoyed the secret support of a number of California state legislators from both political parties. One of his supporters, Tejon County representative Major Walter H. Harvey, "was engaged in raising a company for the purpose of making explorations in the State of Sonora" at the same time that he enlisted to serve with the rangers captained by Harry Love.

The rangers had barely begun scouting when Major Harvey and his company were ambushed and Harvey was killed by Tejon Indians, Stockton newspapers reported. Then came a correction: Harvey was not dead. He had only fallen from his horse while drunk. Shortly after this embarrassing mishap, he was summoned to Benicia. He never did render any real service to Harry Love. Neither did Philomen T. Herbert, G. V. McGowan, Colonel McLane, Willis Prescott, Coho Young, or S. K. Piggott, all of whom must have been in Major Harvey's company.[81] Harry Love replaced them with new recruits in June.

Outraged members of the state legislature who had been absent the night the ranger bill passed reconsidered it the next morning and again voted to indefinitely postpone it, but it was too late. The Herbert and Wade faction had taken all the necessary steps, in keeping with the state constitution, to prevent a reversal from taking effect. They had produced more petitions, proposed an act before the legislature, discussed questionable sections (such as naming only Joaquín Carrillo) with the legislature, and compromised (e.g., limiting the rangers to three months service). As soon as the bill passed they had rushed it to the governor who signed it into law before the assembly reconvened. The vote was final. The rangers set out just as the gubernatorial race was heating up.

The Rangers Bring Back Two Heads and a Hand

Harry Love and his rangers began tracking Mexican horse thieves in Mariposa and Tejon counties where Joaquín Valenzuela and his confederates ranged. Then they went to San Jose to investigate a crime attributed to Joaquín's band and from there followed trails in the San Benito Mountains toward Mission San Juan Bautista. John White of the *Republican* kept abreast of their activities with the help of rangers Captain Patrick Edward Connor and William Howard, both of whom were Mexican-American War veterans. William T. Henderson and John A. White (no relation to the editor) were veterans, too. Captain William "Bill" Byrnes was an Indian-fighter and gambler who had met Joaquín Murrieta at Murphy's Camp in 1850, probably at a monte table. Byrnes's scouting party included Mariposa Deputy Sheriff John Sylvester. The *Republican* cheered them on while a correspondent from Sonora town in Tuolumne County taunted them for political reasons.

Edward A. Pollard, a Whig and supporter of William Walker's filibusters, wrote teasingly to the *Alta*, "Capt. Harry Love appears to have no scent of Joaquin," and then complained that Tuolumne County was having trouble with the Yosemite Indians and that the rangers should "divert themselves from the pursuit of the 'Rawhead and Bloody Bones' hero to chastise the Indians."[82] After all, hadn't the Texas Rangers been founded for the purpose of fighting Indians? Pollard went on to accuse the California Rangers of murdering their prisoners. "I have just been in conversation with a gentleman who had just left the State Rangers . . . [at] Howard's Ranch on Burn's creek, Mariposa," wrote Pollard. "They had . . . captured a Mexican cattle thief, who was surmised to be Joaquin's brother, [brother-in-law, according to Harry Love's July 12, 1853, letter to the governor]. . . . They had also captured two horse thieves. These were at once started, under guard, to Quartzburgh for trial," but they never made it to town. Both prisoners were found "perforated with half a dozen balls each."[83] A few days later he repeated the charge: "Love's Rangers have determined to take the law into their own hands. . . . The two prisoners, who were shot . . . were reported to have attempted an escape. . . . Astonishing accuracy to have emptied a six-shooter into the body of a man in flight!"[84]

Pollard didn't care about the Mexican prisoners. His target was the governor and other Democrats running for office to whom the rangers owed their existence. Independent editors like Edward Kemble echoed what Pollard said about the rangers wasting their time hunting "the fabulous robber chief JOAQUIN" when they could be chastising marauding Indians. "We think their present occupation of scouting for a man whom nobody ever saw, and who, perhaps has no existence except in the imaginative brains of the legislators, and who, if he does exist, is most likely out of the State or in a place of safety [i.e., Sonora, Mexico], is not particularly profitable to the State, or serviceable to the community." The ranger's mission was in vain and yet "the politicians [i.e. Democrats] are shouting loud hosannas to the Joaquin Rangers for their brilliant services."[85] Joaquín was dismissed as a fiction by Whigs who wanted to see the Democrats voted out of office. Joaquín Murrieta and his banded associates were real enough, but opponents of the Democrats did not think their crimes merited the hiring of rangers at the expense of the state.

When news came from Los Angeles that Joaquín Murrieta had definitely been seen in that city in June, an annoyed Kemble joked about how tiresome the subject had become: "'Hang that fellow Joaquin!' exclaims the irrascible old gentleman over his coffee and morning paper; there's been nothing else in the prints for the past five months!—but Joaquin won't be hanged. He still keeps walking at large as ubiquitous as ever. . . . If all rumors are correct, he was in four counties and two townships on the same day."[86] After ignoring the Joaquín band for two months, Edward Kemble found the subject annoyingly prevalent because of the state rangers.

For example the Democratic *Republican* reported that the "untiring efforts of Capt. Love, Lieut. Connor and their brave company of rangers have had the effect of completely ridding . . . [Mariposa] county of desperate murderers and horse-thieves."[87] The rangers were also praised in political debates, the incumbent governor saying they were critical to the security and prosperity of the citizens. Whigs, meanwhile, continued to poke fun, even after rangers Patrick E. Connor and William Howard helped Stockton Sheriff Edward Canavan catch a horse thief belonging to the Dawson gang.[88] Canavan had learned of the arrest of E. Wright and Martin Newell in Columbia, both of whom mentioned Dawson when interrogated. Frank Freeman was arrested with Dawson. Sheriff Canavan then travelled all the way to San Francisco to catch William Anderson. The five Americans from Columbia had "hitherto enjoyed good reputations," until they robbed Adams Express at Mormon Island of seven thousand dollars in March 1853. The Columbia safe crackers had two Mexicans in their company, provoking some journalists to conclude that the gang was part of Joaquín's guerrilla band.[89] A few Whigs suggested that Dawson was the real leader of the so-called Joaquín band.

On July 27, 1853, Patrick Connor received a message from Harry Love and shared it with the editor of the *Republican*: "An organized gang of some fifty horse thieves had been discovered . . . ; for some time past the neighborhood of San Juan [Bautista] has been infested with robbers." Captain Byrnes and company arrested five men and seized the stolen horses they had in their possession. "The prisoners have confessed and pointed out the headquarters of the thieves . . . in the coast range mountains, on the border of the Tulare Valley. They have . . . some three hundred stolen horses with them. They describe their comrades as ill clothed and ill fed, some having nothing but shirts on their bodies."[90]

Cantua Creek empties into the Tulare Valley not far from what is today called Joaquín Ridge. Love's party was moving south from Mission San Juan Bautista while Joaquín Murrieta's band was moving northeast from Los Angeles. The rangers rode at night, as the sun was fiercely hot during the day. The outlaws probably did the same. At dawn the rangers spotted a thread of smoke rising from a bluff to the southeast and headed in that direction. Two Mexican sentries were quietly arrested by

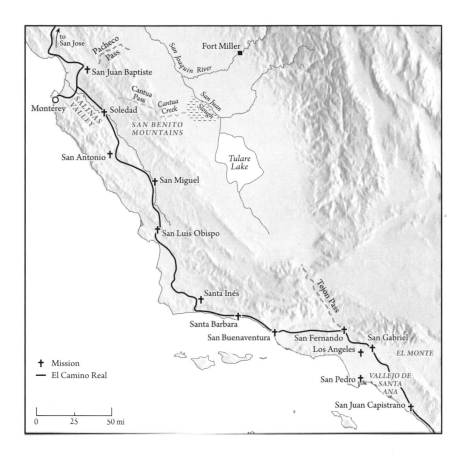

Bill Byrnes before the rangers came upon a Mexican camp. The *Republican* was the first to get the news.

> Capture of the Bandit Joaquin.
> Head Waters of the San Joaquin River, July 26th.
>   Sir: . . . I hasten to inform you of the death of Joaquin, the robber, who has been such a curse to the country for sometime. Capt. Burns . . . and Mr. Silvester arrived here yesterday evening with the heads of Joaquin and one of his band, whom they captured at a place called Singing River [*arroyo cantua* in Spanish], about 140 miles from here. The remainder of the party are expected here this evening with two prisoners. Captain Burns has preserved the heads in spirits in order that they may be the more readily recognized. . . . The weather is very warm,-Thermometer, 115 in the shade.
>   Further Particulars. Snelling's Ranch, July 27th, 1853.
>   Mr. Young, the Government Mail Carrier, just arrived. . . . He stated that Capt. Burns, . . . arrived at the Fort . . . , with the heads of the notorious robbers Joaquin and "Three Fingered Jack," together with two other members of Joaquin's infamous band as prisoners. The Rangers encountered this party of marauders near Panoche Pass, on the 23d instant. . . . They were six in number. . . . Two of the party made their escape unscathed.[91]

The news reached San Francisco two days later. Edward Kemble published two dispatches from *Todd's & Co. Express* that confirmed the report, but he prefaced it with a comment that expressed his continued misgivings: "Of the capture and death of Joaquin there appears to be some doubt, though it is highly probable that the scoundrel is taken." As for the identity of the one with three fingers on one hand, he had no doubts whatsoever as to who that was:

> "Three-fingered Jack" is an old offender; a consummate villain with whose early exploits in California we are quit familiar.

... He was the principal actor in a terrible tragedy, which occurred in the spring of 1846 not far from Sonoma. Two of Fremont's party were captured by a band of native Californians
headed by this "Three Fingered Jack," and their persons hor-
ribly mutilated. . . . One was literally flayed alive! Jack—who
derives his sobriquet from the mutilation of one of his hands,
caused by its having been caught under a lariat against the
pommel of his saddle, while lassoing a bullock—was once
a prisoner of this city. . . . Since his escape . . . we have not
heard of him. . . . The mention made of him in the following
account gives to the report an air of truthfulness that to us is
quite convincing. We hope it may be correct.[92]

Kemble was well-acquainted with the history of the notorious Californio who, in 1847, was identified as Bernardino García. Although the
rangers' prisoners identified the three-fingered Californio as Emanuel
García, not Bernardino García, Kemble was certain there was only one
notorious three-fingered Californio named García.

News of the deaths of Joaquín and Three-Fingered Jack came when the
political battle was at full tilt. One observer said the election was "the
most exciting among the topics of general discussion. . . . The parties
are marshaling their forces; meetings, conventions, speeches, newspaper articles, and the usual weapons for conducting a warfare of this
kind, are now actively employed. Candidates are on the stump, office
seekers prompting from below, wire-pullers managing the scenes, and
the people keeping a wary eye on the whole, that they may check-mate
the game" by voting.[93] Joaquín and the rangers continued to be targeted
in speeches and articles. Edward Kemble wanted the Bigler regime and
those who had voted for the ranger bill voted out of office, so he continued to call Joaquín's existence into question.

The renowned robber chief Joaquin, who has been made a
great hero of romance by newspaper writers and legislators,
has at length been captured by the State troops raised for
the purpose—at least a man supposed to be him has been
taken. The Joaquin war has cost the state a good round sum
of money, and has resulted in nothing more than is accom-

plished by the taking of a thief or robber by a constable. . . .
The Joaquin that there has been so much talk about was purely
a fabulous character, whose exploits of villainy have been announced as occurring on the same day in half a dozen different places. . . . Still, we are glad that the supposed romantic
chieftain has been captured.[94]

It wasn't that the rangers didn't deserve credit for good police work,
but rather that they existed because of political sleight of hand. An unpopular bill had been passed one night, and the governor had signed it
into law that same night. It was a costly bill, and the success of the rangers did not make it any less onerous in view of the state deficit.

John White, of the *Republican*, was quick to rebut the *Alta*'s mocking
words. "Some newspapers," he wrote, "seem to doubt whether the Rangers have really got hold of Joaquin. . . . In our mind there is no doubt that
Joaquin Valancuela , not Carrillo, has been killed. This Joaquin was well
known in Mariposa county as a notorious horse thief, and as the companion of 'Three-Fingered Jack.'"[95] White said that Valenzuela "was well
known to be somewhere among the Tulare mountains," and that Harry
Love was, at that time, following him. Not only did the rangers kill Valenzuela and break up the company he was with, they expected to close
in on Carrillo as well. "A clue we are glad to say has been found to the
whereabouts of Joaquin Carrillo, and there is little doubt that he also
will be trapped. In reference to the fact that Joaquin Valancuela has really been captured, our Mariposa correspondent says, in a private letter:
'He is the Simon Pure Joaquin, and you will see his head in the course of
a week in Stockton.'"[96]

Kemble immediately retorted: "But this 'Simon Pure(?) Joaquin' is *not*,
after all, he that Love's Rangers were organized to make such walking
after. He is not the roving, daring, formidable, murderous, ubiquitous,
sharp-shooting and notorious Mr. Joaquin of whose exploits we have
heard so much. Is he?"[97] That Joaquín, according to the interview at a
rancho in Monterey County, was Murrieta. And had not the governor's
warrant been for Joaquín Carrillo, after all?

The *Alta* editor also reprinted political news clipped from the Whig
Stockton Journal: "Mr. Waldo [the Whig gubernatorial candidate] is cer-

tain of his election, but . . . he must have faithful and able associates, to assist him in stemming the tide of wrongs that threaten to sweep over and subvert the great principles of democracy." As for Joaquín and the rangers, the *Journal* added, "It is remotely intimated that the reported capture and decapitation of the bandit Joaquin may be a humbug. . . . Perhaps some hombre who had the misfortune to be born a Mexican, has lost his head. . . . As an item of interest we may notice a suspicion that is gradually obtaining converts to the effect that the man Dawson . . . was no less a person than the far-famed outlaw [Joaquín] whose deeds at one time filled the country with alarm."[98] The Whig editor did not really care if the rangers got Joaquín or not; his goal was to undermine the Democratic governor who had offered a reward for Joaquín and then signed the ranger bill into law—two moves that were calculated to win over voters at the southern mines.

John White and other editors of Democratic Party papers responded by stuffing their columns with letters voicing strong support for Governor John Bigler. He also published Captain Love's lengthy "official report" which, contrary to White's earlier assertion, identified the Joaquín they had killed and beheaded as Murrieta, not Valenzuela. White's guess— that it was Valenzuela—had been based on what he had last heard from the rangers several weeks earlier. In spite of his error, he believed the official report should silence the "paltry doubtings and ill-natured reflections of some papers in the State, in reference to the conduct of Harry Love's Rangers."[99] White went on to declare that the rangers had killed "the real Joaquin, the murderer of the Calaveras and the horse-thief of Mariposa." This was the Joaquín that his Monterey correspondents had identified in April, the same about whom the *San Francisco Herald* had reported on June 8, 1853, that Joaquin was "frequently called 'Carrillo, Cruz,' etc. but his real name is Joaquin Moriata." This was the Joaquín for whom the governor had offered a reward.

A prisoner the rangers brought back with them had identified Joaquín Murrieta and confessed that "the band was on the road from San Diego to the mines, with the intention of making one more foray upon the Chinese and Americans, and then returning to Sonora." After a gunfight at Cantua, "Joaquin and one of his principle [sic] men were beheaded. . . . The head of Joaquin's lieutenant was spoiled, on account of being shot

23. Harry Love, c. 1856. Courtesy of the Old Timers Museum, Murphys, California.

through the skull, and it was necessary to bury it at Fort Miller."[100] John White's tone was triumphantly confident. He had been defensive after erroneously identifying the beheaded bandit leader as Joaquín Valenzuela. Murrieta's head was by far the better prize, politically. The success of the rangers would contribute to the victory of Democratic candidates who had supported the ranger bill.

Harry Love's report gave a detailed description of Joaquín Murrieta that matched the one published in the *San Francisco Herald* and *Los Angeles Star* in August 1853. Captain Love said he spoke to Joaquín before the shooting started. He noted that Joaquín had a light complexion, was rather well made, and was gentlemanly in his manner. After he was killed, the body was examined; in addition to the scar on his right cheek there was "a scar on the right breast, and another scar describing the course of a bullet across his back just below the shoulders. There were also two scars on his legs, the records of two bullet holes." Love expected to find rich loot, given the amount of gold these robbers had stolen, but the young gambler and those with him had "no money in their possession." However the rangers did collect "five six-shooters and two holster pistols, seven horses and five saddles and bridles." The horses were "four dark bay California horses, two grey California horses, and one dun horse. They were marked with Spanish brands."[101] Andrés Pico was already on his way north to collect the horses that bore his brand.

Love's account of the encounter at Cantua was foreshortened by Kemble into just two sentences: "Joaquin was taken by surprise, being unarmed and just coming into camp, leading his horse. As soon as he got sight of the Rangers, he jumped upon his horse and fled, but was not quick enough."[102] Following this news brief, the Alta reprinted the memoir of Three-Fingered Jack as told by Monterey correspondent Benjamin Kooser. He was glad the rangers killed García but did not wish to trumpet that success because of the election, so he did not comment on the memoir.

On August 11, 1853, the Republican reported the arrival of Captain Harry Love. He brought with him "the trunkless head of the bandit chief Joaquin. The trophy will be ready for exhibition . . . today." Those who went to see it and recognized the features were invited to swear out affidavits. "This renowned bandit has at length, terminated a career unparalleled in the history of crime," wrote John White. He then listed Joaquín's exploits, inserting those that newspapers had earlier attributed to Claudio Féliz and others, thereby paving the way for John Rollin Ridge to expand Joaquín Murrieta's role in history and in legend.

Those who went to see the head in Stockton included some spectators drawn by the notoriety of the man. Others came to see if it was the head of the Joaquín Murrieta with whom they were acquainted. There were, after all, other Joaquín Murrietas in California at the time. Undoubtedly some people did not recognize the head as belonging to the Murrieta they knew, but others did.[103]

Henry V. McCargar carelessly boasted he was "well acquainted with Joaquín the celebrated and notorious robber; and that he has drank [sic] frequently and rode often with him," and yet he was not arrested for being affiliated with the band. A more credible witness was the local Catholic priest, Reverend Father Dominique Blaive, who under oath said he recognized the head as that of a young man he met at the Hotel de Minas in Stockton and "he verily believes the said head to be that of the individual Joaquin Muriatta, so known by him two years ago."[104] Then a group of Sonorans—Clemente Morales, José María Rivera, Bernardo Reyna, and Francisco Rivera—said they were well-acquainted with Joaquín Murrieta and had known him as a boy in Mexico, Francisco adding that he had raised him.[105]

While the Sonorans' affidavit was being taken, George Washington Havens came up and said he recognized the features as those of Joaquín Murrieta, whom he had known for three or four years, having met him up "at the mines," adding that he also "knew and knows his sister and brother-in-law."[106] Two days later Dr. N. B. Hubbell saw the head and recognized it as that of a young Mexican he had seen near Vallecito, between Murphy's Camp and Angel's Camp the previous winter in company with Three-Fingered Jack and two others. "He concluded it was three fingered Jack because on describing the person whom he saw in company with the man to whom the head belonged, . . . Capt. Love . . . instantly pronounced the description as accurate of said Jack." Hubbell said he suspected that the Mexican to whom the head belonged was Joaquín because he had seen him alive when the citizens of Vallecito were in pursuit of Joaquín. Although armed with a rifle, Hubbell said he did not shoot Joaquín because he was with three armed Mexicans. If he had killed the leader, the other bandits would have killed him.[107]

The *Stockton Journal* editors were impressed with these affidavits even though they supported Whig candidates. "The head does not appear natural, being discolored . . . about the mouth," the *Journal* reported. "It is readily recognized, however, by those who knew the bandit, by the deep scar that marks the right cheek. There can be no doubt that this is the Joaquin whose depredations occasioned such terror in Calaveras county last winter." Suddenly the capture of Joaquín wasn't humbug, but this pause in political attacks aimed at undermining the rangers whom Democrats had hired did not last long.[108]

In San Francisco, John Lewis, formerly of the *Los Angeles Star*, stopped by the Alta office and announced his intention to return East. He brought with him several back issues of the Los Angeles Star from the month of July 1853. From these Kemble extracted old news about Joaquín and introduced it as current events. He followed that with a sarcastic remark: "We are glad to hear of the continued health of Mr. Joaquin. His head was never more firmly on his shoulders, it appears. . . . This hydra-headed individual, the Star says, is in the neighborhood of San Fernando, with twenty-five men, all armed with revolvers, double-barreled guns, swords and lances. The robbers have visited several ranches in that vicinity. We give this on the very best authority, to wit, Don Andrés Pico . . . who, by the way, was wounded in the thigh by an Indian arrow one day when engaged in the pursuit of horses stolen by Indians."[109] Indeed Murrieta had been in San Fernando about a week before he died, but Kemble made it sound as though he was there in early August.

The Republican reprinted a clip of the same news but said that one of the Joaquins was "in the neighborhood of San Fernando," according to Don Andrés Pico. Harry Love used the news from Los Angeles to argue in favor of continuing the rangers in service. In an interview published in the Republican, he said the other Joaquíns were still at large. He claimed that "various bands of guerrillas extend from Sonora [Mexico] to Shasta [California] but their principal . . . strongholds are in the coast range of mountains between Santa Clara and the Los Angeles valleys." He also said he was sure that their guerrilla chief, Joaquín Murrieta, "could have raised two thousand desperadoes [and that] such was the bandit's purpose, to scour the entire southern country, sack the small settlements, and before a body of troops could be raised, announce himself at Sonora. The prisoner . . . had intimated as much."[110] Love was confident that he and his men could break up the whole band if continued in service.

Harry Love's appeal for a renewal of contract excited a second round of attacks on the rangers and their integrity, even while the head was carried to San Francisco and exhibited there. Ignacio Lisarraga of Sonora went to see it and said it was definitely that of Joaquín Murrieta: he had known him in life and recognized his head in death. Kemble nonetheless insisted that public interest would be "somewhat modified by the information that this wonderful head was taken from the shoulders on some plebian robber, and that the real hero of so many romances—the veritable

Joaquin is quietly enjoying the fruits of his adventures, at his native home in Mexico."[111] That was what Walker's filibusters wanted people to believe. His friend John Nugent, editor of the San Francisco Herald, who had published the famous "interview" with Joaquín Murrieta and had reported that Carrillo and Cruz were psuedonyms Murrieta used, printed the following during the election—with a disclaimer:

> We have received a letter signed Joaquin Carrillo, the name of the other famous Mexican robber—the same who killed and robbed [John] Foster, the partner of the late Major [James] Savage, and who is known to have been skulking in the valley of San Jose for some years past. The letter reads thus: "SAN FRANCISCO, August 18, 1853. Señor Editor Herald:—As my . . . supposed capture, seems to be the topic of the day, I will, through your kindness, inform the readers of your valuable paper that I still retain my head, although it is proclaimed throughout the presses of your fine city, that I was recently captured, and became very suddenly decapitated." We have no idea that the letter is genuine, but give it for what it is worth.[112]

The letter was probably written by William Walker, who was in town that week. He had just returned from Guaymas, Sonora, where he met with the embattled governor and eagerly offered to assist him in fighting political enemies and guerrilla bands in exchange for land in the under-populated northern frontier. The governor had recently forced out a couple of French filibuster parties from California. He turned Walker down, but the freckle-faced, redheaded adventurer decided it was too late to go back on his plans. His supporters had invested in the mission he had envisioned. When he returned to San Francisco he told his supporters that everything was in order and that it was time to purchase supplies and munitions and load it aboard their ship.

Walker had supporters at Fort Yuma, too, on California's southeastern border close to Sonora. The Alta published a correspondence from one "C. H. P." who was stationed at Fort Yuma. "It is the general opinion that the banditti known as the Joaquin gang, and other robbing parties, can only be exterminated by carrying the war into the enemy's country, Baja California," he wrote. "An expedition of sixty men could easily conquer the whole peninsula, capture San Tomas [sic], and hang every robber therein."[113] This was one of Walker's pronounced goals. He had marketed his expedition as one in which both Sonora and Baja California would be "liberated" and a "free" republic founded with himself as president of the new Sonora, which would control the Gulf of California. He would rescue the good citizens already living there from the bad men that made their lives insecure.[114]

Horace Bell described the filibuster cause this way: "First, the earth is the Lord's . . . , and we are the Lord's people; second, . . . all Spanish-American governments are worthless and need to be reconstructed . . . ; . . . the people of Lower California and Sonora are, or should be, dissatisfied with Mexican rule, and . . . cry out for American aid . . . ; the Sonoreños ought to rise, proclaim their independence and cry for help from the generous Filibuster, who stood ready to help the down-trodden Mexican and to feather his own nest in particular."[115] Filibusters like William Walker talked a lot about freedom and liberty and coming to the aid of a people afflicted by an unstable government, but when raising funds his investors believed the scheme would make them rich. There was all that land, full of mineral and agricultural potential, and there was the Bay of California, an excellent Pacific-based port and fishing harbor said to be rich in pearls.

Meanwhile Whig California gubernatorial candidate William Waldo, whose campaign was losing steam, wrote to the Alta from Sonora town in Tuolumne County about Governor Bigler's visit there. A former journalist, the somewhat reluctant politician signed his correspondences "Walli." Waldo preferred to campaign through the independent press, being a man of independent spirit whom the Whigs had selected because his editorials lambasted the Bigler regime. A talented writer, Waldo turned out to be a mousy public speaker, and that contributed to his declining popularity.

Waldo dubbed John Bigler the "great Hyperscritus" (printer of paper money) and depicted himself as an ordinary miner in his lampoon of Bigler's campaign. After hearing a cannon go off, he wrote, "I dropped the pick and shovel and went to town to see what was going on. When I arrived . . . behold, a string of stages and horsemen were marching down Washington Street, preceded by a band of music and half a dozen flying

Monday Evening, August 8, 1853

WALDO AND REFORM

WHIG STATE TICKET,
For Governor,
WILLIAM WALDO.
For Lieutenant Governor

24. Whig political banner featured in the *Marysville Herald*.

banners." He followed the procession to city hall, where Governor Bigler stood on a wagon to deliver his speech, one that "touched upon his sufferings, . . . [whereupon] a torrent of sympathy began to flow. Many beat their breast in grief, others tore their hair, and a very great many fainted." Americans in the 1850s instantly recognized a parody of the Christian Great Revival meetings that swept through upstate New York in the 1830s. "There stood the Governor, like a patient persecuted Christian. . . . The effect was astonishing throughout, insomuch that an attentive dog, being overcome, gave a spasmodic yelp, pitched a somersault and died."[116] Waldo then offered a depiction of Joaquin and Captain Love that was equally sarcastic about both. "The report of the death of Joaquin is not believed here," he wrote, tongue-in-cheek. "A report was current a few days ago that [Joaquín] was seen swimming the Tuolumne River, carrying his head in his mouth. Another report was about; that Captain Love came upon Joaquin with twenty men—it was in the night . . . and charged down upon them and dispersed them. But alas! What mistakes will happen! The company had wounded and killed seven goats!"[117] This time the reference was to Don Quixote, the delusional knight of Spanish literature who attacked a great army, as he thought. In reality, it was a flock of sheep.

In his closing remarks, Waldo took a more serious tone when revealing the extent to which filibuster activities were being carried out in Tuolumne. "There is a measure on foot in this city and county to raise a company to 'explore,' as is said, the northern district of Mexico for gold. The list of names already counts 534. Some are from other counties. They intend to go well armed, and will take with them several pieces of artillery. Strange prospecting company! Wonder if there's nothing else in the bag besides gold! They intend to start in about three months, and will go down on the eastern side of the mountains, toward the head of the Colorado River. A committee of five are in the county getting names." Committee members, he added, were all friends of "Dr. Walker."[118]

Four days later Edward Kemble published a letter from a Los Angeles–based correspondent who signed with the editor's symbol for "begin new paragraph." This was the letter that caused Joseph Henry Jackson to insist that not just the life and adventures but also the death of the legendary Joaquín Murrieta was based on a conglomerate of outlaws named Joaquín.

> August 16, 1853.—It affords some amusement to our citizens the various accounts of the . . . decapitation of the notorious Joaquin Murieta. The humbug is so transparent that it is surprising any sensible person can be [convinced]. . . . The very act of the Legislature authorizing the raising of a company "to capture the five Joaquins, to wit, Joaquin Carrillo, Joaquin Murieta, Joaquin Valenzuela," etc. etc. was in itself a farce. . . . Does the Legislature soberly and seriously outlaw

five men, . . . whose names not one member in ten had ever even heard mentioned?

At the time of the murder of Gen. Bean, . . . Murieta was strongly suspected of the crime, and efforts were made to arrest him, but he managed to escape; and since then, every murder and robbery in the country has been attributed to Joaquin. Sometimes it is Joaquin Carrillo . . . ; then it is Joaquin Murieta, and then Joaquin something else; but always Joaquin. . . . The very gentlemanly judge of the second judicial district is Joaquin Carrillo, and the boys cry after him in the street "there goes Joaquin!"

A few weeks ago a party of native Californians and Sonorians started for the Tulare Valley, for the expressed and avowed purpose of running mustangs. Three of the party have since returned, and report that they were attacked by a party of Americans, and that the balance of their party, four in number, had been killed; that Joaquin Valenzuela, . . . was killed as he was endeavoring to escape, and that his head was cut off by his captors as a trophy.[119]

Clearly, the action of the legislature was what annoyed this writer most. He didn't really care which Joaquín the rangers killed. What bothered him was that they were about to claim the governor's reward and collect the promised salary of one hundred fifty dollars a month for doing what the volunteer Los Angeles Rangers could have done at no cost to the state. As for the identity of the Joaquín the rangers killed, the first report from Stockton had, after all, said it was Joaquín Valenzuela. The Los Angeles writer went on to say that the head displayed in Stockton was not that of Joaquín Murrieta, "and this is positively asserted by those who have seen the real Murieta and the spurious head." The identity of the Joaquín killed was indeed debated in Los Angeles, as has been seen in La Estrella. Rojo had found it necessary to remind readers that the evidence collected by the rangers was supported not only by numerous affidavits but also by the confession of the prisoner and by General Andrés Pico, who recognized the head.

The Los Angeles–based *Alta* correspondent called the head a fake because he was angry about Harry Love's repeated appeals for continuation in service. "The term of service was about expiring, and although I will not say that interested parties have gotten up this Joaquin expedition, yet such expeditions can be generally traced to . . . speculators."[120] William Walker's expedition was indeed supported by speculators, but the writer saw Harry Love and his company as speculators who were tapping the state treasury. If the filibusters enjoyed more support than the rangers, it was because most of Walker's investors were contributing funds from their own pockets.

The writing style of the Los Angeles correspondence is suspiciously similar to that of Horace Bell, who founded the satirical Los Angeles Porcupine in the 1880s. Bell arrived in Los Angeles in time to witness the condemnation and hanging of Reyes Féliz. He joined the Los Angeles Rangers, a volunteer company which was not compensated for their efforts although local Californios did provide horses and refreshments as needed. The Los Angeles Rangers mustered in July 1853 and went in pursuit of Manuel Vergara in August after he murdered David Porter. The outlaw escaped but met his end at a ferry crossing on the Colorado river, while en route to Sonora.[121]

Horace Bell was riding with the Los Angeles Rangers again in October, when they received word that about seven members of a band of eighteen or so Sonoran youths believed to be part of the Joaquín band had arrived in the vicinity.[122] Probably led by Pancho Daniel, the band had robbed and killed a French peddler in San Luis Obispo. Their trail was found because of items they discarded while heading south. They were pursued by a San Luis Obispo posse which they tried to trap. During a shoot-out, men were lost on both sides. John Rollin Ridge wrote this battle into legend, but placed Joaquín Murrieta and Three-Fingered Jack García in the middle of the clash. The historical band split up that night. A couple of the outlaws were closely pursued. One more was killed. Meanwhile a San Luis Obispo messenger traveled by steamer to Los Angeles to sound the alarm. Californio and Indian scouts conducted a search and soon located a band of seven to ten Sonoran youths who had recently arrived from San Luis and were in possession of the peddler's goods. They were camped under willow trees at Boyle Heights, Horace Bell later recalled. The rangers quietly surrounded them. Then the shooting and shouting started. Two bandits escaped, one was killed, and four were arrested:

Ramón Espinosa, his sister Octaviana "Cayetana" Espinosa, Manuel Olivas, also called Manuel Verdez, and Anastacio Higuera, also called Juan and Ignacio. The young woman remained in custody in Los Angeles but the three young men were taken back to San Luis Obispo by steamer and there they were hanged. The Los Angeles Star reported that when the prisoners were asked if they had any last requests, Higuera said "He would be happy if he could be freed long enough to flog one yankee."[123]

In September 1854 Horace Bell was in Weaverville helping Edward Pollock start the Trinity Times. While there he met Frank Buck, who ran a general store. Buck picked up a copy of Ridge's book Life and Adventures of Joaquin Murieta and sent it to his sister in Maine. In a letter that accompanied the book, Buck mentioned Horace Bell, who had told him that he'd been a ranger during the pursuit of Joaquín, from which Buck erroneously concluded that he had ridden with Harry Love. Buck also told his sister that Bell was with the ranger party that took the bandit leader's sister from a camp to Los Angeles. But it was actually Ramón Espinosa's sister the rangers took to Los Angeles. Either Buck confused the story he had heard or, what is more likely, Bell embellished the story he told. Bell also talked to Buck about Joaquín's reported fate. "As many persons . . . are willing to swear that the head is not his, as the other way," Buck wrote to his sister.[124] Bell had good reason to envy the state rangers and their one hundred and fifty dollars per month payment plus a share of the one-thousand-dollar governor's reward. Mocking them would have felt justifiable. But any doubt Horace Bell may have had about the identity of the head were gone by the time he wrote Reminiscences of a Ranger. By then he had met William Henderson, the ranger who shot and killed Murrieta, and in 1858 he had learned of Joaquín Valenzuela's capture and hanging.

Meanwhile Governor John Bigler was reelected in September. So were James Wade and Philomen Herbert. (Henry Crabb also won.) The Joaquín band and the ranger bill had helped get them reelected. The rangers continued to exhibit the head of Joaquín Murrieta through November. At Mokelumne Hill, Alfred Doten saw a Mexican woman who recognized it break down and cry. A Mokelumne Hill correspondent to the Republican wrote that "to a large number of respectable Americans, besides Mexicans, and Chinese, there is not the remotest doubt in our mind that the

Rangers have got the veritable scoundrel's head." The Chinese in particular whose camps Joaquín and band had robbed "recognized the head instantly and were exceedingly rejoiced at his capture."[125]

From Mokelumne Hill the ghastly exhibit was carried to San Andreas, then to Angel's Camp, and then across the Stanislaus River to Columbia and Sonora. A band of armed Mexicans shot at two stagecoaches in Tuolumne County. One stopped and the band inquired after the head, but it was the wrong coach. The other stage did not stop, and the Mexicans who gave chase pulled away when fired upon. The head was displayed in Sonora, where "the bandit was well known" and where "all concur that it is the apex of the veritable robber," wrote "Mephistophiles" in a correspondence to the Republican. "His old partner recognized his features at a glance; and in fact, all those hereabouts who had the honor of Joaquin's acquaintance testify in the affirmative."[126]

The history would seem to end here, as did the legend, but Joaquín and Jesús Valenzuela, Bernardo and Pancho Daniel, and a good many others associated with the band continued to be active. They, too, are part of the history behind the legend. Between 1854 and 1859 the increasing tension between Hispanics and Anglo-Saxons in California excited new interest in Joaquín Murrieta and his legend, even as various members of the band who had outlived him were hunted down by vigilantes and lawmen.

As for William Walker, his brief stint as "president of the republic of Sonora" ended when he and his company were forced to return to Alta California in defeat, much to the delight of his Mexican pursuers. Walker tried again in 1856, but his target was Nicaragua then. It was Henry Crabb who led filibusters into Sonora next. Crabb's fate and that of his followers overlapped and had an effect on news of the continued activities of Hispanic bandits and the vigilante response they excited.

5. Joaquín Valenzuela and Others in *El Clamor Público*

While the state rangers were pursuing the Joaquín band in the vicinity of Cantua Creek, the *Calaveras Chronicle* reported the murder of Mark T. Howe near Angel's Camp. Howe had been shot in the head, then lassoed and dragged to a secluded spot (a method used by Claudio Féliz and band in 1851). In August a Mexican named Antonio shot at two Chinese miners in the vicinity of Foreman's Ranch, wounding one. They notified local authorities, who formed a posse of armed Chinese miners. Antonio was smoked out of the cabin in which he took refuge and riddled with bullets when he came out and took aim at the posse. He survived the fusillade long enough to disclose information about the band to which he and Howe's killer belonged. They were the remnant of the Joaquín band, described as being "small men, about 5′ 6″ in height, rather slender built, and most of them light complexioned. . . . They dress extremely well and are all gamblers by profession—such as you generally see around monte tables—not one of them is over twenty-four years of age."[1] The band had a few lone wolves still roaming around Calaveras County.

Mariposa County suffered an upsurge in crime after the rangers were disbanded. In October 1853, A. M. Pryor and wife, who lived on a ranch near the Merced River in Mariposa County in the neighborhood where Joaquín Valenzuela had gained some notoriety in 1852, were visited by two Mexicans. They ate watermelon, paid for it, and left, but then returned in company with three others later that day. One of those who had been there earlier grabbed Mrs. Pryor and held her. She screamed. When her husband, who was sick in bed, rose to rescue her, another outlaw shot him. A third stabbed him and slit his throat while the remainder ransacked the house and stole five hundred dollars. The murderers wanted to kill Mrs. Pryor as well but the outlaw who held her protested, so she was left alive, but bound.[2] Similar burglaries would be carried out later by outlaw bands with which Joaquín and Jesús Valenzuela were affiliated.

In December 1853 deputy John "Jack" Wheelan tried to arrest Jesús Senate in Los Angeles on charge of murder. The gambler resisted, drawing a knife and plunging it into Wheelan's heart. Senate was one of the outlaws Teodor Vásquez named in his confession, together with Joaquín Murrieta, Claudio Féliz, and Francisco "Pancho" Daniel, among others. Less than a month after killing Wheelan, Jesús Senate joined Atanacio Moreno and Luis Burgos, "the masked man who often declared himself to be the veritable and terrible Joaquin."[3] They and three other well-armed Mexicans robbed all the guests at a dance in Los Angeles. The masked men claimed the place was surrounded by Mexican guerrillas, and if anyone put up a struggle everyone would be killed. Following the robbery, the band stopped at Martin Delong's house at around three o'clock in the morning. Martin was suffering from ague. He watched helplessly while they looted his home and gang-raped his wife. A week later Moreno killed Senate and Burgos, loaded their bodies on a wagon, and drove back to Los Angeles in anticipation of collecting the rewards offered for each of them.[4] He was received as a hero until he pawned stolen goods.

California in the 1850s was indeed as the journalist from Monterey said it was. In the context of an interview with Joaquín Murrieta he correctly pointed out that the Golden State was in political and cultural turmoil and suffering from acute moral degradation. Men came seeking easy money and indulged in drinking and gambling, there being plenty of alcohol and gambling houses. They brawled over card games and women. Duels occurred over political differences. A strong sense of individual and family honor too often motivated the drawing of weapons and the delivery of hard blows. A fight between two men in a bar could quickly escalate into a general melee between groups of men divided by language or culture. Efforts made by citizens like Alfred Doten and William Perkins to stem the violence through participation in vigilante arrests, "trials," and executions proved necessary. But these measures were typically put into effect only if the victim was a white man. A few brave lawmen and justices of the peace stopped a lynching now and then, but too often angry mobs succeeded in executing suspects on the spot, with and without evidence of wrongdoing.

Not all hangings occurred in response to crime. Some hangings were carried out by outlaws against suspected traitors. In 1855 near Mission San Juan Bautista in Monterey County, when an American storekeeper discovered that two saddles had been stolen from his stable, he went after the Mexican thieves, found their camp, and recovered his saddles when the thieves fled, riding bareback. The posse that went with him pursued the band into a grove of oak trees, where they found a Chilean and a Mexican hanging from tree limbs. One of them had been shot, the other stabbed, and both were strung up with the rope passing through the mouth. They had been dead for at least two days.[5]

Other hangings were senseless and racially motivated. Stephen French told Howard Gardiner that, after losing all of his money while gambling with three Americans, he asked them if they could spare a dollar as he had yet to pay the laundress for washing his clothes. They lent him the dollar and followed him to where the Mexican laundress lived with her husband, who ran a bar. The three gamblers ordered drinks, then made advances on the laundress. When her husband protested, they dragged him outside and hanged him from a tree, "ignoring the pleas of his weeping wife." Stephen French reported the crime but the newspapers did not publish it and nothing came of it.[6] Had he reported it to a Spanish-language newspaper the result would probably have been different. The Spanish-language press, though not very powerful in political circles, was partial to news of unjust acts committed against Hispanics by Anglo-Americans, even as the American press was partial to news of crimes committed by Mexicans against Americans.

The Sacramento Democratic State Journal, for example, reported the cold-blooded murder of one Dr. Marshall and an attempted murder of one Mr. Le Moine, both of San Antonio, which is near Mt. Diablo (across the bay from San Francisco). A Mexican stopped at Marshall's house, asked for a drink of water, received it, engaged in small talk with the doctor, then knifed him to death and left. Le Moine was greeted by a Mexican who asked if he could spend the night. Le Moine turned him down, saying he didn't have room to house a guest. The Mexican immediately drew his revolver and fired, wounding Le Moine in the head. Le Moine avoided death by grabbing the revolver and fighting his assailant while crying out for assistance. Seeing others coming the assailant fled, leaving his horse and gun behind.[7] Neither he nor the one who killed Marshall committed robbery or showed any interest in doing so. American newspapers asserted that the attacks were unprovoked: "It is difficult to account for the prevalence of such a murderous disposition on the part of the natives." Nothing was said of the fact that the "natives" in and around San Antonio were being despoiled of their land and livestock by Anglo-American squatters, tax collectors, money-lenders, and unscrupulous lawyers. That part of the story surfaced in Spanish-language newspapers like El *Clamor Público*, which also covered news about outlaws affiliated with the Joaquín band.

The editor and proprietor of the *Los Angeles* El *Clamor Público* was Francisco P. Ramírez. He began as an apprentice to Manuel C. Rojo in the office of the *Los Angeles Star/La Estrella* when but thirteen years old. In 1851 he went to San Francisco to attend a college for scholars ages fourteen to eighteen. While there he worked on the *Catholic Standard* beginning in May 1853. Fluent in French, Spanish, and English, the teenage journalist often read the French/Spanish *San Francisco L'Echo du Pacifique/* El *Eco Pacífico*, as well as the *San Francisco Herald* and the *Alta*.

The *Catholic Standard* folded in the spring of 1854. Ramírez moved to Marysville and joined the staff at the *Marysville Daily California Express*, the first Republican Party newspaper in California. He was there for a year. Then he returned to Los Angeles and took over as editor of *La Estrella*, M. C. Rojo having left. A couple of months later, Henry Hamilton, who had covered the exploits and pursuits of Joaquín Murrieta and band as editor of the *Calaveras Chronicle*, became editor of the *Los Angeles Star*. He wanted to do away with the Spanish section and encouraged Ramírez to start his own newspaper. Ramírez collected subscriptions, bought a press on credit, set up an office, and in June 1855 published the first issue of El *Clamor Público*. He was eighteen years old.

El Clamor Público Covers Crime

To Francisco P. Ramírez all perpetrators of nefarious deeds deserved to be punished under the law by a just and impartial judicial system, as promised in the U.S. Constitution. Born in 1837 and raised in Mexican

25. Francisco P. Ramirez, 1864. Seaver Center for Western History Research, Los Angeles County Museum of Natural History.

Los Angeles, he had faced the same temptations, pressures, and prejudices all Hispanic youths faced, in that there was plenty of gambling in Los Angeles and plenty of mistrust between races coexisting there. Eager to learn, he picked up languages easily and read books with zeal. If like so many youths he felt a need to prove his manhood and chose to do so by means of wit and wisdom through the medium of the press, rather than by demonstrating physical prowess hunting bears or exhibiting an indifference to fate by breaking the law. Raised as a Catholic in a middle-class family, he believed in justice and in divine retribution. Perhaps that is why he tended to be impatient with those who admired outlaws. Crime was and is by nature cruel and unjust, and Ramírez devoted his newspaper to fighting injustice in all its manifestations. He complained about crime in Los Angeles as much as did Hamilton, but what set him apart from his American colleague was his stand against judicial discrimination and his disgust at the way Anglos so often got away with murder and other crimes when the victim was Hispanic.

For example in March 1855 he reprinted news from the *San Francisco El Eco Pacífico* of how a squatter and cattle thief named John Wilson killed a man on whose land he had settled without permission: "Terrible Assassination—Don José Suñol was murdered in front of his house at San Jose by a Yankee American—unprovoked. No attempt has been made to arrest the murderer."[8] Suñol was the nephew of Don José de los Reyes Berreyesa. He had confronted Wilson, who responded by shooting him dead on the spot. Wilson was never prosecuted.

A similar murder occurred in Los Angeles County. "Horrible tragedy!" reported Ramírez "A young Californio, José de Jesús Lopez, was riding near Mission San Gabriel, all alone, when John Morris gave him a blow to the head with a hoe, killing him instantly. The crime was witnessed and reported but not surprisingly, as we all know, Morris enjoys complete liberty."[9]

Ramírez also complained about news from Amador County (just north of Calaveras County), where three Mexican felons were hanged and all the Mexican residents were forced into exile. "The Mexicans have been expelled for a crime they did not commit solely because of what some of their compatriots did in alliance with various Americans and Chileans. . . . So why don't the Americans purge themselves of their own compatriots who took part in the crime instead?"[10] Ramírez also translated and reprinted a story from the *San Andreas Independent* (edited by Benjamin Kooser) that mentioned Joaquín Murrieta: "In Calaveras County, . . . there is a camp that used to be called Indian Creek but is now known as *Los Muertos* [Land of the Dead]. . . . it was from there that the bandit Joaquín Murrieta embarked on his desperate career. In 1851, 4000 Mexicans settled there but were attacked by 800 Americans and their camp completely destroyed. Thirteen were killed and various others wounded. The graves of the dead are visible to this day on the hillside. From this circumstance it takes its doleful name." To this Ramírez added: "What a sad record for our brothers the Mexicans!"[11] Whenever Mexicans were expelled, the Americans who did so excused the deed by saying all Mexicans harbored and assisted their countrymen, including criminals. Ramírez found this assumption insulting and hypocritical.

> We see that Californios are often accused of hiding individuals suspected of committing crimes. There may be some truth to this, but we are quite sure they do not hide criminals more often than do the Americans.... We saw what happened, for example, when Mr. Hine killed Domingo Jaime some years ago. Who helped him effect his escape from jail? Not Californios! And who hid him so that the authorities could not find him? Not Californios. It is wrong—yes, very wrong—for any citizen to offer refuge to a man accused of a crime; such individuals ought to be judged impartially and according to the laws which all of us ought to obey. Those Californios who hide a criminal, may do so because they do not understand the laws, as they have not yet been printed in Spanish.[12]

He then published a translation of the law defining what it means to be an accessory to crime, willingly and unwillingly, together with an explanation.

Although mob violence was condemned by all newspaper editors, vigilance committees were not. In 1856 Ramírez followed with interest the vigilance committee news from San Francisco. There were arrests, hearings, and an execution. Ramírez translated news clips from both sides of the debate. The San Francisco Herald, which had supported the 1851 vigilance committee, consistently opposed the 1856 vigilante movement. Those who took the law into their own hands, argued Herald editor John Nugent, undermined trust in public institutions and courted anarchy. The Alta meanwhile favored the vigilantes, and so did the Los Angeles Star editor, Henry Hamilton. Hamilton suggested that the people of Los Angeles should form a vigilance committee, too, in response to a surge in crime.

In 1856 Los Angeles residents reported numerous burglaries and robberies. There had been a prison break at San Quentin. A band of fugitives led by Juan Flores joined the Pancho Daniel band in San Jose. When some members of the band ran into trouble there, they headed south to Los Angeles County and stayed in the vicinity of San Gabriel. Using the alias Gomez, the leader of a masked band robbed Don Joaquín Varelas's house. Later that day the house of Vicente Sálcido in the city of Los An-

26. Sonora Town, Los Angeles, 1857. Author's collection.

geles was robbed. "These robberies are being committed . . . with inordinate frequency and each day they occur demonstrates all the more a need to form a Vigilance Committee for the purpose of looking after the interests of our fellow citizens,"[13] reported El Clamor Público, but when a vigilance committee *did* convene, the outcome was not at all what Francisco P. Ramírez had in mind.

The Death of a Chivalrous Musician

On Saturday, July 19, 1856, deputy constable William "Bill" Jenkins picked up a notice at the Los Angeles County Sheriff's office and went to collect a debt of three dollars owed to a Los Angeles storekeeper by a guitarist named Antonio Ruíz. Jenkins found Ruíz at home conversing with his landlady, Doña María Candelaria Pollorena. She was washing a shirt in a basin when the deputy arrived. Others present were also engaged in various small tasks. The deputy approached Ruíz and served him notice. Ruíz said that he did not have the money at present and that Jenkins should come back later that night, after Ruíz had performed and earned some money. Jenkins glanced around the room as if looking for something. Then he walked into an adjoining room and picked up Ruíz's guitar, which represented his livelihood. Ruíz asked him what he was doing. The deputy said he was confiscating it in lieu of the debt.

As soon as he left, Sra. Pollorena began to fret. She told Ruíz to call the deputy. She wished to speak with him—it was important. Ruíz did so and Jenkins returned, but he was suspicious and drew his revolver, holding it ready at his side as he reentered the house ahead of Ruíz. The others in the house, on seeing Jenkins had drawn his weapon, withdrew to the patio, fearing trouble. Through the open patio door they could hear Pollorena ask for the guitar. She said she had put a letter in the sound box and wished to retrieve it. On the table behind her was another guitar, one that had belonged to her son and that a neighbor once heard Ruíz describe as worthless because it did not have a good sound box. Perhaps Jenkins suspected she intended to exchange one for the other. He refused to give her the guitar. When she grabbed it, Jenkins would not let go. While they struggled, Jenkins raised his gun. Ruíz cried out in alarm, "María!" and grabbed the deputy from behind. But Jenkins simultaneously aimed over his shoulder and fired, knocking Ruíz to the ground with a bullet through the heart. Pollorena screamed. Jenkins glanced at his victim, then left, guitar in hand. A doctor and a priest were sent for. The doctor later testified that the amiable musician did not blame Jenkins for what happened, saying he understood Jenkins was only trying to do his duty. But he said he was sorry to lose his life over three dollars owed to a man with plenty of money. It seemed so pointless.[14]

Ruíz died unarmed while performing a chivalrous act, reported Ramírez. The people were alarmed because his killer was afterward seen walking down the street, still wearing a deputy's badge. He had turned in the guitar and informed the city marshal of the shooting, saying it was in self-defense. He was neither reprimanded nor relieved of duty. Disgusted citizens petitioned the city mayor and talked of holding a vigilance committee meeting, arresting the culprit and seeing that justice was done.

Following the well-attended funeral, on Monday, July 21, 1856, Mayor Benjamin "Benito" Wilson went to the sheriff's office and ordered the marshal to put Jenkins behind bars immediately. That night, people gathered for a Vigilance Committee meeting. They wanted to hold a grand jury hearing on the case, but Star editor Henry Hamilton, and Marshal William "Billy" Getman urged the people to wait until the next morning, saying tempers needed to cool. Their Mexican spokesman accused Getman and Hamilton of seeking a postponement because they knew that the prisoner's friends were coming from El Monte and San Gabriel. They feared a jailbreak was planned. Getman said there would be no jailbreak and invited the people to help him guard the jail. The California Lancers surrounded the jail, together with other volunteers. (The lancers, formed in 1850, outlasted the Los Angeles Rangers, who disbanded in 1854.)

Around midnight Jenkins's friends from San Gabriel and El Monte arrived and attacked the lancers. They took the people's spokesman, Juan C. Hernández, and four others hostage, saying that if the Mexicans lynched Jenkins, they would do the same with their prisoners. "Sr. Don Juan Hernández," wrote Ramírez, "more than once was believed dead because they said that he was the principal head of the 'tumult' and they reasoned that it would be best to kill him. Fortunately for Sr. Hernández, a friend [Getman] intervened on his behalf and rescued him."[15] Billy Getman persuaded the "Monte boys" to hand over their prisoners for safekeeping. Hernández and the others were then locked in jail for their own protection.

Next morning Francisco P. Ramírez disconsolately noted that Henry Hamilton of the Los Angeles Star proposed a resolution forbidding all persons of Spanish descent from taking part in the vigilante court proceedings. Hamilton and his friends from El Monte and San Gabriel argued that Mexicans and Californios would be prejudiced against the defendant. Ramírez recognized the insult for what it was, but he attended the trial anyway, hoping for justice. After all the testimony had been heard from María Pollorena and various other witnesses, including the doctor who tended Ruíz, Judge Benjamin Hayes instructed the jurors to be impartial and do what was right. He pointed out that while some of the testimony was contradictory in places, it was clear that the defendant had employed unnecessary force resulting in the death of an unarmed man with no record of violence or interference with the law. His speech had no effect on the El Monte jurymen. They took five minutes to reach a verdict: not guilty. The gross miscarriage of justice excited a mini-revolution that historians have retrospectively dubbed a "race riot." Gambler Jack Powers played a part in the struggle. Joaquín Valenzuela was very likely present as well, being affiliated with Jack Powers, who never went anywhere without Hispanic bodyguards.

French resident Ferdinand Cariergue and Jack Powers led local Hispanics to the old mission convent behind Nuestra Señora la Reina de Los Angeles Church and broke into the mission armory. Antique muskets and shot were handed out. They even commandeered a small brass cannon. Thus armed, they marched toward the jail. Marshal Getman, with a small force of well-mounted deputies and California lancers, watched as the "revolutionaries" approached. Getman sent a lancer out to speak with the leader and offer to negotiate. Cariergue agreed to speak for the people. Marshal William Getman then rode out to meet Cariergue. Suddenly someone in Jack Powers's crowd fired at Getman, the bullet splitting his scalp. He dropped from his horse to save his life and rolled when he hit the ground to avoid three more bullets aimed at him. Chaos followed, with mounted defenders of the city scattering pedestrian revolutionaries and taking twelve men prisoner: Cariergue, Powers, four other Frenchmen, and Powers's bodyguards. All were released on bond the next day and exiled from the county.

Mayor Benito Wilson then called another public meeting and invited people to set aside the anger that haunted streets and darkened eyes. He said that racial violence would cripple their "fair city's" reputation. He accused Ferdinand Cariergue, a former French filibuster, of fomenting the riot and invited prominent Californio and Anglo-Saxon citizens to patrol the streets and insure the safety and security of local businesses and residences against a possible riot. Francisco P. Ramírez agreed with the mayor: Cariergue's role in the mini-revolution was reminiscent of filibuster acts, and Cariergue had, after all, been one of the French filibusters who fought a little "revolution" in the city of Hermosillo in 1852. However, he demonstrated impartiality by reprinting in the original French a letter Cariergue had sent to the San Francisco L'Echo du Pacifique. Cariergue insisted that he had intended to negotiate with the marshal to have Bill Jenkins exiled, for the sake of peace in the community, but someone in John Powers's party started shooting. It was also the Powers party that had urged the people to break into the armory and arm themselves before approaching town hall.[16]

Jack Powers had plenty of riot experience. A former member of a band of thugs called the "Hounds," he participated in a riotous attack on the Chilean neighborhood in San Francisco in 1851, after which the Hounds were forced into exile. In Santa Barbara in July 1853 he fomented a mini-revolution when his Californio landlord accused him of occupying private property without permission, the lease Powers had requested having been denied. Powers rallied Hispanic vaqueros and bandits, built a small canon out of a stove pipe, and thwarted the authorities who were going to forcibly evict him. He thereafter kept a band of Mexican bodyguards around and his ranch became an outlaw rendezvous.[17]

Ramírez also reprinted editorials by José Marcos of *Eco del Pacífico* and John Nugent of the *San Francisco Herald* that blamed Marshal Getman for not taking immediate action against Jenkins. They blamed Jenkins for having shown a lack of sound judgment, and they blamed Mayor Benito Wilson for not acting until petitioned by the people. "An unhappy Mexican named Antonio Ruíz . . . , in consequence of his chivalric comportment toward a woman in distress," wrote Marcos, "was killed by a deputy sheriff. Assassins who are agents of the law are hypocritical enemies of the law." John Nugent agreed. He also condemned the Los Angeles Vigilance Committee trial that acquitted Jenkins. "Our laws were at one time the pillars of our liberty. Now they are a farce. When someone commits an offense, three or four people . . . form a Vigilance Committee and foment murder and mayhem."[18]

Although he was open to other perspectives, Francisco P. Ramírez was not yet ready to give up on vigilantism, but he did give up on being cordial to the editor of the *Los Angeles Star*. Henry Hamilton had repeatedly accused him of inciting the people to riot, saying that it was Ramírez's inflammatory remarks and errant reporting that had provoked the people. The young editor of *El Clamor Público* pointed out that the resolution Hamilton had called for to bar Hispanics from jury duty during the trial of William Jenkins, and the biased speech he gave the night before the trial said more about him than all his editorials inviting cooperation between Anglos and Californios. True cooperation, he argued, meant Americans must trust their Spanish-speaking neighbors to do what was right and not marginalize them so that they would have little reason to cooperate. "There must be *union* in this town in order to have security," wrote Ramírez, so "let there be no differences between those of diverse nationalities and let this hatred that different races profess against one another be transformed into most sincere friendship." *El Clamor Público* did have bilingual American subscribers, too, after all.[19]

The Ruíz-Jenkins case illustrates the kind of unequal treatment under California state law that riled Hispanic residents and made them willing listeners to outlaws like Joaquín Murrieta, who knew how to play the empathy card to his own advantage. Those whom Manuel C. Rojo admonished in his editorial "¿Quién es Joaquín?" against believing that young men with blunted morals were avengers, hungered for someone who could make just the injustices they witnessed and suffered. They were eager to follow a French filibuster and heed Jack Powers's call for revolution because they wanted their grievances to be heard in such a way as to bring about a change in the status quo. In Spanish-language folklore, Joaquín Murrieta has been depicted as fighting oppression, but in history it was Francisco P. Ramírez who did so. He identified with his readers. He became, for a few years, their self-appointed champion, but the hero's mantle proved heavy.

Word Duel: Los Angeles Editors Ramírez and Hamilton Unsheathe Sharp Opinions

Francisco P. Ramírez's editorials reveal familiarity with classical literature, philosophy, Catholic theology, and Mexican revolutionary writings. He had witnessed the coming of the Anglo-Americans. A few dozen settlers came first and married into Mexican families. Then came the soldiers and gamblers, together with a large variety of Europeans. Last came the wagon trains of Anglo-American families from Arkansas and Missouri whose numerical presence brought changes that challenged the culture, language, and Catholic faith of those born in California. Ramírez adapted without abandoning his heritage. Instead he championed it in El Clamor Público. He gave special attention to the Day of the Dead, covered Spanish-language theater events, and reprinted news from Mexican and other Hispanic newspapers from abroad.

Ramírez embraced American democracy and the ideals of the new Republican Party because it opposed slavery and preached equality. (The Republican Party had replaced the Whig Party by 1856.) Aware that his people were without much representation in the state of California, he decided to be their voice and open his columns to their hopes and complaints. In the first issue of El Clamor Público he proclaimed his willingness to be what the legendary Joaquín Murrieta became: the defender of his people. El Clamor Público means "The Public Outcry." An irrepressibly youthful excitement comes through in his early prose. As a teenager

27. Henry Hamilton (on left) with friend and fellow Democrat William McKee, 1864. This item is reproduced by permission of The Huntington Library, San Marino, California.

among men and an Hispanic among mostly Anglo-Saxon colleagues, Ramírez was exuberant, gutsy and alert. He knew that newspaper editors were often attacked, beaten up, even assassinated, but he was not intimidated when Henry Hamilton insulted his intelligence and questioned his integrity, or threatened him and his family.

Henry Hamilton was a formidable foe. Older and more experienced, Hamilton was a redheaded Protestant Irishman from Londonderry who had lived in New York City for a year before he sailed to California in 1849. In 1851 he and Colonel James Ayers founded the *Mokelumne Hill Calaveras Chronicle*.[20] Hamilton's editorials revealed a racially biased view of the Spanish, colored by the same inherited history of the Spanish Armada and the Inquisition that influenced John White of the *San Joaquin Republican*. However Hamilton was also a Southern Democrat and, as such, was willing to acknowledge the Hispanic dons in southern California who were active Democrats. He was also a Mason. The Masons were a nativist fraternity that placed loyalty to "the brethren" (fellow Masons) and, in California, to Anglo-American culture and politics ahead of honesty, justice, and equality. The Californio Democrats understood this kind of fierce loyalty and the chivalric code of honor it inspired. They were nativists, too. They believed their own culture, language, and family ties were more important than honesty or justice, as was demonstrated when the impoverished Cipriano Sandoval was sacrificed for the crimes of one belonging to their own class and connected to them through marriage.

As a Democrat, Hamilton patronized wealthy Californio Democrats like Andrés Pico and Juan Sepúlveda by indulgently patting them on the back for supporting Marshal Getman during the Ruíz riot, then condescendingly correcting them when they dared show solidarity with fellow Hispanics who were at odds with American Democrats. Such tactics excited fight in teenage Francisco P. Ramírez, but he still translated and reprinted Hamilton's sugary calls for cooperation between the races even while Hamilton accused him of sowing division. Ramírez said he wanted unity, too, but *unity with equality*. Hamilton was a conservative. He favored the caste system, as did most prominent Californios. From his upbringing in Londonderry he brought the conviction that some races and classes of men were better than others and therefore most worthy of leadership.

The differing perspectives of the two editors colored the way they covered the news. Of Bill Jenkins's demeanor during his trial, for example, Hamilton wrote that he displayed remorse over the "tragic accident," whereas Ramírez wrote that "his face showed no emotion" throughout the trial. When these two editors witnessed the impact of murder by Californio and Mexican bandits of the Juan Flores and Pancho Daniel band, formerly called the Joaquín band, they both reacted with expressions of horror and outrage. The difference came in how they viewed the vigilante response.

Juan Flores and Band Take Revenge and Vigilantes Respond in Kind

About three months after Antonio Ruíz was killed, Pancho Daniel and band showed up in the vicinity of San Gabriel and began to commit burglaries, their victims initially being "gachupinos" (Spanish immigrants). In November they were joined by a band of San Quentin fugitives led by Juan Flores and called "las manillas"—a sarcastic reference to the shackles with which they had been coupled while inmates.[21] No real effort was made to make arrests even though the newspapers published complaints and issued frequent calls for vigilante action. A French resident would later suggest that inaction on the part of North American authorities in San Gabriel was because they found it amusing when Hispanics fell prey to Mexican robbers.

In December Juan Flores and band left San Gabriel and moved to the Cahuilla ranchería near Mission San Juan Capistrano. Among the fugitives with him was Andrés Fontes. He and Flores were native sons of Los Angeles from poor families. Each of them had been arrested by American officers on charges of horse stealing. Both were convinced that the officers who arrested them had done so to get rid of them because of disputes over women. Fontes had argued with sheriff James "Santiago" Barton over a Cahuilla woman, and Flores had argued with deputy sheriff Charlie Baker over another woman. Flores and Fontes swore they would take revenge. They tried to incite the Indians at San Juan into rebellion. Various warnings came into Los Angeles from neighboring rancheros whose horses were stolen that trouble was brewing, but the warnings were not taken seriously.

Then the band committed a murder in the third week of January 1857. They went to the town at Mission San Juan Capistrano and robbed three stores in succession, the proprietors hiding or fleeing for fear of their lives. As they entered a fourth store, owner George Pflugardt attempted to defend his property and was killed. The gang of six, flanked by twenty or more Cahuillas who wanted a share in the loot, roamed east, stealing horses from José Cota's ranch along the way.

The Californio sheriffs and justices of the peace at San Juan Capistrano apparently did nothing, so local business owners sent a Frenchman named François to the county marshal in Los Angeles with an appeal for help. On January 22, 1857, Los Angeles Sheriff Santiago Barton summoned Deputy Sheriff Frank H. Alexander and constables William Little and Charlie Baker and deputized volunteers Alfred Hardy and Carlos F. Daly. François went with the posse.

They left at night, traveling by the light of the moon and arriving at Don José Andrés Sepúlveda's Rancho San Joaquín at dawn. Sepúlveda offered Barton more men and fresh horses, saying he had heard the band numbered not less than fifty, most of them Indians. It would be dangerous to continue with so few men, he said. Barton thought Sepúlveda exaggerated and did not accept his offer, though a couple of his men did exchange their horses for fresh mounts. They headed out after breakfast, riding between low, rolling hills in single file, probably hoping to surprise the outlaws. Their guide spotted an abandoned campfire and, fearing an ambush, turned back and shouted a warning, but it was too late. Outlaws appeared on both sides and commenced shooting. The guide was killed. Little, Baker, and Barton drew their weapons and fired back, but all three were killed. Alexander, Hardy, and Daly, who brought up the rear, retreated at a run, but Daly was mounted on a mule and soon fell, shot in the back. Alexander and Hardy were chased eight miles, but the bandits pulled away once Rancho San Joaquin came into view. All of the dead were riddled with more bullets and stripped of money, watches, rings, hats, boots, and weapons.

The horrible news shocked the people of Los Angeles. The Star reprinted reports of the San Quentin prison break on October 8, 1856, involving Juan Flores, who had been arrested in 1855. Mayor Benito Wilson sent word of the ambush to the governor and legislators representing Los Angeles, appealing for financial and military assistance. The mayor was responding as though the area had just suffered a guerrilla attack from the Joaquín band. He even sent word to San Diego, asking authorities there to set up road blocks, as it was believed the bandits would attempt to flee south across the border. But in case they went north, as had Joaquín Murrieta, he asked soldiers stationed at Fort Tejon to set up roadblocks, too. Then he authorized a house-to-house search in the city, in case a spy was present. He was in effect declaring war on the outlaw band, as if the county had been attacked by Mexican guerrillas.

Mayor Wilson struck back with everything he had, and since, at the time, Henry Crabb and his filibuster band was in town, he accepted their offers to help. The filibusters had arrived from San Francisco by steamer and hoped to buy horses or oxen in Los Angeles to pull their wagons overland through Fort Yuma and on into Sonora, but they were finding that a scarcity of animals had pushed prices higher than expected. Crabb's well-armed filibusters helped the mayor of Los Angeles with his war on crime by making house-to-house searches for spies and confederates. They made fifty-two arrests. They departed the next day, the story of their adventures appearing from time to time in California newspapers, many editors being friends, participants, and supporters of Crabb's effort to carry out what he and his men believed was their manifest destiny. Crabb believed he would succeed in doing what William Walker had failed to do in northwestern Mexico.[22]

Francisco P. Ramírez expressed alarm at seeing filibusters searching homes. They marched fifty-two mestizos off to jail, but the mayor assured the editor of El Clamor Público that each case would be reviewed quickly and everyone innocent would be released. True to the mayor's word, within a few days, the city had reviewed all cases. Only eleven of those arrested were detained; no one had come forward to vouch for them. Meanwhile Ramírez poked fun at the filibusters who left town with their wagons full of explosives, arms, and ammunition, claiming they were "settlers of Gadsdonia." (Gadsdonia, the southern half of Arizona, was purchased from Mexico in 1853.)[23]

While the house-to-house searches were underway, Marshal William

C. Getman posted a summons inviting every able-bodied man who possessed arms and a horse to pursue the gang. "If an Hispanic commits a crime," wrote Ramírez, "we ought not to defend him just because he is Hispanic; on the contrary let us deal with him severely so that he will know that he ought not to abuse our hospitality and the laws of our country."[24] A dozen parties set out, some composed of Californios and others of German and French immigrants. Marshal Getman led an Anglo-Saxon party. Other Anglo-American parties set out from San Gabriel and El Monte.

Andrés Pico's posse of Californios included Tomás Sánchez and Sr. don Juan Sepúlveda. They departed the morning after Getman's posse left. When they crossed paths with two American posses from El Monte led by Frank Gentry and Bethel Coopwood, the three parties joined forces. Pico had sent Indian scouts out to track the bandits and, if possible, infiltrate the band and learn where they were headed. One scout had already returned with news. The band had split up. He knew where Juan Flores and those with him were camping. The posse followed his lead, while Marshal Getman and his posse visited the site of the shootout and commandeered wagons to carry the dead lawmen back to Los Angeles for burial. A portion of his posse accompanied the dead, while the remainder went with him to San Gabriel, an informant (Antonia "La Molinera"?) saying that the band had departed in that direction.

Less than a week later Marshal Getman and posse returned to Los Angeles. They had not taken any prisoners, but Getman said that he'd learned at Mission San Juan Capistrano that the band had celebrated their victory and that Juan Flores had said that the Americans fought bravely. He was told that Pancho Daniel was the real captain of the band and that he shot Sheriff Barton. Flores killed Charlie Baker. Little was killed by James Silvas, nicknamed "Cotaro" (from *catabo*, wine sampler). With them were Antonio María "Chino" Varelas, Juan Gonzales, Faustino García, an Indian called "Benito," and the twins Lorenzo and Dolores Ruíz. All of this appeared in the *Star* but not in *El Clamor Público*.

Faustino García, Benito, and the Ruíz brothers were never mentioned again. In *El Clamor Público*, Santiago "James" Silvas was listed separately from Juan "Catabo" Sauripa, alias Juan Silvas. Meanwhile the *Star* also listed a Guerro Galindo who was also not mentioned again. Hamilton offered a carefully disguised report from Getman's posse regarding two Mexicans found hanging from a tree and a third dead Mexican who had been shot in the head at a place called "Los Nietos," bordering Pío Pico's property in San Gabriel. "He did not know who killed them, nor what their names were: all is mystery," reported the Star.[25] Ramírez, meanwhile, said he was hearing all kinds of rumors which he could not yet credit and so did not print them—at first.

When Andrés Pico's posse returned, Ramírez related how the lancers had caught up with Juan Flores and band, cornering them on the crest of a ridge the other side of which had fallen away, leaving a concave cliff. The bandits tried to fight their way out with heavy gun fire, but Pico's lancers had no guns so they sat low while the Americans from El Monte returned fire. When the shooting stopped, Pico called to the outlaws and invited them to surrender, successfully persuading three to deliver themselves up: Juan Catabo, a Sonoran nicknamed "Güero ardillero," and the teenage "Chino" Varelas. Varelas asked for amnesty in exchange for cooperating with the posse in helping them locate other members of the band. He said he had been forced to join the gang on pain of death after they robbed his father's home. He also said that Flores had escaped down the cliff using a lariat that was too short. The outlaw had free fallen some twenty feet from the end of the rope onto sliding rubble. José Jesús Espinoza and Bernardo Lopez had followed him. (El Clamor Público called the latter Bernardo Lopez at first and then Lorenzo Lopez. "Leonardo," the name used in the Star, is an Italian name.)

So steep was the terrain that Pico's company lost two horses and a rider during the descent, the ground giving way and one rider's leg breaking under the weight of his horse as they fell. While he was rescuing the wounded man, Jim Thompson, son-in-law to José Andrés Sepúlveda, came with yet another search party. He had known Flores since boyhood and offered to take Varelas as a guide so that he could go cut off Flores's escape. Pico agreed. The men from El Monte and Tomás Sánchez left with Thompson while Pico took the other prisoners, the man with a broken leg and the lancer who had lost his mount, to the nearest ranch. Thompson's role was minimized by the editor of El Clamor Público, who credited Pico and Sánchez with the arrest of Juan Flores. Hamilton printed Thompson's full report in the Star and gave but scant congratulations to Pico and Sánchez.

Jim Thompson and party caught up with Juan Flores and those with him at a cave not far from the cliff down which they had escaped. The robbers, Tomás Sánchez told the editor of El Clamor Público, defended themselves with as much boldness as before, but they were tired and had not eaten for three days. After Flores was wounded in the hand and wrist in an accident involving a carbine, they surrendered. All three were "delivered up to the Americans at Mission Santa Ana. They were confined to a room for the night: their hands were tied, except for Flores, because of his wound. During the night he untied his companions and they struck the sentinel with a hard blow and fled."[26] Thompson had left three volunteers on guard, but two had left their posts. The Star claimed the guards who left their posts were Californios.

The escape was infuriating. Andrés Pico was encouraged to hang "Juan 'Catabo' Silvas and the famous ardillero" on the spot, which he did, lest they, too, escape. Meanwhile, reported the Star, Coopwood and Gentry brought Chino Varelas to Los Angeles and asked him to point out houses he knew had been visited by members of the band in the past. The exercise proved fruitless, as everyone's house had already been searched. Then came good news. Two days after his escape, Juan Flores was arrested again, brought to Los Angeles, and lodged in jail. Coopwood and Gentry told the Star editor that, when arrested the first time, Flores had Barton's gold watch and revolvers. He had no loot on him when Frank "Pancho" Johnson ran into him on the road to San Buenaventura. Flores had brazenly ridden up to a check point and, when stopped and questioned, told the soldiers from Fort Tejon that his name was Juan Gonzales Sánchez and he was a cowboy on his way to a job in San Fernando. He looked so pathetically gaunt and dusty and was so poorly mounted, they deemed him harmless and let him pass. Johnson had no trouble arresting the famished, wounded outlaw. When he led him into Los Angeles, a crowd gathered round to stare at the latest bandit legend.

Another Head Is Severed

The arrest of Flores and the hanging of two of his band by Andrés Pico's party were good news to Francisco P. Ramírez, but he was also hearing troubling news from San Gabriel that he did not believe at first. Then came confirmation. A grief-stricken father stopped by the office wanting to know why his son had been killed by the Americans:

> Events in San Gabriel—Three Men Hanged by the People and One Shot who Died in the Arms of his Wife.
>
> REASON FOR THE ARREST
>
> Last Thursday night [Jan. 29, 1853] four individuals were arrested in San Gabriel on suspicion for having been accomplices in the recent murders; three were hanged and one was shot dead.
>
> GREAT CONFUSION
>
> We heard things that would provoke horror if related, committed by a company of armed men, who under the pretext of having the authority to summarily execute outlaws, had attacked like voracious lions some unhappy victims. . . . But we cannot believe everything that is said, . . . [yet].
>
> THE DEAD
>
> The names of those who were hanged as suspects, . . . are as follows: Juan Valenzuela, Pedro Lopez, Nasario Duarte, and Diego Navarro. . . .
>
> Regarding the death of the last, we have the following account from his aging father: "He was patching his roof with tar and was coming down when some armed men came and without giving any explanation, carried him away . . . , and took him to a tree where they had already prepared three men for execution. They put cords around their necks: they all dropped at the same time: but Navarro's rope broke and he dropped to the ground. Seeing that death had not taken him, he asked . . . what evidence of crime did they have against him, but the bloodthirsty mob did not listen, the greater part of them being drunk. Seeing that he was without recourse, he called to his wife, and she went to him just as he was being shot, and this heroic woman took him in her arms: it was in her arms that he died."[27]

Saddened and perplexed, Ramírez tried to explain the nightmare. "There are times when the authorities do not conduct themselves as they should and the people rise up in all their majesty in order to see that the laws are complied with," he wrote, in an attempt to describe the purpose of vigilantism. Unfortunately, he added, they sometimes ended up "sacrificing, in their furor, innocent victims."[28] This was inexcusable. The innocent should not die like martyrs in place of guilty criminals, but that was what had happened in San Gabriel. A week later Ramírez was happy to print a correction: Nasario Duarte had not been hanged after all.

Henry Hamilton responded to Ramírez's sketch of events with mockery, after which he published a detailed if doctored account of events in San Gabriel. Ramírez translated and reprinted the Star version a week later, following it with a commentary. He accused Hamilton of whitewashing events at the expense of innocent victims whose families were grieving and charged that it was criminal to defame the name of good men by insisting they had connections with outlaws. Hamilton, however, remained confident that his readers viewed Mexicans (including Francisco P. Ramírez) as he did: people incapable of telling the truth. He accused Ramírez of having published "a false report of the events that took place in San Gabriel."

Hamilton's account of events appeared in the February 7, 1857, issue of the Star. Events in San Gabriel, he wrote, started on Thursday morning, January 29, 1857: "Messrs. Cyrus Sanford, Gifford, and Totten, were on their way to the Mission [San Gabriel]. Near the Ranchería [Indian village there], they saw coming toward them on the same road Mr. William M. Stockton, riding along side a Mexican; at the same time there was another Mexican approaching" their own party. Hamilton said the two Mexicans had left San Gabriel together but they had separated. One saw Stockton questioning the other and cut across the field to rejoin him, but in doing so, he came between Stockton and the party Cyrus Sanford led. "Stockton, seeing that the Mexican . . . was armed and of a suspicious appearance, called out [to Sanford]: 'look out for that man, he's a thief.'" Stockton had been asking the Mexican nearest him where he was going. When the Mexican told him, Stockton accused him of inventing his destination. That made the Mexican "turn his horse toward Stockton" in a confrontational manner, wrote Hamilton.

Sanford and party simultaneously turned their horses toward the armed Mexican that Stockton had called a thief. "Seeing this the two [Mexican] strangers spurred their horses and drew their pistols. Sanford and his companions, with Stockton, gave chase." But only Stockton and Sanford were well-enough mounted to keep up with the armed thief. The man Stockton had been questioning was not mentioned again, but when Hamilton listed members of the band who had been killed at Mission San Gabriel, "un tuerto" (a one-eyed man) from Sonora named José Santos was among them. He was apparently leading a pack mule at the time Stockton questioned him.

"During the running fight," Hamilton continued, "Diego Navarro was seen mounted upon a fine white horse." Hamilton accused Navarro of "endeavoring to unite with the other Mexicans." He said Gifford and Totten hailed him and ordered him to turn back, but Navarro "refused to obey" the order and was soon "overtaken at least two miles, perhaps three miles from his house, on which, according to the account in *Clamor Público* he was putting 'brea' [tar]." Hamilton then claimed that Navarro, "when asked why he did not stop when hailed, . . . said one of the men that was running . . . owed him a little money and that he was going to meet him to get his payment. He was asked what was the name of the man, but would not say."

Ramírez rebutted Hamilton's mockery by explaining that Diego Navarro's father had left details out, being distracted by grief. When he went out to the farm at dawn, his son was in fact repairing the roof of his house. While his son worked on the roof, he himself had set about loading the cart with grain that he had come to take to market in Los Angeles. When he was finished loading the wagon, he could not see the oxen anywhere that were needed to pull the cart. That was when his son got down off the roof, saddled his horse, and left. He went to look for the oxen. His father saw him go over the hill and saw him brought back, under arrest. The Americans never explained why they arrested him. They came and made the whole family walk to Mission San Gabriel, and there they waited in front of the church to see what would happen next.

Ramírez continued to quote the *Star*'s account of Stockton's and Sanford's pursuit of the thief. The armed Mexican shot Sanford's horse in the chest several times, and Sanford shot the robber in the thigh. Quoting Hamilton, Ramirez reported that the robber, "being closely pursued and having discharged all his shots, quit his horse and took to the swamp behind Mr. Courtney's mill. The swamp was set on fire by Mr.

[Thomas] Van Deusen . . . , and the Mexican was revealed, covered . . . in mud. At that moment, Mr. [Frank] King of El Monte arrived and seeing the villain, called to him to come out and surrender, which he refused to do, so Mr. King dispatched him with his rifle."[29] The corpse was retrieved and the thief identified as Miguel Soto, an escaped suspect in an assault and robbery case that had occurred in the fall of 1856 in Santa Barbara. This case also involved Miguel Blanco, who was captured and confessed, then escaped. (Blanco would later be implicated in another crime that led to the arrest of Joaquín Valenzuela.)

Ramírez accepted this part of the report as being incontestable. There were lots of witnesses and they all said the same thing, but harmony fell apart when it came to what happened next. The justice of the peace at San Gabriel, Dr. William Osburn, who had been put in charge of Ana Benites during the investigation into General Joshua Bean's death in 1852, was a Mason and a friend of Henry Hamilton. Hamilton naturally printed a sanitized account of his actions: "A general search had taken place and a large number of suspected persons were taken prisoner—among them, Pedro Lopez and Juan Valenzuela. A jury of twelve persons was appointed by the citizens assembled, among whom were some natives and a fair and impartial trial was given them; in proof of which a large number were released."

Ramírez quoted a translation of the above assertion, saying it would be funny in an ironic way, if the truth had been less tragic. "The 'large number of suspected persons'" he wrote, "*were all the Mexicans and others of Spanish race that lived in San Gabriel. All were arrested and lined up in front of the church. That is where they were when the body of the Mexican was brought from the marsh. One of those arrested, in whose veracity we put the greatest confidence, having known him a long time*," described what happened next.

The mud-caked corpse of Miguel Soto was yanked out of the wagon. "The justice of the peace at the Mission drew his knife and cut off the head—though various Americans were opposed to it—and pushed it around with his foot as if it was a stone; after that, he plunged his knife into the body several times" and invited other Americans to do the same, wrote Ramirez. Only one did. Meanwhile Diego Navarro was brought in—no one knew for what. His family joined those standing in front of the church. As for the trial by jury, Ramírez's informant said, "It seemed to me that there was no jury . . . as scarcely 15 minutes passed between the time that prisoners Juan Valenzuela, Diego Navarro, and Pedro Lopez, were taken into the quarters of this justice of the peace and when they were brought before us again with their hands tied. Although it happened before our eyes, we could not believe they would execute these poor men so suddenly and swiftly, . . . without evidence of crimes."[30] Surely fifteen minutes was not enough time to select a jury, hear witnesses, deliberate, and sentence three different cases. Besides a justice of the peace did not have the authority to preside over criminal cases. As for Hamilton's claim that there were "some native sons of California among the jury members, that was impossible as all of them were taken prisoner . . . Or perhaps," Ramírez quipped, "what he meant to say was that the prisoners passed judgement on one another as a new approach to *justice!*"[31]

Navarro, Valenzuela, and Lopez were taken to a tree and hanged by William Osburn and friends, but the cords were cut by sober Americans who were trying to control the situation by agreeing to a mock lynching in hopes of preventing a real one. But a drunk William Osburn wanted revenge. James Barton was not only a close friend, he was a Junior Warden of the Masons. Little and Baker were Masons, too. Osburn and friends had tried to drown their grief in drink, even while they seethed at a people from whom the murderers came, as they saw it. When the cords were cut, Osburn drew his revolver and shot each one through the head. It happened so quickly that no one had time to react and stop the tragedy. "We are prepared to prove that 'the tale of the one who died in his wife's arms' is only too true," wrote a heavy-hearted Ramírez. The wife of Diego Navarro ran up to her husband and "held him in her arms after he was shot, and he expired in her arms."[32]

The whole hellish episode made the young editor wonder: "In what era do we live? . . . In what civilized country does one find a justice of the peace who can condemn men to death?" But he was glad that, "to the honor of the American people who were there, many of them . . . did everything possible to . . . rescue them, and we will never forget their noble efforts." In fact all of the good citizens in Los Angeles had "condemned, with indignation, the murders, with the exception of the editor of the *Star*, who not only approves of such horrible proceedings, but also breaks the hearts of fathers, mothers, wives and sisters, by publishing before the whole world that the victims were criminals of the worst class. . . . How great the infamy and acrimony of that writer!"

The unrepentant Henry Hamilton, himself a heavy drinker and loyal Mason, knew that he did not stand alone in choosing to tell the version he gave of events at San Gabriel. He and Osburn had countless sympathizers, even as Diego Navarro was surrounded—in death—with grief-stricken family and friends. Francisco P. Ramírez saw fit to leave Osburn's name out when detailing the crimes of the "justice of the peace at San Gabriel" out of respect for his anonymity in history. But Henry Hamilton had no qualms about slandering Navarro's good name, thereby sullying the reputation of his whole family. He accused the diligent farmer of being "a man of general bad character and dangerous, if permitted to live in any peaceable community." Ramírez countered, "Navarro was completely innocent. He was born here and those who were acquainted with him assure us that no one can say anything at all bad about his character. . . . The disrespectful assertion that has been made against him is nothing but a fraud and lies!"[33] Angered by these accusations, Hamilton not only slandered Diego Navarro, he also attacked the editor of El Clamor Público. But Ramírez did not let his attack go unanswered:

> Now, we have a word for the editor of the Star. Whenever he mentions us, he has asked the people why they protect and sustain us. Since only he is preoccupied with spreading slander against El Clamor Público, we have paid little attention to his attacks. . . . But if his object is to bring our newspaper down, we expect a more chivalrous method than that of falsely representing us as "incendiary". . . . If he has given us such a label because we have defended the unfortunate souls sacrificed at San Gabriel, then we are honored. . . . This newspaper was established with the singular object of defending our brothers and compatriots, who are everywhere humiliated and oppressed; for as long as there are individual rights, we shall publish those facts that may otherwise be too bitter for this day and age. Yet it may all be in vain, like preaching in a wasteland.[34]

The note of fatalism with which Ramírez closed is the first hint of mounting frustration. He had just turned twenty years old, and already he was weary of the burden he had so eagerly shouldered two years earlier. His fighting words against oppression and in favor of individual rights bear a marked similarity to those of John Rollin Ridge. Ridge wrote of Joaquín Murrieta that "he leaves behind him the important lesson that there is nothing so dangerous in its consequences as injustice to individuals." Barton and Baker were killed by avenging fugitives who felt they had been wrongfully arrested, but that is often true of law-breakers. What made their claims seem valid to fellow Hispanics was that men like Diego Navarro were made to suffer for being of Hispanic heritage and not just for being in the wrong place at the wrong time. The elusiveness of equal rights for mestizos in California troubled Ramírez, but what really smote him was the ease with which Henry Hamilton rallied a loyal following among Anglo-Americans while defaming a good man's reputation. Ramírez was ready to face his foe using a "more chivalrous" method, but he found Hamilton unwilling to do him the honor of fighting a duel. Doing so would mean acknowledging that Ramírez was in some measure his equal. Instead Hamilton flippantly remarked that lately the editor of El Clamor Público, whom he had previously called "soft hearted," turned out to be "soft headed" instead. The challenge was treated like a joke. To Hamilton sacrificing the reputation of Diego Navarro in order to protect that of his good friend and fellow Mason William Osburn was no more nor less than should be expected.

Ramírez began to realize that there was only one way to fight Hamilton's accusations: use words that might win Anglo-Americans to his side. So he wrote editorials insisting he never sought "to cause enmity between the races" or "corrupt the imaginations of easily distracted people," as Hamilton claimed. All he wanted was "to see justice done, so that all the inhabitants of this county may live henceforth in greater peace and tranquility with one another, and in better harmony than heretofore."[35] He acknowledged yet again that there were many good North Americans in Los Angeles, some of them in positions of authority. Justice was still possible, he believed. Patience was all that was needed, patience and a willingness to work with Anglo-Americans.

28. While Juan Flores was hung from a scaffold, Pancho Daniel was lynched from the same gate beam as Lachenais, seen here, who was lynched in 1870 for the murder of Jacob Bell. Author's collection.

"It is important . . . to be open," he wrote to his bilingual American readers the following week. "Let the public be honorably vindicated. . . . It ought not to be overlooked that what may very well have happened is another band of villains arose . . . intent on exterminating malefactors, that sacrificed our best citizens" in revenge for the death of Sheriff Barton and his fellow Masons. "That which we ask we believe to be very just and right," Ramírez insisted, "and in conformance with the equal rights, justice and liberty in our trusted laws and constitution, which extend to all those who were born here."[36] The people wanted an investigation into the deaths of Valenzuela, Lopez, and Navarro of the district of San Gabriel. That was their legal right.

Juan Flores Hanged

In spite of their many differences, Hamilton and Ramírez did agree on two points: Juan Flores deserved to hang, and Antonio María "Chino" Varelas deserved amnesty. Amnesty was granted in May, three months after Flores was hanged. Before the hanging, people had lined up outside the jail waiting their turn to go in and gawk at the "bold desperado whose daring exploits they had heard about," reported El Clamor Público. "One visitor asked him if he was really the captain of the gang," reported the *Star*, "to which he instantly replied, 'become an outlaw and then you'll know.'" Flores was nineteen years old when arrested by Charlie Baker in 1855 for grand larceny. He had sworn he would take revenge, and he did, but vengeance is vengeance's reward. "Juan Flores," reported *El Clamor Público*, "remained in jail until last Saturday, when the people . . . filled the streets all the way to the church and it was proposed that they hang Flores, there being good evidence of all his crimes, to which the crowd, without dissent, gave their firm approval." But then the editor of the *Star* shattered public harmony. *El Clamor Público* reported that Hamilton "stood up on a table and began to harangue the people, demanding that they hang three other Mexicans [then in jail], two for having stolen horses at El Tejon, and the last for having attempted murder. This inhumane proposition was subjected to a vote, resulting in 395 votes in favor of allowing the courts to judge these other cases, and 257 votes in favor of hanging them forthwith, by which the sensible party carried the day."[37] Flores was the only gallows attraction that day.

He was led out "between two priests, and passed through the streets resolutely to . . . where they had built a scaffold." Charlie Baker's riata of braided leather supplied the noose. "How small the heart of those who seek revenge through such insignificant things!" sighed Ramírez. He did not stay to watch. One of his staff members covered the hanging. The young fugitive "spoke a few words, asking for forgiveness, and confessing that he had committed crimes." He died hard because his hands had not been tied tightly due to his wrist wound. His good hand instinctively yanked free and grabbed the noose. For ten minutes he struggled. Finally the executioner stepped forward and pried his hand out of the noose so that he could expire. "How sad that he had committed such crimes so early in life!" reported *El Clamor Público*, "but at last he who had mocked justice for so long is dead."[38] To Francisco P. Ramírez, there was no difference between a bandit who kills a good lawman and a justice of the peace who kills an innocent citizen. They both mocked justice.

The hanging did not satisfy Henry Hamilton and friends. After celebrating the event in local bars, they resolved upon lynching the three Mexican prisoners they had wanted to hang with Flores, and any other Mexicans they found in jail. They scaled the jail yard walls and banged on the jail door, waking up Frank Carpenter, who was on guard duty, and demanding he hand over his prisoners. Carpenter had locked himself in just in case a lynch party called. He refused to open the door, adding that if they broke in, they would have to kill him, for duty obliged him to resist and he would rather die doing his duty than live knowing he'd failed. His nerve unnerved them. They left, disgruntled. "We allude to these circumstances because we would not want to lose any opportunity to commemorate deeds of fidelity and humanity among those that are public servants," wrote Ramírez.[39] But of course, the account of Carpenter's heroics was not acknowledged in the *Star*.

Looking for Non-violent Cures

The day Flores hanged, Sheriff Barton was eulogized at the Masonic lodge. El *Clamor Público* also remembered the sheriff for his honesty and fair-mindedness. "Who does not remember, . . . his gentle patience, as a tax collector, among those people who were discontent, late in paying, or had difficulty understanding the system?" But, for Ramírez, Santiago Barton's "most important trait . . . was his unswerving impartiality. . . . He never distinguished between persons or classes . . . He even spared the life of a young Californio who was armed and had for a long time resisted arrest. . . . *Impartiality!*—such an important trait should be cultivated and maintained in the administration of justice; nay, but it is synonymous with *justice*."[40] If only Barton's fellow Masons could be as impartial and fair as he!

In addition to eulogizing Sheriff Barton, Ramírez printed a "Reminiscence" of Cipriano Sandoval, probably written by Fr. Lestrades. The padre pointed out that the American vigilantes were not the only ones guilty of hanging an innocent. In 1852 Sandoval hanged because he was a poor shoemaker with no friends or family in high places among the Californios; he had been "sacrificed between two murderers where should have been the one to whom prodigals gave amused congratulations, he who had the good fortune to be rich and have influential friends. The very recent lamentations of the latter as he lay dying, revealed . . . the whole truth, if not soon enough to do any good."[41] Felipe Reid, afflicted with smallpox, had confessed on his deathbed that what Cipriano Sandoval said of him was true. He had paid him silence money, had friends and family willing to provide him with the perfect alibi, and got away with murder.

Following this revelation, Ramírez invited his readers, be they Californio, American, or foreign immigrants, to share their thoughts about unity. "In the past there have been innumerable grievances between us—what better time than now for building avenues of good faith? What is the real nature of the sickness from which our social and political body suffers? Is it an incurable cancer, or a tumor that can be cut out with the help of modern science?"[42] Because of the acts of bandits in their midst—bandits who claimed they were responding to injustice—the citizens of Los Angeles were being repeatedly forced to chose between encouraging unity when fighting crime or maintaining the status quo with its inherent mistrust between people of differing races and classes. Ramírez opened his columns to the whole community in an effort to improve understanding and hopefully resolve differences.

A variety of citizens responded to Ramírez's invitation. One Californio said that the local government was too big, there were too many positions, with the result that taxes were too high—the old alcalde system was better. Another complained that the laws were too complex. It was hard to know what one's rights were under these laws. Several said the laws were ineffective; they failed to protect the people against criminal acts carried out by public officials like Deputy Sheriff William Jenkins and the justice of the peace at San Gabriel. Several more called on county officials to live up to the words they spoke when sworn into office wherein they promised to investigate the behavior of those officials who abused their positions in grievous ways.

Town auxiliary Columbus Sims responded to calls for an investigation. Writing in lumpy Spanish, he defended the justice of the peace at San Gabriel by appealing to the heart: "No one needs the sanction of the law to follow the recommendations of the heart—if the heart is good." He insisted that the vigilantes in San Gabriel had acted as they did because they dearly loved the posse men who were murdered, even as brothers: "Life is not weighed in the same balance with property." When a life is lost, "the good and true man . . . finds the courage to go without delay and protect his neighbors and brothers."[43] He also pointed out that in the past, local dons had retreated indoors during popular movements to catch criminals, but not this time. "We have seen with what zeal our citizens have pursued the bandits of San Juan Capistrano." He applauded Andrés Pico for capturing and lynching two of the outlaws. "If only a similar show of force had been shown when the celebrated Joaquín passed through this county. . . . How weakly the people responded to the call of the authorities then! Joaquín robbed us and made fools of us."[44] In closing he argued that no one had set out to hang or shoot innocent men in San Gabriel, "but if it happened, well then, it was for the good of the people." To Sims the intentions of those at San Gabriel who sought the outlaws that killed Barton and his deputies were good. They had sought to serve and protect the community from bandits.

A correspondent who signed himself "Viajero" (visitor) also mentioned Murrieta. The recent assassinations might not have occurred, he argued, if the community at Mission San Juan Capistrano had a justice of the peace and constable. (Apparently the men elected to those posts, Jose A. Yorba and Santiago Rios as justices of the peace, and Brigada Morillo and Francisco García as constables, either viewed their offices as a source of income and nothing more, or else did not fully understand what was expected of them.) "As long as we leave this remote community without a civil government," he complained, "how can we hope, reasonably, that bands of thieves will not make it their rendezvous? The famous Joaquín was not arrested while here, because, they say, no one *ordered his arrest!* Flores considered himself secure in the area extending from Santa Ana to San Juan Capistrano."[45] This prompted Ramírez to write a double column detailing the responsibilities of those filling various county seats and local offices, both what they should do, and what they were not authorized to do—such as carry out executions. Again he called for an investigation into the actions of the justice of the peace at San Gabriel.

The Barreyesa Tragedy

While Francisco P. Ramírez continued to print readers' missives, he also reported the latest vigilante news, tentatively trusting what he read in the *Star* about the arrest of José Jesús Espinosa in San Buenaventura, as reported by Constable Ezekiel Rubottom of San Gabriel. Rubottom's posse had picked up the outlaw trail from where Johnson had arrested Flores, and they continued north. In San Buenaventura they arrested Espinosa, who confessed to Fr. Domingo Serrano of the mission there. Espinosa was then questioned by an investigative committee appointed by the citizens of San Buenaventura. He said he was born in Monterey, California, and was eighteen years old. He deeply regretted having taken to the outlaw trail. He begged forgiveness for theft and said he had not killed anyone. In answer to questions about the gang, he said there were not more than ten in all and that it was Andrés Fontes who shot Sheriff Barton and killed him. Juan Flores was captain of the band. Other gang members included Antonio "Chino" Varelas, Juan "Catabo" Sauripa, Santiago "James" Silvas, Lorenzo Lopez, and someone Espinosa called "Santos" (possibly José Santos). The Sonoran called "El Ardillero" joined them after they left San Juan Capistrano and did not take part in the gunfight. Pancho Daniel, Murrieta's elusive confederate, was not mentioned at all.[46]

Espinosa was tried, convicted, and hanged at San Buenaventura. Ezekiel Rubottom and company then headed back to Los Angeles with a copy of his confession. On the way back they met Encarnación Berreyesa who had a noose scar on his neck. When questioned he said that he used to live in Santa Clara, near San Vicente. Some highwaymen killed and robbed an American on the road near his home there and a posse came looking for the murderer. The posse questioned him, but he knew nothing. They did not believe him, so they dangled him in hopes of forcing a confession, but since he knew nothing, he could not tell them anything, so they left. Rubottom's party either misunderstood or did not believe Berreyesa. They reported to the *Star* that Berreyesa had been hanged for a murder committed in Santa Clara, but some confederates took him down and revived him. They finished the job, hanging him from a tree by the road a few miles outside San Buenaventura. The next day, they arrested a Mexican pedestrian they met on the road and turned him in when they reached Los Angeles.

The news of Encarnación Berreyesa's fate reached his brother, José, in northern California about two weeks later. A grief-stricken Don José sent a long letter to the editor of the *San Francisco Herald*, who cited the tragic misadventure as an example of the terrible consequences of "popular tribunals." Ramírez published the letter on March 28, 1857, together with excerpts from Nugent's commentary. "How many crimes have been committed in the name of justice! All over California innocent men are sacrificed, in a moment of insane fury, and by persons of worse character than the victims . . . Year after year these atrocities are repeated and always with impunity." John Nugent called for an end to vigilantism.

Don José's letter revealed that not only was Encarnación hung unjustly, but another brother, Nemesio Berreyesa, had earlier been lynched for the same Santa Clara murder, and he, too, was innocent. Nemesio had been away at the time of the murder. When he came home a band of masked men burst into the house at night and dragged him away from his pleading wife and clinging children. His wife reported the incident to the sheriff of San Jose next morning. A search was conducted. Nemesio Berreyesa's corpse was found in a secluded spot, hanging by the neck, his hands and feet tied. The sheriff said he could not arrest the murderers as the men responsible had been masked and their identities were unknown. The case was dropped.

After Nemesio's murder Encarnación's wife became distracted. She begged her husband to move away from there, so he took his young family to Martinez (not the mining town but an older farming community northeast of modern Berkeley in Alameda County). When an American squatter shot and killed his cousin, José Suñol, Encarnación's wife begged her husband to move again. This time they moved to San Buenaventura where her parents lived and where she believed they would be safe. Apparently, wrote Don José, there is no safe place in California for *los hijos del país* (those born there).[47] This was the tragic truth Joaquín Murrieta and other outlaws exploited when appealing to Californios for sympathy by talking of abuse at the hands of North Americans. This, too, is why the Joaquín band legend has lasted so long and proved popular during the Civil Rights Movement. This is also why Francisco P. Ramírez called his newspaper El *Clamor Público*.

The Berreyesa epistle appeared in newspapers all over the state, stirring sympathetic editorials everywhere among Anglo-Americans. The vigilantes in Los Angeles suddenly came under statewide scrutiny, prompting a resident of El Monte to compose a report and send it to the pro-vigilante *San Francisco Alta*. It depicted Los Angeles and San Gabriel vigilantes as heroes who succeeded in bringing about justice and an end to crime in their county. Listed among the outlaws who had been captured and dispatched were Diego Navarro and Encarnación Berreyesa.

Ramírez cut this report to pieces, insisting that it "contains grave and devious fabrications, and manifests brutal and savage sentiments" toward all people of Spanish descent. For example it mocked Andrés Pico for having ordered an American to cut off the ears of the bandits he hanged and bring them in as evidence, but it said nothing about the brutal actions of the justice of the peace at San Gabriel. In response Ramírez determined to publish evidence of the crimes committed in San Gabriel. He translated from the French a letter that a local correspondent had sent to the San Francisco Le Phare.

The Le Phare article called San Gabriel's justice of the peace "the beheader." It reported that after he was done executing people and mutilating a corpse, the decapitated head was "carried to del Monte where an older American, a respectable man of good faith," reported seeing several drunk men with filthy hands enjoying a raucous game of ninepins in the large front room of a prominent residence. "On taking a closer look, he realized the ball was a human head, and that empty liquor bottles served as ninepins. It seemed to him they did not know what they did as they were quite drunk."[48] The French correspondent went on to describe how another American posse from San Gabriel followed the route toward Tejon and came upon two Mexican hermits at Los Nietos whom they hanged on suspicion of complicity with criminals. A third Mexican (one-eyed José Santos) was shot dead and his pack mule confiscated, "the posse being in need of provisions." He also said that the people had petitioned the American authorities, asking them to investigate and prosecute the San Gabriel "thieves and murderers," but he sarcastically added that such would never come to pass as "wolves do not eat their own kind."[49] Francisco P. Ramírez, however, did not see Americans as wolves. Their constitutional laws were full of promise. There were good and bad Americans just as there were good and bad gente de la raza. The good people, he was confident, would not ignore the petition asking for an investigation into the proceedings at San Gabriel that he and hundreds of others had signed, some North Americans among them.

In April Ramírez informed his readers that he had had a visitor. "Mr. Norris, an American wheelwright, who previously resided at del Monte in this county" stopped by to talk about Encarnación Berreyesa. It had been his sad fate to find the body, cut it down, and take it to the home of

Berreyesa's widow and orphans. "Mr. Norris knew him quite well" wrote Ramírez, "and had never heard it said of him that he had been . . . suspected of any crime. A $100 relief has been collected for his inconsolable widow."[50] Things were indeed looking up. Concerned Americans were reaching out to those who had suffered cruelly from unjust treatment.

Like Preaching in a Desert

Ramírez rejoiced when Judge Benjamin Hayes announced there would indeed be a court investigation. Clamoring for justice had worked. He enthusiastically reported that a grand jury was being selected to hear complaints about the justice of the peace at San Gabriel and to review the cases of the twelve Mexicans still in jail only because they were poor and had no one to vouch for them. (Eleven had been arrested during the house-to-house search in January, and one had been arrested by Ezekiel Rubottom and company in March.) On April 6, 1857, the grand jury convened. They were a mix of "good citizens," wrote Ramírez, such as Cyrus Sanford and Juan Sepúlveda.

Then came the day of the hearings. The editor of El Clamor Público eagerly attended, full of expectations and high hopes. "Imagine our surprise and indeed, that of all the good citizens present," he groaned, "when they opened the Court of sessions and with bare-faced impudence, the justice of the peace of San Gabriel took his seat next to the County Judge [Benjamin Hayes], he who was notorious for having violated his jurisdiction, hanging three innocent men at Mission San Gabriel! . . . This is a blatant mockery of the people: an abuse of the laws; and what is more, a hideous blot on the American character!"[51]

The disgusted young editor went on to report that, not surprisingly, Judge Hayes announced that the charges of unlawful executions at San Gabriel would not be investigated. "Could it be because some of those presiding had been responsible for the crimes?" he quipped. At least, he said in closing, "we know that our conduct as a journalist, in exposing and denouncing these crimes as they happened . . . had the full support of all good citizens and all our compatriots."[52] There was but one small consolation: all twelve prisoners against whom no charges had been brought were set at liberty.

Crabb's Filibuster Folly and Fate

While the hunt continued for members of the Juan Flores and Pancho Daniel band, once called the Joaquín band, news of Henry Crabb and his filibuster party were covered in the same California newspapers that covered news of vigilante actions and military roadblocks around Los Angeles county and beyond. Throughout the months of struggle with vigilantism in Los Angeles, there came bits and pieces of news about the military struggle between Governor José de Aguilar and former Governor Manuel Gándara in Sonora and hints that filibusters were on their way to exploit the conflict. The American view was that the filibusters would take sides, bring victory to their Sonoran allies, and then persuade them to break with Mexico, become a free and independent republic, which would then seek to join the United States. Henry Crabb enjoyed as much if not more support than did William Walker, especially among Southern Democrats in California.

Unlike Walker, Henry Crabb believed he had a claim to property in Sonora. He had married into a Sonoran family through which he was distantly related to Governor José de Aguilar. Crabb's father-in-law, Augustín Ainza, was a gachupín (Spanish settler) from the Philippines who moved to Sonora when a young man and married the daughter of a wealthy family. The couple raised a large family on a hacienda and ran a silver mine worked by Mayo Indians in the province of Alamos, Sonora. They left in 1842 and resettled in the San Joaquin Valley of California.

Augustín Ainza told Henry Crabb and his other American sons-in-law, Rasey Biven and John Cortelyou, (all of whom came from southern plantations in the United States) that his Sonoran hacienda was looted and burned by Indians and the mines confiscated by the government. He complained about how Sonora suffered from frequent cycles of violence. Indian rebellions and gubernatorial "revolutions" had caused thousands to do as he had: pack up and leave. His sons-in-law had all studied law. They told him they could help him reclaim his property in Sonora. Meanwhile the whole family read with interest various news reports about French and American filibuster expeditions into Sonora. They all failed and yet Augustín and his sons and sons-in-law flirted with the idea of a joint effort with friends and extended family in Sonora to establish a free republic there. In 1855 Mexicans in California had begun to form caravans of settlers and lead them to the northern provinces of Sonora, which were no longer blighted by drought. The Ainza family participated, urging friends to go and plotting to use the resettlement movement to start a filibuster revolution. Augustín and his sons then went to Sonora themselves, ahead of Crabb, and preached revolution. They were arrested and charged with treason.

Henry Crabb didn't know about the arrests when he arrived at Fort Yuma and informed his followers of his real intentions. He had enrolled them as volunteer settlers of Gadsdonia, but now he revealed his true purpose: he was going to Sonora to fight for freedom. Half of his followers quit and left for Tucson, but Crabb was not disheartened. He told the eighty or so remaining followers that nine hundred more recruits would be arriving by sea. They would land at a small northern fishing port not far from the town of Altar, where Crabb was headed. El Clamor Público reprinted a news clip from Mexico claiming that one thousand five hundred filibusters had left San Francisco and were sailing to the Gulf of California. In response the governor ordered the port at the mouth of Rio de la Asumpción blocked and sent troops to Altar, the intended rendezvous point for the filibusters. Four ships came, but not being able to anchor, they all turned back.

Henry Crabb did not know reinforcements coming by sea had been blocked, but he must have heard that Governor Aguilar and General Ignacio Pesquiera had defeated, captured, and executed Manuel Gándara and his brothers. Retreating Gándara supporters who feared retaliatory acts were coming north, passing through Fort Yuma on their way to California. General Pesqueira even published a call to arms, inviting Sonorans to unite and patriotically defend their homeland against American filibusters. The anti-American mood in Sonora was strong, excited by recollections shared by miners and merchants who had returned from California after suffering abuses at the hands of North Americans. The prejudiced behavior of Anglo-Americans had excited Mexican patriotism, but Henry Crabb was blinded by manifest destiny and his own patriotic notions. He and his followers believed that as Americans they were somehow invulnerable, and that Mexicans could not pose any real danger to them.

At Sonoita, Crabb received a letter informing him that Sonoran military forces were prepared to do battle with him should he continue to invade Mexico. Crabb wrote a response, protesting the threat of violence. He claimed that he and his party came in peace and were breaking no laws; therefore the military should cease and desist from making threats. But in the event that he and his party came under attack, he would respond in kind. He then led his ill-fated party to Caborca, where they were attacked and forced to surrender. All but the youngest of them were executed. Dr. Juan Hernández, formerly of Los Angeles, severed Crabb's head after his execution and preserved it in mesquite liquor. (John C. Frémont and wife claimed Juan was the orphan Pablo Hernández whom they adopted in 1841, but by 1887 they forgot about Henry Crabb and remembered "the beheader"—Hernández—as having become the beheaded bandit Joaquín.)[53]

To Sonorans the filibuster leader from California was a brigand chief and consummate villain. During the struggle, Crabb had attempted to blow up the church at Caborca in which all the town's women and children had taken refuge. (He used a four-year-old boy as a human shield while attempting to detonate dynamite, but the wick was wet and the plot failed.)[54]

El Clamor Público was the first newspaper in California to publish news of Crabb's defeat. A May 2, 1857, headline read, "¡Derrota de los filibusteros!" (Defeat of the Filibusters!) The article told a story of brave Mexican soldiers led by capable Mexican officers fighting well-armed freebooters and taking many of them prisoner. There was no mention of executions until the American press in California got the news. Their headlines screamed, "Massacre of Col. Crabb's Party!" The Mexican military was depicted in the same light as the Joaquín band and the continuation of that band under Juan Flores and Pancho Daniel. Los Angeles had but recently mourned the loss of a sheriff, two constables, and a volunteer deputy. Now the whole state mourned six former state legislators turned filibuster: Dr. Thomas J. Oxley, John Henry, Esq., Colonel W. H. McCoun, Colonel Nathaniel Wood, Freeman S. McKinney, and Henry Crabb. (John Cortelyou was also executed.) The North American press also reported that a Mexican cavalry unit had crossed the border into Gadsdonia and murdered four helpless Americans. They had been with Crabb's party but were forced to stay behind as two of them were sick and one had been wounded from an accidental gunshot. The fourth was an old camp cook who volunteered to stay behind and take care of the other three.

Calls for retaliation surfaced all over California, among them Rasey Biven's excited demand for U.S. military intervention. Bands of armed Americans left Calaveras and Mariposa counties and made their way to Gadsdonia with the intention of exterminating Mexicans. Meanwhile armed bands of Sonorans loyal to Pesquiera crossed the border in a euphoric state, as eager as the Americans were to pick a fight along the border. The defeat of the filibusters had proven to them that North Americans were not invulnerable. Because of the Apaches, there had not been any real border conflicts between Hispanics and Anglo-Saxons in what would become Arizona, but that changed. Border conflicts continued into the twentieth century (and, some would say, up to the present). It was during border conflicts when "El Corrido de Joaquín Murrieta" became popular in Spanish-speaking border communities. (The song depicts Joaquín singing defiantly of taking revenge against abusive Americans.)[55]

Francisco P. Ramírez was alarmed when California Senator William Gwin echoed Rasey Biven's call for revenge and a renewal of war with Mexico. He was also troubled by the slant most American newspaper stories took when covering filibuster news. They saw no heroes among the Mexicans who fought to protect their homeland. They called Mexicans "savages" and General Pesquiera a "traitor." Benjamin Kooser, who in 1853 had profiled Three-Fingered Jack García, said that General Jesús García Morales, who was in command of the unit that defeated Crabb's filibusters, was related to the Garcías of Monterey. Kooser charged that the executions of the American filibusters by the Morales unit were in revenge for the deaths of several of Morales's cousins in California, including Anastacio García, who had recently been lynched.

While the Joaquín band never really materialized into a guerrilla war threat and Walker's and Crabb's well-armed little companies did not pose much of a military threat to Sonorans in Mexico, both illuminate the North American view that the war with Mexico was not over. Southerners in the United States coveted more land and felt manifestly destined to take it. By extension, they supposed that Mexicans in California posed a threat to stability and plotted a guerrilla war because they desired to reclaim conquered territory. That mindset saw the Joaquín band that became the Juan Flores and Pancho Daniel band as a guerrilla threat that provoked calls for government and military assistance to local law enforcement efforts and vigilante responses in Los Angeles.

So rife was the prejudice against Mexicans in American papers following Crabb's defeat that Ramírez was skeptical, at first, of reports claiming that four Americans had been dragged out of their beds and killed on American soil, or that Crabb's head was cut off and preserved by Dr. Hernández. However once his own sources confirmed these reports, he translated and published a page full of columns clipped from American papers. Most of them expressed outrage and called for a retaliatory war with Mexico. But others argued that Crabb had knowingly broken international law and that no one could blame the Mexicans for crossing the border and committing a lawless act in view of the fact that that was exactly what Crabb's party had done. They also pointed out that the officers at Fort Yuma failed in their duty when they knowingly permitted heavily armed filibusters to continue on the road to Mexico. To this Ramírez added that the band of renegades who killed the Americans in Gadsdonia were Mexican filibusters who acted without their government's consent or approval.

Ramírez also defended General Pesqueira. How, he wondered, could Americans call him a traitor for defending his country against armed invaders? He had even given Crabb fair warning, issuing a proclamation saying he would give no quarter and having his officers send a letter to Crabb, to which the latter responded with threats and insults. Crabb was given every opportunity to abort the mission, and he did not do so. The executions, Ramírez argued, were the only way the people of Sonora—so often unjustly targeted by filibusters from California—could make it undeniably clear that heavily armed freebooters pretending to be settlers were not welcome and never would be.

Meanwhile Henry Hamilton, who supported Rasey Biven's calls for retaliatory war, dropped by the *El Clamor Público* office. He brought with him Franklin "Pancho" Johnson, the man who had arrested Juan Flores. Johnson had lived in Los Angeles for over a decade before moving to San Buenaventura a few years earlier. Ramírez knew him well. Hamilton said he came because Ramírez had published José Berreyesa's invitation, several weeks previously, requesting evidence of crimes committed by his brother Encarnación. He said Johnson had a letter containing that evidence. Johnson then gave the letter to Ramírez. It was signed "various citizens of Buenaventura."

Ramírez asked Johnson if he knew any of these "citizens." Johnson said he didn't know if he did. Ramirez then asked who gave him the letter. Johnson glanced at Hamilton, prompting Hamilton to say he intended to publish it and hoped his colleague at El Clamor Público would do likewise. Ramírez thanked them and said he was sorry, he could not print a letter unless he knew who it was from. For all he knew, it was composed by the "creative" editor of the Star. Hamilton protested, saying the signers wanted to remain anonymous. Ramírez countered that in his experience those who sought anonymity in the press needed only ask and it was provided. For example he had recently published a letter from "varios Californios," but he knew who wrote it. To remain anonymous even to an editor meant fraud or fiction was being offered. Ramirez said he would be happy to print the "evidence" as soon as the writer revealed himself in private. That never happened.[56]

The fabricated letter appeared in the Star after all sympathy for the Berreyesa family had been drowned in the blood of Crabb and his filibusters, and yet only one northern California paper picked up the story—the San Jose Tribune. Hamilton's cleverly composed "evidence" came complete with a quote in which Encarnación was purported to have said, "about midnight an American passed, riding a mule—we lassoed and dragged him from his mule and I finished him by stabbing him." Such was the fate of "old Mr. McClure of this city," wrote the editor of the Tribune. He then noted that, according to the Star, Encarnación Berreyesa had been "executed" in San Buenaventura "chiefly on account of his connection with Pancho Daniel's gang."[57] A San Jose posse was out hunting for Pancho Daniel at that very moment.

Pancho Daniel and the Mysterious Lorenzo Lopez

Pancho Daniel had kept a low profile since being mentioned in Teodor Vásquez's confession in January 1852. He was wanted for crimes committed in Tuolumne County in association, no doubt, with Claudio Féliz,

Joaquín Murrieta, and Pedro Sánchez. He was also wanted for horse thefts committed in the vicinity of San Jose and Santa Clara. In July 1856 he boldly galloped up to a fellow thief who had just been arrested in San Jose and spoke to him before fleeing under fire, but that was the only piece of sensational news about him to surface in newspaper columns until he was named as one of those who killed Sheriff Barton. The governor's offer of a one-thousand-dollar reward for Daniel's capture, dead or alive, prompted bounty hunters in northern California to follow every clue and tip they heard. A reward of five hundred dollars was offered for "Leonardo Lopez" (Lorenzo), who had been arrested with Juan Flores. Flores had untied him and Espinosa, all three fleeing north.[58]

According to Teodor Vásquez, Pancho Daniel sharply reprimanded his brother Bernardo for robbing and killing a Sonoran peddler, insisting that killing Sonorans was strictly forbidden (though robbing them was not). In 1856 Bernardo Daniel was arrested in San Luis Obispo as a suspect in the murder of two more peddlers. Although he escaped from jail during a staged fight between inmates (the guard unlocking the door in order to break up the fight), young Bernardo was soon recaptured by an ad hoc citizens' posse that immediately lynched him.[59]

Pancho Daniel was in San Jose in the spring of 1856 and in San Gabriel in early fall of that year. He and the outlaw that the Star listed as "Leonardo,(Mejicano,) un chapo pelón [shaved head]" left Los Angeles County at different times, each of them passing through Santa Barbara and San Luis Obispo counties quietly. Lorenzo joined a band of horse thieves in the Salinas Valley, Monterey County. Pancho Daniel may have been there, too. Local Californios tired of being robbed formed a posse led by Sr. don Pedro Chabolla. During a wild shoot-out conducted on horseback, Lorenzo Lopez was shot through the jaw. He went down and was left for dead, but on regaining consciousness he crawled under a shrub where he waited for night. Then he rose and managed to travel forty-plus miles to a small tent at Guadalupe Quicksilver Mines (also known as New Almaden Mines).

The mine lay six miles south of San Jose in Alameda County. In 1851 there was a shootout between Mexican miners and an Anglo-American posse when a local sheriff tried to arrest the German foreman. An American lawyer who claimed that he owned the mine had provoked the foreman into striking him. The lawyer then charged the man with assault and demanded that the sheriff arrest him. Given that Lorenzo sought sanctuary at Guadalupe, it is probable he once worked at the mine and had participated in a shootout with the sheriff and his posse in 1851. (The German foreman later turned himself in).[60]

On November 16, 1857, a Monday morning, constables Jasper D. Gunn and Jacob L. Miller followed a tip provided by local citizens and found Lorenzo in bed in a tent, "but thinking on a first view that they were mistaken in the individual, did not attempt to arrest him." On being assured by their informants that there was no mistake, they returned. This time Lorenzo threw off his blanket and "springing up, presented a Navy revolver and fired. The ball took effect in the left arm of Mr. Miller. . . . Miller instantly presented his gun at Lopez's head and pulled the trigger, but the cap exploded without discharging."[61] The constables retreated outside and took cover. Lorenzo kept shooting until he ran out of ammunition, then sliced open the back of the tent and fled up a ravine under a shower of bullets. His path was cut off by a young man on horseback who had come to assist the lawmen. Seeing there was no escape and feeling his life ebb away, the outlaw threw away his knife and surrendered.

The prisoner was taken to San Jose where his wounds were dressed. "Besides the bullet in his head, we counted eight buckshot and pistol ball holes in his back and limbs, several of them very dangerous. On his right arm he has the initials, in India ink, J. C. [Joaquín Carrillo?]; and on the left, C. L. A. U., with an eagle and other figures." His back was also scarred by a flogging. His weapons included a "large holster pistol, a very heavy butcher knife and a dangerous looking short sword [or machete]. At the time of the affray he did not expect or desire to be taken alive."[62] However, the doctor said his wounds, though grave, were not fatal.

When Marshal William Getman went to San Jose by steamer to take the wounded prisoner back to Los Angeles with him, the San Jose police were still looking for Pancho Daniel. They were so confident of their impending success, they prematurely sent word to a Stockton newspaper of his demise. El Clamor Público printed the erroneous report on November 28, 1857: "A newspaper from Stockton says that Pancho Daniel, a confederate of Juan Flores, was killed recently in Santa Clara County. He would not surrender and it was necessary to kill him in order to disarm him." But Daniel was not dead, only wounded.

Meanwhile in Los Angeles, El Clamor Público reported that "Luciano Tapia alias Lorenzo Lopez has been tried and convicted by the testimony of numerous witnesses, of having been one of those that last January and February, murdered a German resident of San Juan Capistrano named George Pflugardt."[63] Sentenced to death, he was not scheduled to be executed until February 16, 1858, the same day when Thomas King, an Anglo-American who had also been tried and found guilty of murder, was due to hang. While King and Tapia waited, a wounded Pancho Daniel suddenly joined them. San Jose County Sheriff John E. Murphy had captured him at last and sent him to Los Angeles.

On Saturday, January 23, 1858, both the Star and El Clamor Público reported that Pancho Daniel had surrendered. Henry Hamilton reprinted the full-length San Jose Tribune account of January 20, while El Clamor Público limited coverage to a single short paragraph. Sheriff John Murphy, with his eye on the governor's reward, sent spies out to learn of Daniel's whereabouts. On being informed that the outlaw intended to go to a dance at a Monterey residence that night, the sheriff and his men disguised themselves, took up positions, and watched the house. At around eight o'clock in the evening, two young Mexicans dressed in three-piece suits approached the house on foot, stepped inside, looked around, and then left, walking away leisurely. No one paid them much attention as the pair looked docile and did not appear to be armed, but Murphy recognized Pancho Daniel and hailed him. The two Mexicans immediately darted off in different directions. Murphy pursued Daniel, his surprised and excited posse joining the chase. They fired a hail of bullets at the fleeing outlaw as he splashed up the Guadalupe River and disappeared into a grove of willow trees. From there he returned fire. The posse fired back until the outlaw stopped shooting. They were sure he was dead and withdrew to celebrate. However when they returned to the willow grove at dawn the next day there was no corpse. They did find a blood trail, though.

The trail led to a Californio farm house several miles away. Murphy asked the farmer where Daniel was hiding, but the frightened man said nothing. Murphy ordered one of his men to throw a lasso around the farmer's neck, take him to a fruit tree and haul him up and down as many times as it took to get information out of him. That made the farmer blurt out that the robber was in the haystack. Murphy called on Pancho

Daniel to surrender or burn with the hay, whereupon the wounded bandit stepped out and surrendered his weapons. "He is accused of having committed numerous crimes," reported Francisco P. Ramírez, "among them, of having been party to the murder of Sheriff Barton."[64]

Like Juan Flores before him, Pancho Daniel became a popular jailhouse attraction. Daguerreotypes and tintypes were taken of him in San Jose and Los Angeles and marketed as curiosities. Visitors stopped in to stare and ask questions. The Los Angeles court scheduled a trial, but the court-appointed defense attorney, Colonel Edward J. C. Kewen, resigned when his client insisted on pleading not guilty. Kimball H. Dimmick, Esq., was appointed next. He petitioned to hold the trial in Santa Barbara County, arguing that his defendant could not get an impartial hearing in Los Angeles. The court declined, whereupon Dimmick resigned. Columbus Sims was appointed next, but he fell gravely ill, and when he did not recover after several months of waiting the district judge began to look for yet another replacement.[65]

In April 1858 the *San Jose Tribune* reported that the "trial of this notorious individual, which was to have taken place at Los Angeles" had been postponed for four months. A correspondent had gone to see the famous desperado and said, "Pancho has been kept in double irons since his arrival. He says he can prove by parties in San Jose that he was . . . [there] at the time of the murder of Sheriff Barton [in Los Angeles], and a long time afterward." The writer then inserted what a correspondent to the *San Francisco Alta* had written of a still more recent visit with the prisoner:

> After so long a confinement in a narrow and dark cell, heavily ironed to the floor, he was naturally thinner and paler than he appears in the daguerreotypes that have been taken of him. He was neatly and well dressed in a black suit, with silk vest, and . . . looks like a well-bred Mexican gentleman. He informed me he was born in Hermosillo and is 24 years of age.—He of course did not touch upon his case, except to complain of the suffering occasioned by his wound in the leg and his inability to move about in his cell. . . . Soon after, he was removed to the Court room, where I had a better opportunity of viewing him. He sat quietly and modestly, occasionally passing

his hand to his wounded limb as though it gave him pain;
but I thought a nervous anxiety . . . could be detected in the
compression of his lips and occasional trembling of the facial nerves.[66]

A famous tintype on display at Old Timers Museum at Murphy's Camp,
Calaveras County, shows a young man with Sonoran facial features who
is about twenty-four years old and wears a dark suit and silk vest. He sits
with his hands resting against one leg as if controlling pain. The photograph on the *cartes de visite* of the once-famous Francisco "Pancho" Daniel must have looked something like this tintype. However the museum
display assigns another identity to the image—that of Joaquín Murrieta.
By the time the display was installed in the mid-twentieth century, Pancho Daniel had been forgotten.[67]

The Crime Investigation that Snared Joaquín Valenzuela

While Pancho Daniel awaited trial, newspapers throughout the state began reporting news of yet another band of outlaws and the vigilante response in San Luis Obispo. John Nugent criticized the San Luis Obispo
vigilantes, as did Ramírez—following Nugent's lead—but the San Luis
vigilantes, unlike their Los Angeles counterparts, did not sever heads or
ears, stab corpses, or leave bodies hanging from trees alongside roads.
However they did lynch one prisoner. Others were hastily tried before
vigilante juries, condemned by their own confessions, and hanged. The
first one hanged was Joaquín Valenzuela of the famous Joaquín band.

The crime that led to Valenzuela's arrest occurred on May 17, 1858.
Seven armed horsemen stopped at a newly established ranch in a remote part of the San Joaquin Valley about forty miles east of Mission San
Luis Obispo. The ranch was owned by two Frenchmen, M. Josef Borel
and Bartólome Baratié (also spelled Bartolo Baratier), the latter having
his wife Andrea with him. They had two hired hands: a Chilean named
Ysidro Silvas and a young Mexican named Luis Murillo. They welcomed
the seven visitors who said they were vaqueros. The visitors dined, paid
the host, and spent the night outside. They left the following morning—
or so it seemed.

About an hour later, one of them returned and asked if he might stay
a day longer. His name was Miguel Blanco, the same that together with

29. Tintype, c. 1858, of a young, well-dressed Sonoran with a grave yet stoic countenance. Courtesy of the Old Timers Museum, Murphys, California.

Miguel Soto had assaulted and robbed William Twist of Santa Barbara in the fall of 1856. Blanco now sat on a hill and watched the Frenchmen dig a well. Silvas and Murillo were mowing hay with machetes. At around noon, Murillo started toward the house and Baratié followed him. Blanco stood up, walked down to the well, and shot Borel in the head. The shot caused Silvas to look at him. He smiled and fired into the air, causing the Chilean to think he was just fooling around, but he was not. The second shot was a signal. The other bandits suddenly stormed the ranch.

Silvas dropped his machete and put up his hands. Murillo and Baratié began running toward the house. Murillo got there first, but a bandit reined his horse in and fired through the open door, hitting Murillo in the hip. Baratié reached for his gun near the door and was shot in the shoulder, then knocked to the ground with a blow to the head. His wife ran out and knelt beside him, pleading for mercy. They asked her where the moneybox was hidden and she told them. They took all the money, horses, and other desirables. Then the captain of the gang ordered his men to kill Baratié, overruling all objections. Andrea, Murillo, and Silvas were bound and taken to an outlaw camp where a couple of others waited. Along the way the ruthless leader saw a poor American farmer plowing his field and killed him lest he bear witness to their presence.

At camp the loot was divided and the prisoners condemned to death. Froilan Servin, alias Nieves Robles, and an Indian, Luciano "el Mesteño," were ordered to march Silvas and Murillo out of camp and kill them. Murillo and Silvas begged for mercy, causing Mesteño and Robles to argue over their assignment. Finally Robles headed back to camp while Mesteño shot over the heads of the kneeling prisoners. He gave each a little money and a riata with which to catch a horse. Then he walked back to camp, proclaimed the task accomplished, and offered to take charge of the woman. She was delivered up to him when the band broke camp and split up, departing in different directions.

Mesteño was expected to kill the woman but he did not do so. Instead he took her to a cave and lived with her there until their provisions ran out. Then he took her to a house in Sunol Valley where she could catch the stagecoach to Oakland, where she had friends. He also gave her the six hundred dollars and two Baratié horses that were his share of the loot, asking in return that she wait a couple of days before going to Oakland.

Meanwhile Ysidro Silvas lassoed a horse and carried the wounded Murillo to Estrella Inn. He left him there and rode on to Captain David Mallagh's ranch to report the crime. The captain took Silvas to San Luis Obispo, where he told the same story to Sheriff Francisco Castro. Castro and a couple of his deputies took Silvas to the gambling houses in town on the hunch that one or two members of the band may already be wasting their ill-gotten gains. Silvas recognized Santos Robles, alias

Santos Peralta, a Sonoran. He was escorted to jail. A lynch mob hanged him there. Santos was believed to be party to another double homicide and robbery that had occurred two months earlier. He was also said to have been with the Flores band when they attacked Sheriff Barton's posse in Los Angeles.

Sheriff Castro, Captain Mallagh, and vigilante leader Walter Murray urged people to form companies and search for the rest of the band. Ysidro Silvas went with Mallagh's posse to the outlaw campsite. From there they picked up the trail of four outlaws on the run, drawing near enough at one point for Silvas to recognize Desiderio Grijalva, Miguel Blanco, Froilan Servin, and the ruthless "el Güero" who was identified in El Clamor Público as Rafael Money of Los Angeles.[68] He was associated with Jack Powers, about whom Silvas had heard the outlaws talk in camp as if he was the real chief of the band. A Californio named Pío Linares was at the camp and acted like he was the captain in Powers's absence. With Linares was a Sonoran named Jesús Valenzuela, brother of Joaquín.[69]

Joaquín Valenzuela had not participated in the Baratié triple homicide and burglary, but when the posse led by Walter Murray ran into him while searching for Pío Linares and Jesús Valenzuela, Joaquín was taken into custody. When asked if he knew Jack Powers he said he knew him well, realizing too late that he should not have said that. Murray took Joaquín Valenzuela to town, where he was tried on May 18, 1858. Those who testified against him said he was also known as "Ocamorenia" and that he was therefore actually two of the "five Joaquíns" Harry Love and his rangers had been looking for in 1853.[70] Murray himself testified that when Love first pursued Joaquín Valenzuela in the spring of 1852, Love suspected him of having played a part in a number of murders and robberies that took place in Mariposa County. He also mentioned the little girl Harry Love found in Valenzuela's house. Murray had met the girl and her mother in Stockton, where they were still living.

Another witness for the prosecution said that in July 1856 the aged Don Tomás Romero of Rancho de Las Cruces, Santa Barbara County, was shot and killed, and his sixty-year-old wife was bound and raped. Their house was robbed and their horses stolen. A little later an American was killed and robbed on a road near there. The sheriff of Santa Barbara arrested

Joaquín Valenzuela and Juan Sálazar. Romero's widow identified Sálazar as the one who raped her, but she said Valenzuela must have been the one who stayed outside and held the horses while acting as lookout.[71] She did not recognize him as one of those who raped her. Found guilty of participating in these and other crimes, Joaquín Valenzuela was sentenced to death. Murray allowed him to dictate letters to his wife and his employer and to confess to a priest. A telegraph line sent word of the hanging to newspapers everywhere.

Because Valenzuela was mentioned as a member of the Joaquín Murrieta band in the *Sacramento Daily Union*, the editor there reprinted what the *San Francisco Herald* had shared from a private letter: "He [Joaquín Valenzuela] never flinched once; he smoked a cigar, and drank liquor until the rope was placed on his neck. I never saw such nerve in a man before. He told his countrymen to leave this country as soon as possible, for it was no place for them to remain in. He also told them to die before they should reveal a secret." He then asked the executioner to "tie his hands and feet tight, for he was a strong man, and he wished to die easily."[72] Perhaps he had seen Juan Flores struggle.

The day after Joaquín Valenzuela's execution, news came that Andrea had turned up in Oakland. She said she had been taken on a long, arduous journey that lasted seven days and then abandoned at a house where two women lived. But when a "Spaniard" was later seen with two of her horses and questioned by local constables, he said she and a companion had arrived at his house "several days ago." Andrea did not seem to be distressed, so he did not realize that anything was amiss. She had a handkerchief full of gold pieces and paid to stay two more nights after her companion had left. Before she left by stagecoach she paid him to bring the horses to her in Oakland. Andrea was afterward called "a woman of bad reputation" and faced accusations to the effect that she had master-minded the brutal crime. A search for Mesteño led to his arrest. After Andrea identified him, he confessed his part and cleared her of all blame. He was then tried, condemned, and hanged.[73]

While John Nugent and Francisco P. Ramírez consistently denounced the San Luis Obispo vigilantes, Henry Hamilton applauded them. When a lynch mob seized and hanged Santos Peralta, Ramírez reprinted John

Nugent's denunciation and added his own emphasis. "This is how they achieve justice in this country, where they pretend to have laws, and where there are rights and liberty! They lie! . . . here, when they pretend to punish a crime, they commit a worse crime than the one punished!"[74] El Clamor Público also repeated a refrain found in Nugent's editorials which called on the state legislature to outlaw lynching and vigilantism. Vigilantes, Nugent insisted, were too often reacting to a passionate thirst for revenge and not performing a public service out of a love of justice, duly guided by evidence and reason as Walter Murray claimed. Francisco P. Ramírez even used the hanging of Joaquín Valenzuela as evidence of this. Joaquín, after all, had nothing to do with the crime being investigated and yet he was tried by vigilantes and promptly executed. If they wished to prosecute him for old crimes, they should have delivered him up and left it to the criminal justice system to try, sentence, and execute the prisoner.[75]

Ramírez also attacked Walter Murray's posse for actions taken while pursuing outlaw Pío Linares. Linares, he admitted, was well-armed, a good shot, and prepared to die fighting. That made him a very dangerous target, but setting his house on fire was inexcusable. The outlaw's wife and six children were in that house and they were innocent of crime. Thankfully they had escaped injury, "but their home was reduced to ashes and they were left with nothing, nor was any aid afterward offered them," complained Ramírez. "How sad that there are not laws in our penal system that would castigate those who dispose on a whim the life and property of the first person they lay hands on! . . . Nor are there laws castigating he who robs the public treasury and goes marching off to another country to enjoy the fruits of his [filibustering] rapine."[76] Francisco P. Ramírez saw the filibuster actions of Walker and Crabb as part of the same American mindset that led to the establishment of state rangers when the Joaquín band was being pursued and to the rise of vigilante posses when the band was led by Juan Flores and Pancho Daniel, or Rafael Money, Pío Linares, and Jack Powers.

Francisco P. Ramírez was not alone: John Nugent and several other American editors of independent newspapers saw vigilantes and filibusters alike as opportunists who trampled the law while pretending they defended "the people" in the name of "security" and "liberty." Their campaigns were always accompanied by appeals for public funds to compensate them for their lawlessness. And they were always exempt from prosecution in the United States. Although the critical editors were a minority, their voices began to influence the thinking of state legislators and the governor, but not the vigilantes in San Luis Obispo. Walter Murray defended his posses' actions. They killed Pío Linares after he had killed three members of their company, and when Miguel Blanco and Desiderio Grijalva surrendered, they were tried before they were hanged. The rest of the band seemed to have escaped, until El *Clamor Público* and the *Star* reported the capture of Froilan Servin at Mission Santa Ana after Jesús Dominguez pointed him out. Only Rafael Money and Jesús Valenzuela disappeared completely, the suspicion being that they had successfully crossed the border into Sonora. Jack Powers also escaped to Sonora, but he soon moved to Gadsdonia where he was murdered in 1860.[77]

For Pancho Daniel, a Lynching, for Joaquín Murrieta, a Legend Revived

Throughout the San Luis Obispo excitement, Pancho Daniel sat in jail, rubbing his wounded leg and slowly becoming crippled. When Captain Cameron E. Thom, Esq., was assigned Daniel's case in July, he insisted on his right, as defense attorney, to examine each juror in order to determine whether each one could give an impartial judgment. This jury was found wanting, and Judge Benjamin Hayes was forced to dissolve it and appoint a new one in August. That one was also found wanting and was also dissolved. A third jury was dissolved in October. Thom now insisted that Los Angeles jurors were incapable of rendering an impartial judgment and requested that his client be tried in Santa Barbara County. The court was forced to concede, but the people were not.

Early in the morning of November 30, 1858, the jail keeper was on his way to the store to buy some breakfast when he was struck from behind and knocked out cold. When he came to, his keys were missing. He ran back to the jail and found the gate ajar. Pancho Daniel was hanging from the gate beam, still in chains. The lynching caught Francisco P. Ramírez by surprise. He expressed shock, for even while "everyone in Los Angeles considered Daniel a criminal," there was no need to hasten his death with yet another criminal act.[78] Did anyone seriously doubt he would pay for his crimes if tried in Santa Barbara?

California Governor John B. Weller agreed. He offered a reward of one thousand dollars for the arrest of those responsible for the unlawful execution of Pancho Daniel, calling those who lynched him "a gang of bandits." Ramírez published the governor's reward and warned all citizens against protecting outlaws—a charge so often levied against Californios only. It was all in vain. No one came forward to reveal the culprits.

> The barbarous and diabolical execution that was perpetrated in this city has been followed by silence. One of those crimes that features a lower order of man—. . . has been committed in this city—and will doubtless be forgotten as have many another atrocity and horror. But what can be done when murder is the order of the day! California has been stained from one end to the other with the blood of innumerable victims of this type of violence. If nothing is done to repress these acts, they will spread their perverse principles of brute force, and our laws and those who administer them will only serve to cloak the gross and barbaric immorality. Though the governor . . . has taken the first steps toward reform . . . we fear that his proclamation will not produce the desired effect.[79]

Francisco P. Ramírez not only railed against Americans guilty of criminal lynching, he also railed against his own people. An election had occurred. He had argued in favor of the Republican candidates, who promised equality and justice, and he had spoken of abolishing slavery. But the people his newspaper sought to serve had become a political *farce* instead of a united political *force*. For four years he had explained how elections work and pointed out the power and purpose of the ballot box, but he forgot his manners after witnessing the behavior of the local Hispanic electorate on election day:

> We are tired of saying "open your eyes! It is time to defend your rights and interests!" . . . you have become a satire; for when the time comes to exercise your rights, you . . . go chasing after the carriages of candidates in the streets, saying you will

not vote unless they buy your vote! Ignoble traffic! You make us blush with indignation. Have you no idea what honesty is, or are you damned by God as well as men? . . . you live in wretchedness and poverty and seem to want nothing more than to end up like murderers and thieves at the gallows. Have you forgotten that you are citizens and . . . have an incontestable right to govern matters of public interest?[80]

It was hard, fighting for what was right in a society that romanticized wrong.

A year later, when Ignacio Pesquiera became governor of Sonora and invited Francisco P. Ramírez to serve as editor of La Estrella de Occidente, he accepted the job. He was twenty-two years old when the last issue of El Clamor Público came off the presses in December 1859. That same month a newly reestablished California Police Gazette published a book: The Life of Joaquin Murieta, the Brigand Chief of California; Being a complete History of his Life, from the age of sixteen to the time of his Capture and Death at the hands of Capt. Harry Love, in the year 1853. John Rollin Ridge accused the anonymous author of plagiarism, and indeed, the work fairly duplicates much of his 1854 original, but there were differences, too.

The Gazette version has a more coherent and continuous storyline and is less didactic with regard to injustice to individuals. It proved very popular. Within a decade, French, Spanish, and Portuguese versions appeared in Europe and Latin America. Joaquín Murrieta was immortalized, while Luciano Tapia and his tattoos, Miguel Soto and his fiery ordeal, Pancho Daniel and his souvenir portraits all disappeared, and Joaquín Valenzuela became a minor character in legend. Juan Flores and Pancho Daniel resurfaced in a few published California pioneer recollections, like those of Horace Bell. They were left out of California history, but the legendary Joaquín Murrieta became the historical symbol of Mexican banditry as rebellion against unjust laws and actions. Meanwhile Francisco P. Ramírez, whose struggle for justice was overlooked by historians up until the 1990s, lived a long, productive life and died of natural causes.[81]

6. Of Tiburcio, Procopio, Mariana, and Oral Tradition

During the 1860s the Joaquín legend inspired popular fiction and poetry at the same time that the last of the horseback-riding Californio and Mexican bandits preoccupied the lawmen who were patrolling the scattered valleys of the Coast Range from Alameda County to Los Angeles County.[1] The area had been quite familiar to Joaquín Murrieta and Claudio Féliz and even more familiar to Joaquín Valenzuela, Lorenzo Lopez, and Pancho Daniel. It was a good place to round up wild livestock and hide stolen horses because most of the land belonged to Indians and rancheros and was not closely watched. The area continued to be good pickings for bandits after much of the land had fallen into the hands of whites after it became U.S. territory. Anglo-Americans established small, isolated towns with a combination general store and post office at the center. Often there were also an inn and restaurant, a bank, one or two saloons, a barber shop, a stable, a blacksmith and wheelwright shop, a church, and a schoolhouse. These towns were targeted by Tiburcio Vásquez and Procopio Bustamente and their bands because they were isolated and had few sheriffs between them. Rounding up a posse of volunteers took time—enough time to allow the robbers to escape.

In an effort to reduce the crime rate, the state government under Governor Bigler approved the construction of a state prison at San Quentin beginning in 1852. Called "the dungeon" by prisoners, breakouts occurred frequently in the 1850s, but improvements in prison security resulted in fewer escapes in later decades. Meanwhile the governor's decision to outlaw vigilantism had sharply reduced the number of deaths caused by lynch mobs (although lynching did still occur now and then). Meanwhile the American anti-foreigner focus shifted from Mexicans to the Chinese, in part because Mexico was for the first time witnessing a period of relative peace and prosperity. Migrations from Mexico to California slowed down while migrations from China increased dramatically due to word-of-mouth job advertisements: Chinese immigrants proved to be excellent railroad track, tunnel, and bridge builders.

The number of Mexican bandits in California decreased in the latter half of the nineteenth century, in part due to changes in law enforcement methods. Lawmen began using mug shots and sketches to identify fugitives and ex-convicts. They used telegraphs to send immediate warning of outlaw movements to distant counties and trains to travel long distances and cut off bands in retreat. Those who were caught were duly tried, sentenced, and imprisoned. However when released from the dark, vermin-infested dungeons at San Quentin, where floggings and other forms of abuse frequently occurred, former prisoners generally reentered society embittered and unprepared to make amends and become good citizens.

Among those who returned to banditry after release was Tiburcio Vásquez. He was first arrested for horse-stealing in Los Angeles in the summer of 1857. He escaped from San Quentin in 1859 (together with others), but was recaptured and finally released in 1863. He soon returned to a life of crime and was arrested again in 1867 for burglary, for which he served three more years in San Quentin. He undoubtedly met Procopio Bustamente while in prison.

In 1871 Alameda County Sheriff Henry "Harry" Morse wrote an article for the *Monterey Republican* about Procopio Bustamente, alias Tomás "Red Dick" Redondo, alias Joaquín Murrieta. Bustamente had just been released from San Quentin after serving seven years. Sheriff Morse warned readers of his release. Procopio, he said, had been the leader of "an organized band of robbers and cut-throats," and he would undoubtedly return to his old habits. After all, he was "the nephew of the infamous Joaquin Murieta, whose deeds of crime constitute so bloody a chapter in the history of California, being the son of Joaquin's sister."[2] (That same year John Rollin Ridge's widow, Elizabeth Wilson Ridge, took advantage

30. Procopio Bustamente, 1871. Courtesy of William Secrest.

of the publicity Murrieta's nephew, Procopio, received and published an edited reprint of her late husband's book about Joaquín.)

Procopio had not been at liberty a month when he was implicated in a robbery, together with Tiburcio Vásquez and band. Sheriff Morse succeeded in arresting Procopio in 1872 and sent him back to San Quentin for five more years. When released in 1877, Procopio immediately went south, out of Morse's reach, and gathered en route a band of about a dozen Hispanics. They robbed various small community banks and stores in the San Joaquin Valley, all within about a hundred-mile radius of Bakersfield. Pursued by a determined posse, the band split up. One company of six, led by Procopio, was located, surrounded, and arrested, except for Procopio. He escaped by killing one of the posse, snatching the fallen lawman's revolver as he ran and using it to open an escape route.[3]

In the fall of 1880 a teenage Eugenio Plummer and his brother saw three weary travelers leading pack mules through Rancho Cahuenga (where the Hollywood Bowl is today). The boys invited the strangers to the ranch house for refreshments. As soon as the men entered the house, Sra. Guadalupe Valdez de Rocha greeted Procopio by name, but he told her to shush as he was afraid of being discovered. Before leaving, Procopio paid his hostess for the repast and gave Eugenio a couple of souvenirs: a horn cup and British revolver he said had once belonged to his uncle, Joaquín Murrieta.[4] The three travelers headed south, Procopio surfacing next in Hermosillo, Sonora.

Meanwhile Tiburcio Vásquez and band began to commit a series of robberies in isolated rural towns. After several townspeople were killed during one such robbery, the band split up. Harry Morse and posse followed Tiburcio Vásquez and band member Clodoveo Chávez all the way to Los Angeles. There, Morse left matters in the hands of local law enforcement. Vásquez was wounded while trying to escape the Los Angeles posse that arrested him.[5] Clodoveo Chávez succeeded in escaping. He learned through newspaper stories that Vásquez did not want him to attempt a rescue, so he retreated to a border town in Sonora, Mexico.

The wounded Tiburcio Vásquez, meanwhile, became the subject of several souvenir photo cards, booklets, and long newspaper articles that compared him to Joaquín Murrieta. One of those who wrote about him was a young journalist named George Beers. Unlike John Rollin Ridge, Beers had a lot of firsthand knowledge about his subject. He had joined the posses that pursued Vásquez, was present when he surrendered, and interviewed Tiburcio several times while the jailed outlaw awaited trial. He even had access to court records of Tiburcio's trial. But George Beers was not the only one to take advantage of Tiburcio Vásquez's romanticized notoriety. Newspaper articles about Vásquez were compiled and reprinted in the 1874 edition of John Rollin Ridge's book about Joaquín, even while George Beers published his memoir of Tiburcio Vásquez.[6]

Beers described how, when he was with Harry Morse's posse, they stopped to question a Mexican woman living in a little shepherd's cabin at Three Rocks, near upper Cantua Creek. She was forty-three years old and plump but well-proportioned. Her round face was scarred on one side from nose to ear by a knife wound, but it did not mar her sensuous lips, perfect teeth, and sparkling dark eyes. She said her name was Mariana Higuera (also known as Mariana Andrades). She claimed to be Joaquín Murrieta's widow. She also said that the cabin in which she lived had been Joaquín's hideout and that he was only fifteen years old when he came to California, and only nineteen years old when he was killed (a description that matches that of Claudio Féliz).

When Sheriff Morse asked Mariana about Tiburcio Vásquez, she shrugged. One of the posse members offered her his flask of rum. The beverage loosened her up. Asked about the scar on her face, she said she had had an affair with Charlie Baker while Joaquín Murrieta was away. She described how he tearfully forgave her that indiscretion, but when she left him for Charlie, he came back to kill her lover. Finding her alone, he shot her twice, cut her thigh and face, and left her for dead. (Charlie Baker was the deputy sheriff whom Juan Flores shot dead in revenge, he and the deputy having argued over a woman a week or so before Juan was arrested for horse theft in 1855.)

The more rum Mariana drank, the more animated she became: "Her eyes, head, and gracefully-shrugged shoulders assist to convey her ideas," wrote Beers, "while, under the exciting influence of her stories, her swinging arms and her small feet stamping the earth, . . . gives strong emphasis to her assertions." When George Beers asked her about Joaquín's fate, Mariana said that the rangers found him and his men at Cantua and shot him, but he sprang on his horse, bareback, and escaped to her cabin, only to die in her arms two days later from the effects of his wounds. She pointed to a small oak tree on which she had carved a cross and insisted that his unmutilated body was buried there on the banks of Cantua Creek. As for the head that was still on exhibit at a museum in San Francisco, she claimed it was that of an Indian named Pedro Venda, another member of the band. Beers was not willing to assert that Mariana's claims were true, only that they were entertaining.[7]

Unlike Claudio Féliz, Juan Flores, Pancho Daniel, and even Procopio Bustamente, Tiburcio Vásquez was never eclipsed by the ever-lengthening shadow of the legendary Joaquín Murrieta. However the latter remained a literary and folkloric favorite, probably because there was far less documentation available, giving storytellers like Mariana more lee-way to mix exaggerations into spotty recollections.[8]

Renewed Debates over the Identity of a Head

Tiburcio Vásquez was tried, condemned, and hanged in 1874. The gover-nor, however, continued to offer a reward for the capture, dead or alive, of Clodoveo Chávez. Chávez, meanwhile, had moved to Arizona Terri-tory and lived there quietly. Although various Mexican Americans recog-nized him, no one attempted to collect the reward money—that is, until he became a bad influence on Luis Raggio's thirteen-year-old younger brother. Raggio warned his brother to stay away from the outlaw but the boy would not listen. He admired Chávez, even though Chávez had threatened to kill Luis if he betrayed him. Luis Raggio decided that the only way to be free of the threat to his life and the threat to his broth-er's morals was to kill Chávez, but he knew he could not do it alone. He offered to split the reward with two friends if they came with him. The trio caught the outlaw off guard and shot him dead, then took the body to Fort Yuma to claim the two-thousand-dollar reward. They were told that they would have to take the evidence to the governor of California. A physician at the fort severed Chávez's head from the body and stored it in a can of alcohol so that it could be taken to various towns in Cali-fornia for identification purposes.[9]

Clodoveo Chávez's fate provoked a fresh debate about Joaquín Murrie-ta's fate. In 1879 a newspaper correspondent called the head of Chávez "bogus" and compared it to the one brought in by the rangers in 1853. Alfred A. Green responded to the article, saying he agreed. He then pro-ceeded to tell a story, complete with quoted dialogue between himself and a nameless "young priest" he met at Mission San Buenaventura in October 1857.

In the spring of 1857 José Jesús Espinosa was captured and hanged in San Buenaventura for his part in crimes committed by the Juan Flores and Pancho Daniel band, but Green confused the vigilante actions that occurred that year. He claimed the young priest walked him to the spot where Andrés Pico had lynched five (instead of two) bandits in San Buena-ventura. This same priest, Green claimed, also shared a "secret" with him (as if Catholic priests were in the habit of sharing secrets with mere acquaintances). Green quoted the priest as saying that he had recently performed a wedding in Los Angeles and that the groom's last name was Murrieta. When the priest asked the groom if he was related to the famous outlaw, he said yes. Then he showed the priest a letter from August 1857 that was signed "Joaquin Murieta" and that had been sent from Magdalena, Sonora. This letter purportedly said that the writer (Murrieta) knew that the Americans thought they had severed his head "and [he] requested that his family would sanction the story and keep up the illusion, for otherwise they [the Americans] might follow him into Mexico."[10] The whole family had complied and told the Americans who showed them the head that it was that of the famous outlaw.

"I leave it to the reader to judge or form his own opinion," Green added, as if he had reason to believe he would be doubted. He then offered, as proof, the real reason he thought that Joaquín Murrieta had escaped to Mexico. In 1857, while in Mazatlán, Sinaloa, Mexico, he had heard that Murrieta "had been in that part, but that he lived in the state of Sonora." And Green's brother, while surveying for a railroad company in Sonora in the 1870s, had heard that Joaquín had lived at several places along the Sonora River and that he had died but recently, at a ranch in Arispe. Therefore it was now safe for Green to share the "secret."[11]

Green and his brother may well have heard about Joaquín Murrietas in Sonora. There were others. But the California *bandolero*, Joaquín Murrieta, did not die in Arispe in the late 1870s. Albert Owen and later Frank Latta, when they visited Sonora in 1872 and 1935, respectively, did not meet anyone, not even members of the Murrieta extended family in Sonora who claimed that Joaquín "El Famoso" had returned to Sonora after the encounter with the rangers at Cantua Creek. Everyone insisted that they had heard he died in the fight at Cantua or soon thereafter. In any case he was never heard from again.

A letter responding to Green's article was penned by lawyer and historian Oliver Perry Stidger. It appeared in *The Pioneer* on November 29, 1879, and was signed "Old Marysvillian." Stidger confirmed Green's claim with regard to Joaquín Murrieta's fate. He then told a story that also included a quoted conversation, one he said he had overheard. He was in Marysville in "1853, or early in 1854" when Harry Love exhibited the head. Stidger had gotten in line to see the head and stood right behind Joaquín's sister, he claimed. Like the brother and the priest in Green's story, this sister was not named. Stidger said she smiled at the gruesome exhibit and whispered in Spanish to a nameless "Mexican gentleman and lady" who were with her that it was not her brother's head, it was that of Joaquín Gonzales. She told them to say nothing and let the rangers think they had killed her brother. Stidger said he told Captain Love about it, and Love responded, "I know this to be the head of Joaquin Murietta, and she says it is not because she is too proud to own it."[12]

Like Green, Stidger offered additional proof of his story. Some years later he had spoken to Harry Love again in a bar in San Jose. To show that his memory was sound, he named the bar and gave a detailed description of its exact location. He then said that he had asked Love about Ridge's claim. Had he killed Joaquín Murrieta? Love told him he did not kill Joaquín Murrieta, nor was he present when Murrieta was shot dead. Indeed Harry Love never did say he shot Joaquín. He gave full credit to ranger John Henderson from the beginning. He also never claimed to have witnessed the death of Joaquín. After all, Henderson took off in pursuit of Murrieta and both had ridden several miles west, disappearing behind some hills, while Love exchanged fire with Emanuel García and other members of the band.

Stidger's story is at odds with earlier records. On August 24, 1853, the *Marysville Herald*, of which Stidger was a proprietor, printed this editorial:

> It is a great pity, after all that has been done and said, that the death and decapitation of Joaquin should still remain a "vexed question". . . . The last and, apparently, the most reliable information, relative to the affair, is that the head . . . was once the property of Joaquin Valenzuela. Muriata and Corillo . . . , are still alive. . . . The question now arises: "As there are or were three Joaquíns—will the head of any of the trio be sufficient to claim the reward?" This may prove a very pretty nut for the logicians and metaphysicians [words Democrats used to describe John Bigler's oratorical style] to crack—. . . we shall have nothing to do with it.

This was followed by a story about a meeting that ended with "three tremendous cheers for WALDO & REFORM!" and was preceded by a story claiming that the new Board of Land Commissioners had been inactive because an election was underway and the commissioners were afraid "their decisions may operate to the injury of Gov. Bigler." By 1879 O. P. Stidger had forgotten all about the political climate in which Joaquín and the rangers became fair game for mockery in editorials. All he remembered was that some editorials had questioned Joaquín's fate at the hands of the rangers, a memory that was jogged by Alfred Green's correspondence.

Stidger did indeed see the head in mid-September 1853, *after* the election was over and the ranger's term of duty had ended. Harry Love and James Norton brought the head of Murrieta and the three-fingered hand of Emanuel García to Marysville. They used the same building in which the Whigs had held their "Waldo & Reform" meetings, a detail Stidger recalled correctly in 1879. Everyone was welcome to take a look free of charge. Stidger's newspaper reported in 1853:

> There is no doubt that the head on exhibition is that of Joaquin Muriata. Capt. Love has any quantity of affidavits from men who were well acquainted with Joaquin in his lifetime, to substantiate the fact, besides numerous Mexicans who knew him well, certify that the decapitated head belonged to him. We saw and conversed with a Mexican this morning, who said he knew Joaquin well, and that the head . . . was that of Joaquin. Many of our citizens recognize this head as belonging to one of the men who shot Sheriff Buchanan a couple of years ago."[13]

No mention was made of a sister, and no hint of any doubt as to the identity of the head was expressed. Had a newspaper proprietor been aware of Joaquín Murrieta's sister's presence in 1853, not a newspaper in the state would have missed an opportunity to feature her response. And if Stidger had doubts about the identity of the head in 1853, he would have expressed them in his columns. As for his recollection of Love's remark to the supposed sister's assertion, that was probably influenced by a letter Love sent to the *Alta* in 1855: "Mr. Editor: I observe in your issue of the 24th inst., a letter from San Ramon signed 'H.', in which he . . . asserts that the notorious Joaquin Murieta was *alive* and had just returned from Sonora with eleven men, well armed &c., and was going to

... revenge the death of a poor devil called Gregorio Lopez, who having some slight resemblance to him had fallen victim to Love's thirst for a reward. . . . Now this is to state . . . that Harry Love knew Joaquin Murieta, and *knows he is dead*—which fact is certified to by some of the most reliable men in the State."[14]

Francisco P. Ramirez made fun of the stories Harry Love felt compelled to attack:

> The San Francisco *Chronicle* says that according to a trustworthy source, Joaquín the scourge of the Americans, dead and resurrected fifty times by means of that powerful agent known as the "fib", has just appeared in southern California (we do not know if he has come here from this world or the next), and that it is certain he has arrived safe and sound, together with a dozen of his companions, with the object of avenging here the death of one of his dear comrades who has probably been killed unjustly, because to tell the truth, the conduct of all of them has been most honorable and no less worthy of the noose. Capt. Love . . . , has manifest his astonishment when he learned of the ease with which the dead are raised.[15]

Both Stidger and Green had been in California when the rangers were exhibiting the head, and both of them remembered that there had been expressions of doubt back then, but they failed to remember *why*. They forgot about the political race that motivated some editors to mock the rangers and their "trophy." That is understandable, given how often elections occur. They also sensed that the evidence they had was shaky. A lack of confidence resulted in the introduction of more compelling "evidence," such as conversations with relatives of Joaquín Murrieta. Their stories are not invented after the manner of a fiction writer, but rather, they reflect an effort to come to terms with incomplete and confused memories in the context of recent news about yet another severed head, that of Clodoveo Chávez.

Oral Traditions: History versus Folklore

It is through the rearranging of recollections influenced by recent events that memories feed folklore. Folklore usually recounts as authentic, and finds entertainment value in, various sketchy and retrospectively revised recollections of events. Unlike history, folklore does not try to be consistent or cohesive beyond what is thought necessary to make a doubtful claim sound convincing. A good example is the collection of accounts disputing whether the head repeatedly identified as that of Joaquín Murrieta really belonged to him; these accounts preferred to assign the head to someone else, but never the same optional candidate. First, it's the head of Joaquín Valenzuela, then Pedro Venda, then Joaquín Gonzales, and in Frank Latta's book it is that of an Indian called "Chappo."[16] The candidates change because each lacks supporting evidence.

When Hubert Howe Bancroft sent Thomas Savage and Henry Cerruti out to interview Spanish, Mexican, and North American pioneers he found that some of what they collected was confirmable and some was not. He selectively trusted Californio *testimonios* based on objectivity, modest confession of errant memory, and ability to correlate with other sources. Bancroft was looking for recollections that could be used as historical sources, but five decades later, when Walter Noble Burns interviewed "old timers," he knew that most of what he heard was folklore presented as recollections of nominally historical events. Both he and Bancroft were collectors of *oral tradition*, but they used it differently.

Oral tradition encompasses all forms of spoken tradition handed down or shared from memory, whether cultural, religious, familial, or historical. Historically inspired folk activities include Fourth of July fireworks, Cinco de Mayo songs and dances, and annual parades in Caborca, Mexico, commemorating the defeat of Henry Crabb and his filibusters. Historian Paul Thompson, in his book *Voices of the Past: Oral History*, traced the use of oral tradition in history and found that in the late eighteenth and early nineteenth centuries, most historians had turned their backs on oral tradition, discounting such sources as unreliable. They preferred to cite documentary sources found in various archives, but as Thompson points out, archival sources have errors, too. Indeed archival sources are sometimes purged of anything that might reflect badly on those in positions of authority. For example the California State Archives files pertinent to Governor John Bigler's administration are scanty, undoubtedly because his administration destroyed any and all evidence of illegal activities conducted by his staff, such as pocketing state funds for private use.[17]

Oral tradition, with all its imperfections, can and should be used in history, but as with documentary sources, comparative analysis should be applied in order to verify reliability. For example an 1879 interview with William T. Henderson can be broken into two parts: one that is easily verifiable, and one that is not. Henderson is introduced by the journalist interviewing him as the man who killed Joaquín Murrieta. In response to questions (left out of the transcript), Henderson described, from memory, what happened at Cantua Creek on that hot July morning twenty-six years previously. His recollections of events match the 1853 report filed by Captain Harry Love and other 1853 newspaper accounts. The only noteworthy difference is that Henderson retrospectively came to regret having killed the robber chief, not because he thought doing so was wrong, but because of the way journalists and others questioned the identity of the head. If he had been able to bring Murrieta in alive, the dispute over his identity would never have arisen.

The second part of the Henderson interview contained information about Joaquín Murrieta that is more difficult to verify. He shared what he had since learned from William Acklin. He shared it in order to refute romantic claims made in legend. Joaquín, he said, did not become an outlaw because his wife was raped and murdered. He did not even have a wife, Henderson said. However Joaquín did suffer unjustly, he admitted. Joaquín used to live with "Col. Acklin" in the vicinity of Sonora Camp in the "early days" and worked a very rich claim there, but his claim was confiscated by Anglos-Americans. "He gave it up without a struggle" and began working another claim nearby. Again he was ordered off, but this time he refused to go. A fight broke out during which an Irish-American struck Joaquín in the face with a bottle, leaving a ghastly wound. Acklin tended the wound, but Joaquín "seemed a changed man" after that.[18] He left, and afterward, outlaw bands began plaguing the mines.

What makes this second part of Henderson's interview credible, even though it is more difficult to verify, is the straightforward, unembellished manner in which it was shared. Also enhancing the believability of his account are Henderson's willingness to name his source, the account's consistency with historical sources overall, and the fact that Henderson spoke of Joaquín in a way that admitted provocation, an admission that is at odds with Henderson's antipathy toward Mexicans in general.[19]

Unlike the Henderson interview, multi-generational oral histories like those collected by Frank Latta are handed down within a family that may vary the account from generation to generation. The further-removed the teller is from the source, the inherently less reliable the account. The Yokuts Indian accounts recorded by Frank Latta were removed from the original source by one generation. They told with modesty a simple story that they had heard often repeated by their parents. Their accounts were also consistent with other sources. The Yokuts oral tradition is an example of historically useful recollections.

In addition to Yokuts oral tradition, there is that of the Ruddle family, which passed down the story of the murder and robbery of Allen Ruddle from generation to generation. The family account consistently insisted, generation after generation, that Joaquín and band had been suspected because they were known to have been in the vicinity at the time of the murder. Indeed both Joaquín Murrieta and Joaquín Valenzuela were within a sixty-mile radius of Stockton at the time. The Ruddles also consistently mention that Harry Love went after Allen Ruddle's killer(s) and that it was his rangers that eventually killed Joaquín Murrieta and several members of his band.[20] Descendants of Sheriff Robert B. Buchanan likewise blamed the Joaquín band for the tortured and slow death of the sheriff, his wound never fully healing.[21]

Questionable oral traditions that do not make good history sources are those that contradict what should be supporting evidence. Frank Latta was so determined to find out the truth about the Joaquín band that he collected everything he could find, especially interviews—with and without questionable content. The result was a vast body of material full of contradictions. In an effort to remedy this problem, he disregarded some sources and favored others, but he based his decisions on what he himself found most convincing and he consistently favored select oral traditions over other sources, even when certain oral traditions were without supporting evidence.

For example Frank Latta became convinced that the oral tradition shared with him by the widow of Procopio Bustamente was historically accurate. Procopio had told his wife that when he was a boy, he witnessed the solemn burial of a relative in the dirt floor of the tack room at the family's adobe home in California. That recollection may well have been true. After all, he also said that he did not know who was buried in the floor but that he later came to believe it must have been Joaquín Murrieta. Latta discounted anything that disagreed with this story, including the 1879 interview with William Henderson and Harry Love's 1853 report.

The Diminutive and Talkative Sharp-shooter, Avelino Martinez

Among those whom Frank Latta interviewed was Avelino Martinez, a Sonoran immigrant to California who, it was said, had belonged to Tiburcio Vásquez's band. Latta first profiled Avelino Martinez in 1935 for his regular column in the *Fresno Bee*. He described Martinez as a short, wiry, toothless pioneer who claimed to be one hundred years old. He said he was born in Sonora about 1835, the son of Juan Martinez and Antonia Juarez. He also said that his father immigrated to the "placeritas" (gold placer mines) in 1848. Two years later his mother received word that her husband had been killed "by some American robbers while he was mining on the Stanislaus River." Shortly after that a "revolution" (or militia clash over who was the rightful governor) broke out in Sonora. The revolutionaries attacked the Martinez home and "killed two of his brothers and forced the family to scatter like quail." Avelino never saw his mother again after that. He joined a caravan headed north to San Diego, California, and found work with a party of horsemen. He lived in the vicinity of Tehachipi (about thirty miles southeast of Bakersfield) in the 1850s and herded sheep in the 1870s.

Martinez carried a six-shooter in his belt and had become a local legend for his shooting skills. "There have probably been more wild stories told about Avelino Martinez than any other San Joaquin Valley pioneer," wrote Latta. He could still shoot the head off a bottle and had often shot the heads off snakes while herding sheep. Asked about Murrieta, he told Latta he was convinced "that the noted bandit, Joaquin Murieta, was not killed, but escaped to Mexico." He said that once, while herding sheep at Rancho La Liebre, he met Murrieta, in about 1877. He was camping when "approached by an old man who was riding one horse and leading another." Avelino invited him to join him for a repast, which he did. The old man claimed he was Joaquín Murrieta and that he had returned to California to recover some gold he had buried in the vicinity of Cantua Creek.[22]

During later interviews, Latta asked Avelino Martinez leading questions about the Murrieta band. At first Martinez denied affiliation with the Joaquín band, but being repeatedly asked about it, he decided to say what he knew Latta wanted to hear: He belonged to the band. When asked why he had not said so earlier, he replied that he was afraid of "the soldiers," and Latta assured him he had nothing to fear. The trouble with the "soldiers" is that Martinez had long been said to have ridden with Tiburcio Vásquez. He had already acknowledged association with bandits. The fear of "soldiers" was a statement designed to satisfy Latta's curiosity and open the door for more interviews focusing on the activities of the Joaquín band, as Avelino Martinez described them.

Frank Latta is not the only one to quote an interview that was designed to satisfy the interviewer's need for evidence. Journalists Charles Hanley, Sang-Hun Choe, and Martha Mendoza, all members of the Associated Press, won the Pulitzer Prize in 2000 for investigative journalism. They published, that year, their joint report on the Korean War No Gun Ri Massacre. They had interviewed dozens of American veterans and Korean civilian survivors, studied documents, and visited and photographed the site. Edward Daily was among the American veterans they interviewed, and, like Avelino Martinez, he offered the most details of the very sort the journalists sought. As a result Daily was often quoted. He told the young journalists he was a gunner during the war, had committed the massacre, and was haunted by it. He also said he had been promoted, during the war, from corporal to sergeant to second lieutenant in two weeks time, and he remembered being captured and escaping.

Members of the *U.S. News & World Report* staff (who had studied the same event and reached different conclusions) doubted Daily's story and decided to look into it. They discovered that Edward Daily was a mechanic with a company at the rear of the battle zone, not a gunner at the war front. He had been promoted to sergeant but was never a lieutenant. He was never a prisoner. He never even saw the bridge at No Gun Ri, although he described it well. Upon being confronted with these research results, Daily was at first confused and withdrawn, then he publicly recanted. He had gone to veterans' reunions every year for decades, he said, and he had heard a gunner with the Seventh Cavalry describe the massacre of civilians at No Gun Ri. The depiction was so vivid it gave him nightmares, and the nightmares seemed so real, he came to believe that he had done the deed himself. He also said he had been on medication for some time and that it may have had an effect on his mind.

Edward Daily's confession forced three brilliant young journalists to admit that they had believed him, but they argued that they had done so because his description of events closely matched the valid recollections of gunner Norman Tinkler of the Seventh Cavalry. Daily had not invented the story, they insisted, he had only invented his role in it. What the Edward Daily case reveals is that, as Paul Thompson points out, comparative analysis and sensitivity to contradictions or withheld information are not enough. The historian wishing to cite oral tradition as a primary source must also ask: does this story fit too perfectly? If it does, it may have been unconsciously tailored. Avelino Martinez tailored his descriptions of the Joaquín band's activities to fit Frank Latta's preconceived notions based on what he had learned from other sources.[23]

Leo Carrillo and the Moral Dilemma:
Folklore that Borrows from History

The Joaquín band stories Avelino Martinez told Latta are examples of oral tradition that must be designated folklore. Martinez simply told Latta what he wanted to hear. Like the journalists who interrogated Edward Daily, Latta could only cite other oral traditions as supporting evidence (but in Latta's case he often cited them without quoting them). What Martinez and Edwards offered was the missing link to a history that fit the interviewer's preconceptions. Those preconceptions were influenced by personal perspectives and enlarged by what select sources said of the subject being studied.

Curiously the first story Martinez told about Joaquín Murrieta—in which he met an old treasure-hunter by that name—was completely ignored by Latta when he wrote his book about the Joaquín band. The treasure hunter is a typical folklore subject. Perhaps he dismissed it as a folktale told to Martinez by an old man pretending he was the legendary bandit.

Popular folklore like buried treasure stories include accounts of miraculous healings, survival against great odds, seeing or hearing ghosts or other fabulous beings, and, yes, embellishments of witnessed historically significant events involving famous individuals, including bandits and pirates. Even though folklore borrows from memories of real historical events, the teller feels free to change details in the retelling. Like Mariana, the speaker may also employ gestures, winks, pauses, facial expressions, and changes in tone of voice to communicate events in a way that captures the imagination of an audience.

One example of Joaquín band folklore that illustrates just how flexible folklore can be (versus the inflexibility of historical accounts) is tucked inside the memoirs of Leopoldo Antonio Carrillo—better known as Leo Carrillo. A fifth-generation Californio with a sense of humor, Carrillo became a successful comic actor on stage and screen. In 1939 Leo Carrillo starred as Joaquín Murrieta in a stage comedy titled *The Red Bumble-Bee*. Based on *The Taming of the Shrew* by William Shakespeare, *The Red Bumble-Bee* script was weak in wit, said critics, but Leo Carrillo's delightful performance redeemed it. However he is best known for his role as the comical "Pancho" in the 1950s television series, *The Cisco Kid*. The show's title was borrowed from a short story by William Sidney Porter, better known as O. Henry. The literary Cisco Kid was a cold-hearted killer, but Hollywood's rendition was a romanticized California vigilante or lone ranger based on a justice-seeking Joaquín Murrieta.

When Leo Carrillo sat down to write his autobiography late in life, he found he had no desire to write about himself. Instead he wrote a "love letter" to California, the land he treasured for its beauty, ecological diversity, sunshine, and Hispanic history. A part of him wished the "Yankees" had never come to California, for they exploited everything they touched, and his beautiful homeland was (and still is) suffering the consequences. He hoped his humble effort might cause readers to ponder those consequences and seek to preserve what was left.

After sketching the state in poetic phrases, he inserted his family history, with its deep California roots. Leo was born in 1881 at his parents' adobe home in downtown Los Angeles, not far from the town plaza. He was the great-great-grandson of José Raimundo Carrillo, who had settled in Los Angeles in 1769 during the Spanish colonial era. His great-grandfather served as governor during the Mexican era, and his grandfather was a city judge during the early American era, when Manuel C.

LEO CARRILLO AS JOAQUIN MURRIETA
A flamboyant bandit of the 1850's in "Red Bumble Bee"

Red Bumble-Bee*

31. Leo Carrillo as Joaquín Murrieta in *The Red Bumble Bee*. Author's collection.

Rojo worked for the *Los Angeles Star*. The family prospered then, making it possible for his grandfather to send his father, Juan José Carrillo, to a Catholic university in Massachusetts. However when Juan José returned to California with a law degree, got married, and started a family, he soon found he was unable to stop American real estate brokers from snatching away, piece by piece, the family fortune in land and livestock.

In his memoirs Leo also recounted stories that he had heard from his father, among them one that focused on Joaquín Murrieta and band. It is an oral tradition that instructs, one which, when seen in light of what Manuel C. Rojo wrote in his editorial decades earlier, is culturally revealing. Hollywood films about Joaquín no doubt influenced what Leo recalled his father saying, but at the heart of his father's account was the spiritual dilemma Rojo had discussed in 1853, one that Hollywood oversimplified.

Leo Carrillo began recounting his father's story by reproducing the setting in which he had heard it as a boy. He remembered that he and his father were sitting on the veranda of their home in Santa Monica, looking out toward the ocean and watching the sun set. It was 1890. The quiet was interrupted by the "sweet-toned bell in the church tower" ringing the hour in which vespers begins. Leo perked up and listened. His father tussled his hair and asked, "Did I ever tell you about the bell that never rang?" Leo shook his head, and his father recounted on an adventure he said he lived through "before you were born."[24]

In spite of his education, Leo's father had found it difficult, at first, to find work to support his growing family. That was how it came about that he hired himself out to some American businessmen who wanted him to go inspect mining properties in Sonora. He took the train to Tucson, Arizona, then rode south on horseback, crossing the border at noon and continuing on toward the town of Magdalena. It was early spring and the cactus were in bloom. The sun was warm. There was plenty of time to ponder.

"It occurred to me," he told his son Leo, "that it was from this very region that there had come a young man of whom we had heard a great deal in California." He was the most feared outlaw in the state. Everyone in California knew the story of Joaquín Murrieta and how, in revenge for abuses suffered, he began to "exterminate the gringos, the hated Americans, the damned scoundrels who committed the crimes" against his wife, his brother, and himself. But revenge killed his soul: "He lost all feelings of mercy."[25]

"Father," wrote Leo, "felt a great compassion for Murrieta . . . as a person who . . . had been driven out of his mind by the horrors heaped upon him," especially when his own fortunes were so nearly desperate. Yet Leo's father could not feel any compassion at all for the man Murrieta became. During the long ride through the Sonoran desert, while "thoughts of Murrieta kept coming to him" he was troubled by the moral dilemma the Murrieta legend posed. How could Murrieta's desperate deeds be justified? "Yet how could the crimes committed against Murrieta and his bride be overlooked?"[26]

Juan José Carrillo told his son that he was still pondering this dilemma when he reached Magdalena at around sunset. He stabled the horse and went into a smoke-filled bar to inquire about the men he was supposed to meet there. While he waited, an old Mexican approached and said he could tell he was Californian by the way he was dressed. He, too, was Californian, he said. He was born at Mission San Miguel, in the North. "In those days California was unsafe," the old man said. "Bandidos were ranging up and down the state," and Joaquín Murrieta was their captain. Three-Fingered Jack was his lieutenant. Robberies and murders were committed daily. "Horsemen were shot, women attacked in their homes and the whole region was in terror," he said. His depiction of the Joaquín band was not of one that targeted Americans only. The outlaws were ruthless and cruel to everyone they robbed.

So the day came, said the old man, when news was brought to San Miguel warning them that Joaquín and his band were going to raid the place. Cattle, horses, and stores of grain were all put in the mission buildings, and when a wounded messenger arrived saying that Murrieta and his band were on the way, all of the women and children ran to the church for sanctuary (just as the civilian residents of Caborca did in April 1857 when Henry Crabb and his filibusters arrived). The women "huddled inside praying, while the men loaded rusty old muskets" and prepared to defend their homes. The siege began, and the fight was fearful. In the midst of the battle, a young woman holding a baby—afraid that the bandits would break into the church—looked for someplace to hide her infant. She spotted an old bell sitting on the floor. It had never been hung. She shouted to an Indian boy present, "¡Levante la campana!" (lift the bell!). She put the baby underneath and propped the bell up with a stone. "With tears streaming down her face . . . she seized a gun and took her place beside the men defending the mission."[27]

Soon afterward the bandits broke in and behaved like blood-thirsty demons, not justice-seeking avengers. First they shot every man they saw, then they raped the women and murdered them and the children. After killing everyone, they looted the place, set the buildings on fire, and galloped away. "The silent crucifix looked down . . . upon bodies . . . desecrated by the horrible bandits." The old man paused for effect, then said that the vigilantes came, they saw, and they were horrified. They pursued and finally caught up with the desperadoes. Some of them they lassoed and dragged "screaming and kicking into the [ocean] surf until they were drowned." Joaquín Murrieta and Three-Fingered Jack were killed near Pacheco Pass by Captain Harry Love and his rangers. So in the end the bandits paid for their crimes, but Joaquín Murrieta's death "could not erase the memory of the massacre at the Mission of San Miguel . . . one of the most horrible moments in California history."[28]

There was only one survivor—the baby saved by the bell—the bell that never rang. "I am that baby" said the old man. It was love that saved him, he added, a mother's love. And it was righteous indignation that caught up with the men who orphaned him.

The old man's story answered Juan José Carrillo's moral dilemma. Crime cannot be justified, not even in the case of the afflicted Joaquín Murrieta. By taking bloody revenge and turning outlaw, Murrieta became as bad as the men against whom he retaliated. He and his band butchered people, and the crucifix—representing divine judgment—witnessed the desecration.[29] The story made such a deep impression on young Leo Carrillo he passed it on to his children, and to anyone who takes the time to read his memoirs.

Closing Thoughts

I have used an unusual approach to the subject at hand, jumping from American diaries at the gold mines to Los Angeles newspaper sources, then back to the mines as depicted in northern California newspapers and south again to Los Angeles for another look at sources there. Why not integrate these sources to tell a continuous story? Because if I had done so, the story line in this history would have taken precedence. The voices that tell the story from specific points of view would have been necessarily marginalized in order to keep them from interrupting the story.

I chose to marginalize the story in order to feature the voices of sources I encountered. I have focused on what people in the past wrote, and why. It seemed to me the only way that I could expose individual perspectives and political points of view that have not been taken into account before now. For the reader's sake, I arranged content chronologically, but I also imposed a geographical arrangement in order to show the contrast between mostly Anglo-American voices in northern California and mostly Hispanic voices in southern California.

Hispanics saw outlaws as a threat except when there was a family connection; then those lawbreakers became wayward sons that were to be reprimanded. Or else the family had to be protected from the shame of the death penalty by providing assistance in escape, as with Solomón Pico, or by providing an alibi, as with Felipe Reid. (And actually, as Francisco P. Ramirez pointed out, Anglo-Saxons had the same tendencies.) Some Hispanics saw bandidos as avengers of Anglo-American wrongs against them and their countrymen, until they fell victim to banditry themselves. Some admired outlaw leaders for their daring, an attitude they shared with North Americans. They also mourned the fate of young outlaws in that it was a pity a life was lost at such an early age, but grief was tempered with an acceptance that such was their due under the law and under Heaven.

North Americans saw Mexican bandits as eminently exploitable in a political or filibustering context. They also saw bands of outlaws, whatever their race, as a symptom of the chaos that occurred when the gold rush brought too much gambling and alcohol in the midst of tens of thousands of young men from all over the world competing for too few women. Democracy was being tested in the newly acquired territory, even as it was in Mexico, where at times it looked as though it had failed. Some North Americans felt manifestly destined to force their own idea of democracy on Mexico via filibuster invasions, even as they forced it on Mexicans living in California.

The behavior of Mexican highwaymen at the mines reminded some North Americans of the guerrilla bands in Mexico, as described in popular travel books of the day. Travelers recorded how Mexican military and political leaders dismissed guerrillas as outlaws and treated them as such. During the war U.S. officers heard the same thing, but when defending supply lines from guerrilla attack they did not see bands of outlaws, they saw calculating mercenaries often numbering in the hundreds.[1] These two perceptions resurfaced in California's English-language newspapers during the gold rush, with the guerrilla band threat being exploited by American politicians. Spanish newspapers never depicted the Joaquín band as a guerrilla threat. A guerrilla threat was like an Indian revolt. Bandits did not take part in revolts or issue manifestos. However California Indians often participated in the adventures of outlaw bands and augmented their numbers.

California's gold rush outlaw bands did have something in common with Mexico's guerrilla bands. Guerrilla bands formed in Mexico after a military coup, a regional mini-revolution, or a harsh tax law displaced large numbers of people. The Foreign Miners Tax Law in California displaced thousands of mostly Sonoran miners, and it was afterward that outlaw bands formed at the mines. California's gold rush bandits targeted travelers more than any other group, which was also how Mexico's guerrilla bands operated.[2] In addition the perceived threat that a Mexican "guerrilla" band posed in California became a useful political tool, even as making war on bandits proved a useful move among politicians in Mexico. Both Mexican and Californian political candidates promised voters security and peace. In Mexico the number of guerrillas and outlaws made the fight a daunting task. In California, local citizens rallied to support the law, the state constitution having provided them with the right to do so. For example when the Foreign Miners Tax of 1850 was passed, the bill authorized U.S. citizens to take up arms and assist tax collectors, the expectation being that the (unjust) law might excite active and violent rebellion. Anglo-Americans became vigilantes when fighting crime and took matters into their own hands whenever they deemed it necessary. (In the 2000s Mexican citizens likewise became vigilantes and fought crime, but without government approval.)

Both politics *and* prejudice helped shape the Joaquín band legend. Contrary to what Joseph Henry Jackson concluded, the legendary Joaquín and band did not *initially* arise out of any need for a regional folk hero. The inconsistent and even invented accounts of Joaquín and band originated with newspaper writers who exercised a sense of humor in the context of an election in a racially biased setting. The politically punchy news stories about the Joaquín band and the sheriffs and rangers who went in pursuit provided John Rollin Ridge, in a post-election setting, the groundwork on which he built an enduring myth. It was favorably received, especially after the death of Joaquín Valenzuela. That is when Jackson's point about a needed folk hero began to apply.

It has been proposed by John Boessenecker and others that what makes outlaw legends popular is the way in which the hero (usually a male figure) does as he pleases with bravado and independence. He is his own master. He acts outside of existing social and moral constraints, as if free to delineate his own constraints on his own terms. Historian Chris Frazer, in his book *Bandit Nation, A History of Outlaws and Cultural Struggle in Mexico, 1810–1910*, notes that the bandit hero of Mexican corridos is a representation of the masculine *macho* ideal in that the bandido takes risks that most men are not willing to take. When they get away with it, the natural response is to applaud their success, however illegal their methods.

Frazer also found that some Mexican-bandit corridos and folklore feature bloodthirsty, cruel villains. These also take risks in order to do as they please. They even get away with it for a time, but because of the immoral and cruel nature of their actions, they disgust the audience. The villain, therefore, is not applauded, however macho he may seem. He is abhorred, a "raw head and bloody bones" nightmare conjured up to frighten children into doing as they are told. The villain always faces judgment, be it earthly or divine, but then, so do bandit heroes, the difference being that heroes are mourned and villains are not.

The legend of the Joaquín band offers both: Murrieta is a bandit hero and Three-Fingered Jack is blood-thirsty and cruel, a villain who casts a shadow on Joaquín. The presence of Three-Fingered Jack in the Joaquín band makes the rangers who come after them look like the real "good guys" in the end. Good must triumph over evil in legend, but in real life and, by extension, in history, even the history that inspires legends, "good guys" like William Jenkins and Ezekiel Rubottom can make bad choices and outlaws like Luciano "el mesteño" surprise us with good deeds. Jenkins and Rubottom killed Ruíz and Berreyesa, respectively, in part due to racial bias. Luciano was unbiased when he spared the lives of a Chilean man, a Mexican man, and a French woman, then gave away all his loot. He paid with his life for those choices but he was prepared to risk it for his soul's sake.

The Joaquín band legend as literature is invitingly complex. The characters have proven delightfully malleable to creative writers over the decades. Although many oral traditions surrounding the band are romanticized and blandly formulaic, others attempt to grapple with racial tension, classism, and questions of justice versus vengeance. All of that is in the history behind the legend, too. The difference is that history really happened. It is a true story of pleasure, pain, and posturing, of honest, dishonest, and criminal acts, a story of real people in actual time and place with strong opinions and colorful senses of humor. That reality makes history, with all its comedy and tragedy, more compelling than mythology and literature.

One of the books that provoked me to examine the different ways in which a history can be influenced by sources, and even by the writer's preconceptions, was Susan Lee Johnson's *Roaring Camp: The Social World of the California Gold Rush.* In the introduction to her book, she reminds readers that they, too, will inevitably bring with them their own perspectives when interpreting history. Each of us, she pointed out, is shaped by what we have already read of gold rush history, or viewed in television documentaries, western movies, museum exhibits and on trips to California historical sites. Thus my interpretation of the history of the Joaquín band is inevitably influenced by my having been born and raised in California, the great-granddaughter of a gold miner, by my having done mission work at El Calvario with my family, and by meeting César Chavez while in junior high school and demanding that my family boycott grapes. I also studied Latin American history and Spanish in college, and even lived in Mexico City briefly.

When researching this book I intentionally shaped my own perspective by visiting Cantua Creek in July heat and making repeated trips to mining towns and historical sites in Calaveras, Tuolumne, and Mariposa counties. I panned for gold, drove along old stagecoach roads at stagecoach speeds, walked on dirt roads and trails, picked blackberries to slacken thirst and hunger, and worried about meeting the wrong kind of stranger after sunset. I wanted to touch the past by visiting places I had read about in history even though much has changed in those locations. Fresh-water estuaries now fill gulches and valleys, and suburban neighborhoods sprawl around downtown Sonora, Angel's Camp, and San Andreas.

Then the terrorist attack of September 11, 2001, affected me in unexpected ways. Suddenly I read the word "terror" in 1850s California newspapers and intuitively felt alarmed at the bloody deeds of Mexican bandits. I was disgusted when I read that some Chicanos in California called for solidarity with Islamic extremists in 2006. Strong and dark emotions were awakened in me by September 11th that helped me understand the raw feelings which moved friends of murder victims, in the 1850s, to seek swift retribution. Nonetheless the vigilante and lynch mob reactions to the Joaquín band in 1853 and to the Juan Flores and Pancho Daniel band in 1857 remained grotesque, even as the use of torture and humiliation at Abu Ghraib prison during the war in Iraq in 2003 was grotesque. Both events were misguided reactions that occurred because of an inability or

32. Indian Creek meandering toward Six Miles Creek one mile south of Angel's Camp, where Los Muertos was located. Photograph by the author.

unwillingness to curb vengeful tendencies in violent settings. Innocent people have suffered as a result, and that is always tragic.

Susan Lee Johnson is right. Historians cannot help but interpret history from where they are in the historical continuum. No one can slip back in time and live in the past as if the intervening years never happened. However we can see the past in new ways that lead to a deeper understanding of our historical heritage, and that, after all, is what history is all about.

In addition to discovering the influence of politics on what became the legend of Joaquín Murrieta, I learned that when rumors of a Mexican guerrilla chief and band first surfaced in 1850, the only famous guerrilla chief named Joaquín was a Cahuilla Indian chief who had died in 1846. I also found that the Joaquín band outlived Joaquín Murrieta. Unlike in the legend, in history the band included the deeds and fates of Joaquín and Jesús Valenzuela, Bernardo and Francisco "Pancho" Daniel, Juan Flores, Luciano Tapia alias Lorenzo Lopez, and many others, most of whom died in the 1850s. I also found that, while John Rollin Ridge saw the story of Joaquín as a way to highlight a truth about the consequences of injustice to individuals, there is, in the history behind the legend, a

33. The dry bed of Cantua Creek. Photograph by the author.

complex morality play. It is full of men—be they outlaws or vigilantes—who justified ugly acts and blamed others for their own moral weakness. They appealled for sympathy and acceptance without seeking pardon. They manipulated or invented evidence in an attempt to change history's inevitable judgment of their actions.

Historians are trained to be as objective as possible, but we can't help but judge the past in the light of the present. When we study history and then represent it in new light we are deciding what is morally acceptable and what is not, from the point of view of our current generation. In effect, all of history is about what is deemed morally acceptable or unacceptable, laudable or reprehensible, even the history of a legendary outlaw band.

Appendix

Outlaw Band Members Named in 1850s Newspapers

Among Those Named in the Confession of Teodor Vásquez (Hermosillo) in January 1852

Juan José (Sonora)

Bernardo Daniel (Hermosillo): lynched in Santa Barbara, October 1856

Francisco "Pancho" Daniel (Hermosillo): lynched in Los Angeles, November 1858

Trinidad—? (Sonora): killed by fellow outlaw in San Francisco, December 1851

Miguel Luches (Sonora): killed in San Francisco, 1851

Ignacio "Macho" Salsio: fate unknown

"San Lorenzo" (California) [Lorenzo Lopez?]

Sefarino [Chevarino], real name Mariano Flores (Sonora): lynched with brother

    Cruz Flores at Jackson, June 1852. Arrested with them:

      Pedro Morales (Mexico): paid bribe and escaped

      John Hart (United States): escaped

Claudio Féliz (Sonora): killed in Monterey County, October 1852

Reyes Féliz (Sonora): arrested, convicted, hanged in Los Angeles, November 1852

Soliz—(Chile): fate unknown

Gabriel [Soto?]: arrested in Martinez, Alameda County, November 1853,

    together with:

      Rafael Soto

      Miguel Nevara [Navarro]

      Antonia ["la Molinera"?]

      Miguel Sasuelta (Sonora)

      Manuel Peña (Sonora): wounded at Camp Seco in 1851, escaped

Jesús Chenate [Senate]: killed by fellow outlaw, together with Joaquín impersonator

    Luis Burgos, in San Diego County, January 1854

Joaquín Gurrieta [Murrieta] (Sonora): killed and beheaded at Cantua Creek, July 1853

David Hill alias Jim Hill (New York) [alluded to but not named]: captured and

    lynched at Sonora, Tuolumne County, June 1851

Named in the Confession of Reyes Féliz in November 1852

Pedro [Morales?]: shot dead by Harry Love, June 1852
Ana Benites (Santa Fe, New Mexico)
Joaquín Murrieta [see above]
Pedro Lopez: arrested, tried, and hung, December 1852

Others Named as Members of the Band by Newspaper Stories

Manuel Rosas: arrested at Jackson, January 1852, escaped
Pedro Sánchez (Sonora): killed by Alvino Leyva at Martinez, June 1853
Juanito Ramírez (Los Angeles): arrested, June 1853, with:
    Thomas Whitney
    one Gonzales
Pedro Lopez (San Gabriel): shot dead, January 1857
Jesús Lopez: arrested in Marysville, July 1853, with:
    Palonio Sánchez: taken to Jackson, tried, and hanged, July 1853
Manuel Vergara (Mexico): shot dead near Yuma, September 1853
Juan Valenzuela (San Gabriel): suspected of aiding Vergara, flogged, August
    1853; suspected of aiding Pancho Daniel's band and shot dead, January 1857
José "Chapo" Valenzuela (California): arrested in San Diego, April 1852
Octaviana "Cayetano" Espinosa (Sonora): arrested with:
    Ramón Espinosa (Sonora): Octaviana's brother
    Manuel Olivas, also known as Manuel Verdes (Sonora)
    Anastacio Higuera alias Ignacio and also called Juan Ygarra (Sonora)
    [All four arrested in Los Angeles, October 1853, the last three were transported
    to and lynched at San Luis Obispo.]

Named During the Pursuit of Joaquín Murrieta in
Calaveras County, January–February 1853

Cruz Ramos (Mexico): arrested at Camp Seco, jailed at San Andreas, January 25
Joaquín Medina (Mexico): same fate as Cruz Ramos
"Big Bill" (Mexico): lynched at Yaqui Camp, January 17
No name (Mexico): lynched at Cherokee Flat, January 17
No name (Mexico): shot dead at Cherokee Flat, January 17
Ignacius Moretto: jailed at San Andreas and hanged, January 20
No name (Mexico): arrested at Los Muertos, tried, convicted, and hanged at San
    Andreas, February 20
Antonio Valencia (Mexico): arrested at Ophir, tried, convicted, and hanged at
    Jackson, February 15
Juan Nevis [Nieves]: tried, convicted, and hanged at Mokelumne Hill, February 15

Named in the California State Ranger Bill in May 1853

Joaquín Carrillo, the name on Governor's reward posted February 28, 1853; said to be an alias used by Joaquín Murrieta

Joaquín Murrieta [see above]

Joaquín Valenzuela, also known as Joaquín Ocomorenia or Nacamoreño: hanged at San Luis Obispo, June 1858

Joaquín Botillier (Botilleras): arrested in Monterey, 1852 and 1855

Named by the California State Rangers as Being among Those Encountered at Cantua Creek Pass in July 1853

Joaquín Murrieta [see above]

Antonio Lopez (Mexico): arrested, drowned in the Tulare sloughs of the San Joaquin river while attempting to escape

Salvador Méndez alias José María Ochoa (Sonora): arrested, cross-examined at Quartzburg, jailed at Mariposa, transferred to Martinez, and there lynched, September 1853

Emanuelo García, also known as "Three-Fingered Jack," a nickname given to Bernardino García (California): killed in gunfight with the rangers, beheaded, and his three-fingered hand severed. His head rotted and was buried.

Captured Members of the Juan Flores/Pancho Daniel Band in 1857–1858

Pancho Daniel [see above]

Luciano Tapia alias Lorenzo Lopez: arrested in Santa Clara, convicted December 1857, hanged February 1858 at Los Angeles

Juan Flores (Los Angeles): lynched in Los Angeles, February 1857

Antonio "Chino" Varelas (Los Angeles): arrested and pardoned, January 1857

Juan "Catabo" Silvas: lynched, January 1857

Miguel Soto: burned, shot, stabbed, and beheaded at San Gabriel, January 1857

José Jesús Espinosa (Sonora): arrested, convicted, and hanged in San Buenaventura, February 1857

Santiago Silvas: fate unknown

Andrés Fontes (Los Angeles): fate unknown

José Santos (Sonora): killed at San Gabriel, January 1857

Santos Peralta alias Santos Robles: lynched in San Luis Obispo, June 1858

Miguel Blanco (nephew of Pío Linares): killed in San Luis Obispo, July 1858

The Jack Powers/Pío Linares Gang

Pío Linares (San Luis Obispo): killed in June 1858

Jack Powers (New York): escaped to Sonora, Mexico, in 1857, moved to Gadsdonia in 1858, killed in November 1860

Jesús Valenzuela: fate unknown

Joaquín Valenzuela [see above]
Luciano "el Mesteño" (California Indian): hanged in San Luis Obispo, June 1858
Santos Peralta alias Santos Robles [see above]
Rafael "el Güero" Money (Los Angeles): fate unknown
Miguel Blanco [see above]
Juan José "Pantellon" Salazar (California): killed in Watsonville, October 1856
José Antonio García (Californio): arrested in San Buenaventura, convicted and
    hanged in San Luis Obispo, June 1858

Possibly Affiliated with the Band

James "Mountain Jim" Wilson: arrested at Stockton, October 1851, with:
    Frederick "Flat Foot" Salkmar [also "Soltmore"]
    James Cochrane
    [All three sentenced to jail.]

Latecomers

Tiburcio Vásquez: arrested, sentenced, and hanged, 1874
Procopio Bustamente alias Tomás Redondo alias Joaquín Murrieta: escaped to
    Sonora, Mexico

Innocent Men Erroneously Named as Band Members

Cipriano Sandoval
Diego Navarro
Encarnación Berreyesa

Notes

1. The Legend and History

1. Louise K. Smith Clappe is one of those who described a trading post that carried everything from crowbars to sewing needles. The proprietor's "collection of novels is by far the largest, the greasiest, and the 'yellowest kivered' of any" she'd seen. Clappe wrote newspaper correspondences under the pen name "Dame Shirley"; see Clappe, *Dame Shirley Letters*: Ninth Letter.

2. Parins, *John Rollin Ridge*, 45–46.

3. Parins, *John Rollin Ridge*, 14–18.

4. Parins, *John Rollin Ridge*, 19–21.

5. For more about Ridge's family and their struggles on behalf of the Cherokee people, see Wilkins, *Cherokee Tragedy*.

6. Parins, *John Rollin Ridge*, 54.

7. Parins, *John Rollin Ridge*, 94.

8. Hazera, "Joaquin Murieta"; Mondragon, "History and Disguise"; Christensen, "Minority Interaction"; Huerta, "California" and "Murieta el Famoso"; Paz, *Vida y aventuras*; Ridge, *Life and Adventures*.

9. Ridge, *Life and Adventures*, 7.

10. Ridge, *Life and Adventures*, 9.

11. Ridge, *Life and Adventures*, 8.

12. Ridge, *Life and Adventures*, 10.

13. Ridge, *Life and Adventures*, 10.

14. Ridge, *Life and Adventures*, 12–14.

15. Friar Celedonio Jarauta of Zaragoza, Spain, was a young, energetic missionary to the Indians in Vera Cruz at the time war broke out between the United States and Mexico. As a guerrilla leader he raided American supply trains and attacked some of their camps. Jarauta refused to recognize the Treaty of Guadalupe Hidalgo. He published a manifesto denouncing the central government for signing it and then led a revolt in Jalisco. Gen. Anastacio Bustamente sent troops against the guerrilla leader. Jaruata was captured and executed on July 18, 1848. See Bancroft, *History of Mexico, 1824–1861*,

531, 548. See also Frazer, *Bandit Nation*, 77–78, 150–51. In Spain, Celedonio Jarauta was known as Francisco Jarauta. As for the purported name "Vulvia"—it is Italian.

16. James "Mountain Jim" Wilson associated with bandits in the vicinity of Mission Dolores and Stockton, one Frederick "Flat Foot" Saltmore (also spelled "Salkmar" or "Soltmore") among them. Four of the band were arrested at Stockton in June 1851 and tried and condemned in October of that year. The nickname "Mountain Jim" was mistakenly assigned to Frederick "Soltmore" in the *San Francisco Herald*, June 1, 1851. See *San Joaquin Republican*, June 28, 1851.

17. Ridge, *Life and Adventures*, 20.

18. Ridge, *Life and Adventures*, 30–32.

19. Ridge, *Life and Adventures*, 33.

20. Ridge, *Life and Adventures*, 35–42.

21. Ridge, *Life and Adventures*, 45–49.

22. Ridge, *Life and Adventures*, 50–68.

23. Ridge, *Life and Adventures*, 83–91.

24. Ridge, *Life and Adventures*, 155–56.

25. Ridge, *Life and Adventures*, 158.

26. Bancroft, *Works* consists of thirty-nine volumes that include various separately titled works. For example, *The History of California* is contained in vols. 18–24, and *California Pastoral*, originally published in 1888, is in vol. 34. (See Bibliography for complete citation list of the *Works* volumes consulted for this book.) The original California narratives Bancroft collected are located at the Bancroft Library Archives, University of California, Berkeley, together with biographical notes about Spanish, Mexican, American, and other early pioneers. The California narratives were the basis for much of the content found in Pitt, *The Decline of the Californios*, and Sanchez, *Telling Identities*.

27. *Cholo* means "mixed-blood" or "mestizo" but carries a derogatory connotation similar to "half-breed." In the nineteenth century, cholo also meant "soldier." Blanco, *La lengua Española*, 349, lists "chola" as "soldier's wife." Miller, *Juan Alvarado*, 99, quotes Antonio María Osio as saying cholos were men who had belonged to "chain gangs, made up primarily of thieves and assassins from different jails" in Mexico, an opinion Governor Juan Alvarado shared. In Pico, *Historical Narrative*, 44, cholo means "peasant" or "soldier." A new meaning can be found in Rojas, *Joaquín Murrieta, El Patrio: Truthful Focuses*, 21: "A century later the term Cholo would be claimed as a way of identifying being from the barrio" in California and embraced with racial pride. Modern Spanish-English dictionaries define cholo as *mestizo*, but the two words are not used as if synonymous in Latin American countries. Cholo is still viewed as a grave insult, whereas mestizo is descriptive of a class of people.

28. Bancroft, *California Pastoral*, 641–42.

29. Bancroft, *California Pastoral*, 641–42.

30. Rosenus, *General M. G. Vallejo*, 148–53.

31. Ramón Carrillo's death was reported in the *Santa Rosa Democrat*, June 4, 1864. See also Bancroft, *History of California*, 22:162n; *Los Angeles Star*, May 28 and August 20, 1864; Secrest, *Dangerous Trails*, 104–6.

32. Sanchez, *Telling Identities*, 288.

33. See Coronel, *Tales of Mexican California*. The translator and editor made the content accessible to young readers without oversimplifying. Regarding the value of Coronel's recollections, see Bancroft, *California Pastoral*, 778–79. See also Scanland, "Joaquin Murrieta," 530–39n. Scanland used more of what "La Molinera" told Coronel than did Bancroft.

34. Coronel, *Tales of Mexican California*, 57–58.

35. Coronel, *Tales of Mexican California*, 70–71. See also "Reminiscence of Cipriano Sandoval," *El Clamor Público*, February 21, 1857. The article says that Sandoval was hanged largely because of the testimony of "the Indian women" who were believed because "they had no motive for lying." Antonio F. Coronel probably wrote the article.

36. Coronel, *Tales of Mexican California*, 58. See also Bancroft, *California Pastoral*, 666.

37. Coronel, *Tales of Mexican California*, 71.

38. Coronel, *Tales of Mexican California*, 73.

39. Bancroft, *California Pastoral*, 643.

40. Ridge, *Life and Adventures*, 7.

41. Hittell, *History of California*, 3:712–26. Theodore Hittell was formerly editor of the *San Francisco Bulletin*.

42. Hittell, *History of California*, 3:712.

43. Hittell, *History of California*, 3:712.

44. Hittell, *History of California*, 3:712.

45. Hittell, *History of California*, 3:719. See also Lang, *History of Tuolumne County*, 207.

46. Lang, *History of Tuolumne County*, 211.

47. Lang, *History of Tuolumne County*, 214–15. See also "San Joaquin News; an affray in Tuolumne," *Alta*, April 11, 1852; Varley, *Legend of Joaquín*, 26.

48. Lang, *History of Tuolumne County*, 215–16. Dorsey's recollections were also published in Lang, *Early Justice in Sonora*, 81–83.

49. Hittell. *History of California*, 3:725.

50. Hittell may have also met Y. P. Villegas, stationmaster for the Southern Pacific Railroad at Soledad whose father worked on don Francisco Pacheco's ranch. When Villegas was about twelve years old, Joaquín Murrieta stopped by the Pacheco ranch. He said, "I always thought and so did my father, that Murrieta was killed." See *Joaquin Murrieta Scrapbook*, 13.

51. Guinn, *State of California*, 191–92.

52. Guinn, *State of California*, 191–92.

53. Ridge, *Life and Adventures*, 4–5, 7. See also Jackson, *Bad Company*, 3–40.

54. Among the papers covering this story were the *Herald*, April 13, 1852, and the *Republican*, April 14, 1852, both of which cite the Sacramento and Marysville news exchange and the Mokelumne Hill *Calaveras Chronicle*, all sources to which John Rollin Ridge had ready access. James Varley retells this story well in *Legend of Joaquín*, 25.

55. *Republican*, May 1, 1852. See also the *Herald*, April 28, 1852. Probably the *Calaveras Chronicle*—of which no copies have survived—provided Ridge with the story of Joaquín jumping up on a monte table.

56. Ridge, introduction by Joseph Henry Jackson to *Life and Adventures*, xxvi.

57. Burns, *Robin Hood*, 5.

58. Burns, *Robin Hood*, 5.

59. Burns, *Robin Hood*, 28–39. Frank Marshall's story also appeared in Wood, *Tales of Old Calaveras*, 84. Wood included an event Burns left out, in which Ben Marshall saw Joaquín Murrieta in Mokelumne Hill one night in 1852 and ordered him to stop. Murrieta stopped and turned, revolver in hand. He refused to put his weapon up when ordered to do so. Marshall then bade him leave town. Murrieta did. John Boessenecker examined the typescript diary and found that a key Joaquín Murrieta entry was copied, word for word, from a poem by Cincinnatus "Joaquin" Miller. See Boessenecker, *Gold Dust and Gunsmoke*, 342n31.

60. José Antonio ("Tony") Águila told Frank Latta that he remembered hearing Yrenero Corona and Ramón Soto talking about how Murrieta and band stole horses from Rancho Orestimba when Soto had been one of the thieves. Yrenero Corona pursued the thieves. Decades later, after Soto was hired by Corona as head vaquero, the two of them used to reminisce and laugh at life's ironies. See Latta, *Joaquin Murrieta*, 377–88.

61. Latta, *Joaquin Murrieta*, 388.

62. Latta, *Joaquin Murrieta*, 390.

63. Latta, *Joaquin Murrieta*, 391–92.

64. Latta, *Joaquin Murrieta*, 391–92.

65. Latta, *Joaquin Murrieta*, 390–93.

66. Latta, *Joaquin Murrieta*, 390–93.

67. Latta, *Joaquin Murrieta*, 394, 396.

68. Latta, *Joaquin Murrieta*, 621–22.

69. The movie *The Firebrand* with Valentin De Vargas as Joaquin Murieta (Hollywood: 20th Century Fox, 1962) offered a somewhat sympathetic version of Murieta until he turned criminal. A spaghetti western variously known as *Murieta, Joaquín Murrieta*, or *Vendetta*, with Jeffrey Hunter as Joaquin Murrieta and directed by George Sherman (Spain: Pro Artis Iberica S.A., 1964), was also sympathetic with the main character at first, but the film depicted Murrieta as becoming irreversibly cold-hearted after committing murder. A Mexican western, *El Último Rebelde* (Mexico: Hispano Continental, 1961), depicted Joaquín as a guerrilla war leader who laid waste to American mining camps and settlements until ambushed and killed by American rangers.

70. Gonzales, *I Am Joaquin*. This epic poem was originally published in Colorado in 1967.

71. Secrest, preface to *Return of Joaquin*.

72. Varley, Appendix A: "Confession of Teodor Basques," *Legend of Joaquín*, 174–79.

73. Varley, *Legend of Joaquín*, 19–22.

74. Monterey correspondence signed "H. L. B." and dated September 18, 1852, *Republican*, September 29, 1852. See also "A Villain Shot," *San Francisco Daily Alta California*, September 18, 1852. In the *Sacramento Daily Union*, June 2, 1874, Henry Cocks recalls his encounter with Claudio Féliz that fateful night. John Boessenecker shared the latter source with me.

75. Varley, *Legend of Joaquín*, 129.

76. See *Life of Joaquin*, ix–xii. See also Wood, "New Light on Joaquin Murrieta," 62.

77. Pitt, "The Head Pickled in Whiskey," Chap. 4 in *Decline of the Californios*; Castillo and Camarillo, "Joaquin Murieta," Chap. 2, in *Furia y Muerte*. Although the title of *Furia y Muerte* is Spanish, the text is in English.

78. Thomas Gordon's findings are in his master's thesis, "Joaquin Murieta: Fact, Fiction and Folklore." He cites a diverse collection of Joaquín Murrieta lore and oral tradition not found elsewhere.

79. Gordon, "Joaquin Murieta," 89–95, 120–44.

80. Gordon, appendix in "Joaquin Murieta." The property included a butcher shop and shed on a lot facing Main Street, in San Andreas, plus a 160-acre ranch and 260-acre pasture. When this Murieta came to Calaveras, what his full name was and where he came from could not be discovered.

81. Steiner, "On the Trail," 54–56, 66.

82. Steiner, "On the Trail," 54–56, 66.

83. Steiner, "Murieta or Murrieta," 782–83. See also "El Patrio," Steiner Papers, Stanford University.

84. Steiner, "On the Trail," 66.

85. Steiner, "On the Trail," 66. In Ramos, "Murieta, Joaquin," the author cites the baptismal document mentioned by Arnold Rojas to Stan Steiner. It is also cited in Boessenecker, *Gold Dust and Gunsmoke*, 73. I contacted Ramos and Boessenecker about this and both said they were not aware of Steiner's fruitless search. Ramos could not remember where he got the baptismal reference from; Boessenecker said he knew someone who had seen it. Microfilms of randomly selected Sonora church records filmed for the Sociology Department at the University of Arizona, Tucson, for use in statistical studies of pioneer society in Sonora and Arizona did not include Murrieta's baptismal record. I did find a Joaquín Murrieta christened in 1808 who married María Rosalia Munoz and had children by her in the 1830s, among them José Antonio Blas Murrieta.

86. Rojas, chapter 2 in *Joaquín Murrieta: El Patrio*. Rojas published second and third revised editions in 1989 and 1990 but the first edition is the best, having about it a youthful energy and bold presentation. Later editions are argumentative and didactic. They do introduce new material but nothing of consequence. An English version, *Joaquín Murrieta el Patrio*, was designed for use in grade school classrooms. It is a sharply abridged version that includes an interesting introduction by Alfredo Figueroa, one of the founders of the Associación Internacional de Descendencia de Joaquín Murrieta (which should be called "Descendencia de la familia de . . ." as the outlaw never fathered any children).

87. Hobsbawm, Bandits, 181.

88. Boessenecker, "California Bandidos," 419–34.

89. For Albert Huerta's definition of el vendido see Huerta, "California."

90. See image online at http://www.stanford.edu/group/resed/stern/zapata/07-08/Murals/mural024.htm. Stanford has a striking and extensive collection of wall murals by Central and South American students with Chicano and American Indian themes. For a slide show go to http://www.stanford.edu/group/resed/stern/zapata/07-08/Murals/murals.htm (both URLs accessed August 17, 2010).

2. Joaquín and his Countrymen as Depicted in Diaries

1. See Mexican Adaptation, an influential and oft-cited thesis by Richard Henry Morefield. He argues that North Americans—from gamblers to politicians—were motivated by economic factors when dealing with Mexicans in California. While there were racial, cultural, and language differences that contributed to the tension, at bottom the Americans feared losing control of highly coveted wealth in California.

2. As to when the Felíz brothers reached the mines, see Stoddart, Annals, 84–86. In 1849 Claudio was fifteen years old and his brother Reyes thirteen. In the Expositor, November 12, 1879, William Henderson said in an interview: "Joaquín lived in Sonora in the early days"—the early days being 1849.

3. Stoddart, Annals, 84–86. See also Scanland, "Joaquin Murrieta," 530. Scanland cites Coronel as his source for when Murrieta arrived in Los Angeles.

4. Perkins, El campo, chapter 5. William Perkins settled in Rosario, Argentina, in June 1852. A decade later he hand-copied his California diary into a manuscript divided into chapters, probably intending to publish it. But it was not published until more than a century later, in Perkins, Three Years. The book, published in 1961, has an excellent introduction by Dale L. Morgan and James R. Scobie, but the Perkins manuscript was edited for this edition. My citations of the diary are from Perkins's unedited, unabridged manuscript, preserved in microfilm at the Bancroft Library. As the microfilmed manuscript's page numbers are often illegible or cut off, I cite only the chapters, but they are short.

5. Perkins, El campo, chapter 5.

6. Taylor, appendix to El Dorado, 2:237.

7. Perkins, El campo, chapter 5.

8. Perkins, El campo, chapter 5.

9. Perkins, El campo, chapter 5.

10. Perkins, El campo, chapter 5.

11. Taylor, El Dorado, 1:87.

12. For an example of a conflict caused in part by liquor consumption, see Stoddart, Annals, 81–82.

13. Perkins, El campo, chapter 5.

14. Taylor, El Dorado, 1:102–3. This is exactly what happened in New Echota, Cherokee country, in the 1830s. Georgians encroached on Cherokee land and confiscated and

auctioned off Cherokee homes and goods (and abused or lynched occupants), claiming that the property—with all its improvements—belonged to the state of Georgia and that the Cherokee had no rights under Georgia law. See Wilkins, Cherokee Tragedy, 164.

15. Perkins, El campo, chapter 5.

16. Taylor, El Dorado, 2:244–45.

17. For a firsthand account of the February 1850 meeting, see Edward Gould Buffum, Six Months in the Mines (Philadelphia: Lea & Blanchard, 1850), 113–20. See also letter dated September 11, 1850, in Myrick, Letters of Thomas Myrick, 25–28.

18. For an excellent account of the Foreign Miners Tax Law and its impact in the southern mining district, see Dale L. Morgan and James R. Scobie, introduction to Perkins, Three Years, 34–44.

19. Perkins, Three Years, 36; Perkins, El campo, chapter 10. See also Pitt, Decline of the Californios, 60–62, and Boessenecker, Gold Dust and Gunsmoke, 268.

20. Perkins, El campo, chapter 10.

21. Besançon was permitted by law to keep $3.00 for every $20.00 he collected, but instead he kept $7.00 for every $20.00. Newspaper editors complained about this, but Besançon was never prosecuted. With regard to those who tried to become U.S. citizens, see Morefield, Mexican Adaptation, 8.

22. Morefield, Mexican Adaptation, 9.

23. Christman, One Man's Gold, 169–70.

24. Feigning friendship with an intended victim happened often. The outlaw Rafael Money surreptitiously dropped his revolver, pretended he lost it, and lured his intended murder victim into helping him look for it. See Angel, San Luis Obispo, 296. In another case, after dining at an inn, a band of outlaws called for cigars. When the proprietor brought them, he was grabbed and bound. His inn was burglarized and his family murdered. Many more such examples can be found in early California newspapers and vigilante records. See Sacramento Daily Democratic State Journal, October 25, 1854, Republican, October 30, 1854, and Alta, October 28, 1854.

25. Christman, One Man's Gold, 172–73.

26. Christman, One Man's Gold, 174–75; Perkins, El campo, chapter 12.

27. Christman, One Man's Gold, 175.

28. More about Joaquín Murrieta, Juan Flores, and Pancho Daniel will come in the following chapters. With regard to Claudio Féliz, see the Alta and the Republican, September 4, 1852, the Stockton Journal, September 14, 1852, and Varley, "Appendix A" in Legend of Joaquín, 177–78.

29. Christman, One Man's Gold, 175–77.

30. Christman, One Man's Gold, 178.

31. Secrest, Man from the Rio Grande, 53–54; Varley, Legend of Joaquín, Appendix A, 174–79.

32. Perkins, El Campo, chapter 4.

33. Perkins, El Campo, chapter 21. See also Perkins, Three Years, 226n, and the Republican, June 14, 18, and 25, 1851.

34. Alfred Doten's seventy-volume personal journal was printed in a necessarily fore-shortened, more manageable set of four heavy volumes titled *The Journal of Alfred Doten*, with introduction and notes by Walter Van Tilburg Clark. See 1:99.

35. Doten, *Journal*, 1:99.

36. Doten, *Journal*, 1:103.

37. Doten, *Journal*, 1:104.

38. Perkins, *El campo*, chapter 20. The *Herald* reference is in Secrest, *Man from the Rio Grande*, 59–60.

39. Perkins, *El campo*, chapter 20.

40. *Journal*, June 7, 1851.

41. Varley, *Legend of Joaquín*, 177.

42. Perkins, *El campo*, chapter 35.

43. Perkins, *El campo*, chapter 35. Although Perkins did rewrite his diary in 1862 with the idea of publishing it, the legend could not have influenced this entry, for if it had, he would have written "Joaquin Murieta."

44. Perkins, *El campo*, chapter 35.

45. Perkins, *El campo*, chapter 36.

46. Doten, *Journal*, 1:122. The dance performed was the Yaqui deer dance, "with Coyote accompaniment."

47. Doten, *Journal*, 1:122.

48. Doten, *Journal*, 1:124.

49. The word "greaser," in the *Compact Edition of the Oxford English Dictionary* (1979), means "one who greases" wagon or mill wheels. Mariano G. Vallejo ran into this definition and concluded that greaser referred to overland North American immigrants who came to California in covered wagons and greased their wagon wheels en route. In French, English, and Spanish literature a greaser was someone who asked others to "grease" his palm, meaning pay bribes, a usage applied to Mariano Vallejo's brother, Salvador, in 1846. (See Pitt, *Decline of the Californios*, 27.) Greaser was also used by U.S. sailors working on trade vessels who visited Monterey, California, in the early 1840s and bought hides and tallow from *graseros*. Graseros cut the fatty suet off butchered cattle and processed it to make a base for soap and candles. By January 1852 the word was applied to Mexicans in a derogatory way, just as "Yankee" was used in a derogatory way by Southerners to mean abolitionists. Mexicans throughout the Southwest picked up the latter slur from Texans.

50. Clappe, *Dame Shirley Letters*, 166–68.

3. The Perspective of the *Los Angeles Star* and *La Estrella*

1. Manuel Clemente Rojo is mentioned in the following works: Newmark, *Sixty Years*, 53–54, 56; Kemble, *California Newspapers*, 373; and Bell, *Reminiscences*, 6–7. M. C. Rojo wrote a history of Baja California for Hubert Howe Bancroft in 1879. It was translated and edited by Philip O. Gericke and published under the title *Historical Notes on Lower Cal-*

ifornia, *with some Relative to Upper California Furnished to the Bancroft Library* (Los Angeles: Dawson's Book Shop, 1972). He was in Sonora, Mexico, in 1856, according to *El Clamor Público*, January 17, 1857. In 1857 he left for Baja California, where he became a judge, husband, and father. He retired to Mexicali and died in 1900 at age seventy-seven. Regarding Rojo's literary talent, see Blanco, *La lengua española*, 339. See also Rice, *Los Angeles Star*, 14, 15, 52, and Franklin Walker, *Literary History of Southern California* (Berkeley: University of California Press, 1950), 78–79.

2. *Alta*, August 10, 1853, features a colorful story about Ogier.

3. Newmark, *Sixty Years*, 53–54.

4. Newmark, *Sixty Years*, 30. Harris Newmark devoted chapters 4–7 to his recollections of what Los Angeles was like when he first arrived in 1853.

5. *Republican*, May 5, 1852; *Herald*, May 13, 1852.

6. Correspondence from Mariposa dated April 28, 1852, and signed "Responsible," *Republican*, May 5, 1852. See also *Alta*, May 15, 1852.

7. *State Journal*, September 16, 1853. Harry Love recounted this adventure while in Marysville exhibiting Joaquín Murrieta's head. See also Varley, *Legend of Joaquín*, 152, and Secrest, *Man from the Rio Grande*, 220.

8. *Republican*, May 22, 1852, and *Herald*, May 28, 1852.

9. *Herald*, June 26, 1852, *Alta*, June 26, July 3, 1852, and Los Angeles *Star*, June 12, 1852.

10. *Star*, June 19, 1852. The *Star* gave the name "Harry Lull" and then on June 26, 1852, printed a correction: "Mr. Harry Love (not Lull) was the name of the man who shot the Sonoranian prisoner while conveying him to this place."

11. The name Carmello is spelled "Carmillo" in the English section of the *Star* and "Carrillo" in Ross, *Devil on Horseback*, 41–44. I have chosen to stay with the spelling found in the *Los Angeles La Estrella*.

12. See *Alta* and *Herald*, February–April 1851. To learn more about California vigilantes see Bancroft, *Popular Tribunals*. See also Mullin, *Let Justice be Done*.

13. *Star/La Estrella*, July 31, 1852.

14. *Star*, August 7, 1852.

15. *La Estrella*, July 31, 1852.

16. *Star*, September 18, 1852.

17. For more about Joshua Bean see Jack Skiles, chapter 1 in *Judge Roy Bean Country* (Lubbuck: Texas Tech University Press, 1997). See also Varley, *Legend of Joaquín*, 34–41, 188–89n31, n36, and on the Web, "To Trial for Trying to Steal the Courthouse," a selection found under "Life and Times of Col. Cave Couts" at http://www.coutsfamily .com (accessed August 17, 2010). (Joshua Bean, with Cave Couts's militia support, tried to take possession of the town hall and courthouse in San Diego while Bean was alcalde there. Bean wanted it to be his private residence as well as his place of business.)

18. *Republican*, December 4, 1852.

19. *Star*, November 13, 1852, partially reprinted in the *Alta* and the *Herald*, November 30, 1852, and the *Stockton Journal*, December 3, 1852. The *Star/La Estrella* editors guarded the

Reid family name by never printing it in connection with the investigation into the death of Gen. Bean. For more on the Reids, see Dakin, *Scotch Paisano*. Dakin wrote that Felipe was briefly affiliated with the Joaquín Murrieta band. He died of smallpox in 1857.

20. *La Estrella*, November 13, 1852.

21. The *Star*, November 20, 1852, is lost to posterity, but excerpts from the English section were reprinted in the *Alta*, November 30, 1852, and the *Herald*, November 30, 1852.

22. *Star/La Estrella*, November 27, 1852, reprinted in the *Alta*, December 6, 1852. The *Alta* reprint is followed by a note from the editor about how the steamer that brought news from the South had departed from San Pedro, after the vigilance committee had tried and found the prisoners guilty "and condemned them to death. The others were turned over to the people." A motion had been made to take all those in jail and hang them with Benito Lopez and Cipriano Sandoval, but few supported the proposal.

23. *Star*, December 4, 1852, reprinted in the *Alta*, December 15, 1852. *Padrino* means godfather, patron, sponsor, protector, employer. The *Alta*, February 14, 1852, land claims column reported that the State Board of Commissioners received a claim from "Sebastin Nunez [sic], to the 'Ranchero de Orestimba' six leagues in extent, in Tuolumne County." Rancho Orestimba bordered Rancho Pexcadero in San Jose County, which belonged to Antonio María Pico, father of Solomón Pico. It also bordered Francisco Pacheco's land on the south; see Varley, *Legend of Joaquín*, 187n16.

24. *Republican*, December 18, 1852, quoting the *Herald*, which in turn had quoted the *Star*, December 4, 1852.

25. The fascinating story of the Lugo brothers has been preserved in a stirring little book by W. W. Robinson, *The People versus Lugo: Story of the Famous Los Angeles Murder Case and its Amazing Aftermath* (Los Angeles: Dawson's Book Shop, 1962). See also Joseph Lancaster Brent, *The Lugo Case, a Personal Experience* (New Orleans: Searcy & Pfaff, 1926), reprinted in *Mexican California after the U. S. Conquest* (New York: Arno Press, 1976). Brent served as the defense attorney.

26. *Republican*, December 18, 1852.

27. *Star*, December 4, 1852, reprinted in the *Alta*, December 15, 1852.

28. *Star*, December 4, 1852, reprinted in the *Alta*, December 15, 1852.

29. *Star*, December 4, 1852, reprinted in the *Alta*, December 15, 1852.

30. *Star*, December 4, 1852, reprinted in the *Alta*, December 15, 1852.

31. *Star*, December 4, 1852, reprinted in the *Alta*, December 15, 1852. James Varley and other historians appear to have deduced that "Cristóbal" is a misspelling or misprint of Cipriano, but Cipriano was not wounded, nor did he ask for a confessor until after he was sentenced to death. As he accepted five dollars from Felipe Reid because he needed the money desperately, he could not have had a sister who was prosperous enough to house and feed an Indian servant. Cristóbal Duarte's sister, however, could afford to keep a Cahuilla servant girl, who was sexually violated by an inebriated Joshua Bean. This girl was also Felipe Reid's mistress. See Bell, *Reminiscences*, 10.

32. Bell, *Reminiscences*, 28–29. See also *Republican*, December 18, 1852. Felipe's sense of loyalty to his people. the Cahuilla, and the sting to his honor in that the girl who was raped was his mistress, gave him the strongest motive.

33. *La Estrella*, October 22, 1853. Rojo's editorial reveals that many people did not think Benites told the truth concerning Sandoval.

34. *Republican*, December 18, 1852.

35. *Star*, February 26, 1853.

36. The original *Daily Whig* profile of "Joaquin the Mountain Robber" was probably printed on February 13, 1853. Reprints appeared in the *Daily Union*, February 14, 1853, and the *Republican*, February 23, 1853. Villa Real de Catorce is and always has been in northeastern San Luis Potosí, not Jalisco. Walker was editor of the *San Francisco Daily Whig* in 1854 after being acquitted of charges related to his filibuster invasion of Baja California and Sonora and after the paper's name had been changed to the *Daily Commercial Advertiser*. John Lewis, at that time, was working for the *San Francisco Chronicle*. See Kemble, *California Newspapers*, 111, 357, 387; Varley, *Legend of Joaquín*, 191n25.

37. "¡Gran Alarma en Jackson Ville! ¡Persecución de Joaquín!" *La Estrella*, February 26, 1853.

38. As for why five Joaquíns were listed, that is addressed in chapter 4, which also discusses at some length how the ranger bill came about.

39. *La Estrella*, June 4, 1853.

40. *Star*, June 11, 1853.

41. *La Estrella/Star*, June 18, 1853.

42. *La Estrella/Star*, June 18, 1853. Pedro Sánchez's fate was also published in the *Alta*, June 14, 1853. A Mexican named Albino Leyba shot and killed Pedro Sánchez over a gambling dispute.

43. *La Estrella/Star*, June 18, 1853.

44. *La Estrella*, June 25, 1853.

45. Regarding the spiritualists at Mission San Gabriel, see the *Star*, July 17, 1852, and September 18, 1852. For a description of spiritualist "science" in the 1850s, see "The Rationale of Spiritualism, Abridged for the use of Californians," *Alta*, July 31, 1853.

46. For Benito Wilson's account of his encounter with Cahuilla chieftain and marauder Joaquín, see Dakin, *Scotch Paisano*, 122–24.

47. *Star/La Estrella*, January 28, 1854.

48. *Herald*, August 19, 1853.

49. *La Estrella*, August 6, 1853.

50. "La cabeza de Joaquín," *La Estrella*, August 20, 1853.

51. *Star*, August 20, 1853.

52. *La Estrella*, September 3, 1853.

53. Regarding other outlaws known as "Three-Fingered Jack" see Varley, *Legend of Joaquín*, 197n46. Richard Laughlin's nicknames are in Dakin, *Scotch Paisano*, 10.

54. *La Estrella*, September 3, 1853.

4. Northern Newspapers and the Politics of Bandit Hunting

1. Samuel Brennan and party left New York City in February and reached San Francisco six months later. They learned that America had gone to war with Mexico while they were en route. In the fall of 1849 Kemble and Gilbert imported presses and type from New York to sell in California, but Gilbert's politically sharp-edged editorials resulted in duels. He survived one, but died in the second, on August 2, 1852. As a tribute to his friend, Kemble left Gilbert's name under the Alta masthead. See Kemble, foreword by Helen Harding Bretnor to California Newspapers, 9–41.

2. Kemble, foreword by Helen Harding Bretnor to California Newspapers, 28.

3. Kemble, California Newspapers, 109, 153–54, 169, 172, 179–80, 390. For more about John White, see Varley, Legend of Joaquín, 63, 76, 98–100, 115–19. Obituaries were published on March 24, 1871, in the Alta and the Daily Union. The Stockton Times was started in January 1850. Six months later White and Radcliffe purchased a better press and type from Kemble and White used the old press to print the Sonora Herald. Enos Christman carried the first print run of the Sonora Herald from Stockton (where it was printed) to Sonora town in Tuolumne County on horseback. He covered sixty-four miles in four to five hours. John White arrived by stage, persuaded Judge John Gage Marvin to become co-proprietor, and hired Dewitt Clinton Atkins to help Christman set up a print shop in Sonora. He then returned to Stockton and sold his share of the Sonora Herald to district attorney James R. Reynolds. As for why the Democratic Party named their newspaper the San Joaquin Republican, this was because in 1851 "Republican" meant being a citizen of a democratic republic such as the United States of America. Texas and Vermont were independent democratic republics before they became states. William Walker and Henry Crabb, as filibuster captains, sought to establish democratic republics in Sonora, Mexico. The Republican Party was not founded until 1854 and had a tiny following until the Whig Party ceased to exist in 1856.

4. Even prior to the Spanish Armada, the "Black Legend" was spread among Protestants due to the activities of the Spanish Inquisition in the Netherlands.

5. The Regulators made the news in the Stockton Journal, July 2, 9, 29, 1852, and in other newspapers, same month.

6. "A TRUE AMERICAN," letter to the editor, Stockton Journal, July 29, 1852.

7. Alta, July 17, 1852.

8. Alta, July 17, 1852.

9. Alta, July 22, 1852.

10. Lang, History of Tuolumne County, 212.

11. Alta, July 22, 1852.

12. Alta, September 18, 1852

13. Alta, October 11, 1852.

14. Alta, December 29, 1852; Stockton Journal, December 31, 1852.

15. Republican, January 26, 1853.

16. Republican, January 26, 1852, citing Calaveras Chronicle, January 22, 1853. See also

"Peregrine Pilgrim [John Judson Ames]," "Letter from the Mountains," *Alta*, January 26, 1853; "Ames," letter to the editor, *Alta*, January 29, 1853; and Varley, *Legend of Joaquín*, 44, 190n7.

17. Ridge, *Life and Adventures*, 110–28; *Republican*, February 2, 1853.

18. Varley, *Legend of Joaquín*, 46–47, 190; *Republican*, February 2, 1853.

19. If the spelling of Ignatius Moretto's name is correct, he was Italian, not Mexican. It is possible Judge Taliaferro misspelled the name.

20. *Republican*, January 26, 1853.

21. Doten, *Journal*, 1:140.

22. Varley, *Legend of Joaquín*, 49.

23. An abridged version appeared in the *Alta*, January 29, 1853. The chronology does not match what the *Calaveras Chronicle* belatedly provided in an effort to clear up the confusion. For example, it was not on Friday, January 21, but on Sunday, January 16, that Akop's body was found, etc.

24. *Alta*, February 10, 1853.

25. Ross, *Devil on Horseback*, 42.

26. W. M., letter to the editor, *Republican*, January 29, 1853, and *Alta*, January 31, 1853. Juan Nevis was tried March 15 and hanged a month later. See *Alta*, March 20, 1853.

27. *Republican*, February 2, 1853.

28. For more about Walker and his 1853 filibuster campaign see Young, *Journalism in California*, 20–22, and Stout, *Liberators*, 81–102.

29. *Alta*, January 29, 1853.

30. Varley, *Legend of Joaquín*, 49. Varley cites the San Francisco *Herald*, February 8, 1853.

31. *Republican*, February 16, reprinted February 23, 1853.

32. *Republican*, February 19, 1853, and *Alta*, February 21, 1853.

33. Justice Beatty's adventures were recounted in bits and pieces in the *Republican*, February 2, 5, 12, 16, 19, 23, 1853, and in the *Stockton Journal*, February 8, 19, 1853. He probably crossed paths at Jackson Gate with bounty hunters motivated by a $1000 reward offered by the Chinese at Big Bar. Bill McMullen led the bounty hunters. See Nadeau, *Real Joaquin*, 40–42, and Varley, *Legend of Joaquín*, 50–52.

34. *Republican*, February 23, 1853.

35. W. M., letters to the editor, *Republican*, February 16, 1853, abridged versions in *Alta*, February 21, 1853.

36. *Republican*, February 19, 1853.

37. W. M., letter to the editor, *Republican*, February 19, 1853. Prisoner's name published in *Alta*, March 2, 1853.

38. *Republican*, February 19, 1853.

39. *Alta*, February 21, 1853.

40. *Republican*, February 23, 1853; *Sacramento Daily Union*, February 26, 1853.

41. *Republican*, February 23, 1853.

42. Varley, *Legend of Joaquín*, 73. Varley suggests that Ditson's informant was describing Reyes Féliz.

43. *Republican*, March 2, 1853.

44. *Republican*, February 26, March 2, 1853; *Alta*, February 28, 1853.

45. *Republican*, March 2, 1853.

46. *Republican*, March 2, 1853; *Alta*, March 4, 1853. The unnamed prisoner was executed February 20, 1853. See Varley, *Legend of Joaquín*, 59.

47. *Alta*, February 24, 1853.

48. "Sydney Ducks" refers to Australian penal colony immigrants, many of whom came to California from New York City. Some of them were arrested by San Francisco's vigilantes in 1851 and hanged. The most notorious of these was James Stuart. See Bancroft, *Popular Tribunals*, 36:286–96.

49. *Republican*, March 2, 1853.

50. *Republican*, March 2, 1853.

51. *Republican*, March 2, 1853.

52. The Agua Fria correspondent signed his letters "A. J. L." The initials matched those of Frank Latta's uncle, Andrew Jackson Latta, who, according to family tradition, sometimes wrote correspondences to Stockton newspapers. However historian James Varley found a much more convincing candidate: A. J. Lasterer, sometime doctor, judge, and county clerk, who signed the petition calling for the state to fund rangers led by Harry Love. See Latta, *Joaquín Murrieta*, 55, and Varley, *Legend of Joaquín*, 62, 74.

53. *Republican*, March 12, 1853. Another correspondent from Agua Fria wrote, on the same day, that Joaquín had visited Hornitos "some two weeks ago" or during the last week of February. He left "unmolesting and unmolested" but returned a week later.

54. *Republican*, March 12, 1853.

55. *Republican*, March 12, 1853.

56. *Alta*, March 11, 1853. See also W. M., letter to the editor, *Republican*, March 12, 1853, in which he says that things were quiet in Calaveras County.

57. Letter to the editor, *Republican*, February 26, 1853.

58. *Republican*, March 12, 1853.

59. A Whig single-sheet weekly, the *Placerville El Dorado News*, reported that a Mr. Pomeroy of Mokelumne Hill saw the Joaquín of Calaveras at Upper Ranchería on March 17. Article reprinted in *Alta*, March 27, 1853.

60. *Alta*, March 21, 1853.

61. *Republican*, April 2, 1853, reprinted from *Shasta Courier*. Doten and Christman both made the sixty-four-mile trip between Stockton and Sonora on horseback in four to five hours. Adams & Co. express rider Sam White covered 61 miles in two hours, fifty minutes, the *Alta* reported on September 9, 1853. John "Jack" Powers made a bet that he could ride 150 miles in eight hours without changing horses, and he won. See introduction, Ross, *Devil on Horseback*, xiv–xv. The Sacramento River bends north to Colusa; the natural direction to go from there, for Sonorans, would be toward Marysville, there being a Sonora town about a mile outside Marysville. The Clarksville story came from

a Democratic single-sheet weekly, the *Coloma Miner's Advocate*, and was reprinted in the *Republican*, March 30, 1853.

62. *Republican*, April 2, 1853

63. *Republican*, April 9, 1853.

64. *Alta*, April 9, 1853.

65. *Alta*, April 10, 1853.

66. "Report of the Committee on Military Affairs on the activities of Joaquin: April 14, 1853—presented by J. M. Covarrubias, Chairman of the Committee" Joaquin Murrieta Papers. Facsimile in Latta, *Joaquin Murrieta*, 330–32.

67. "Report of the Committee on Military Affairs."

68. "Report of the Committee on Military Affairs."

69. It is possible that George R. B., California-based correspondent for the *New York Tribune*, was the author. His correspondence to the *Tribune*, dated May 16, 1853, was published in the *New York Tribune*, June 14, 1853. This source is listed in Gordon, "Joaquin Murieta." George R. B. wrote that Joaquin "is one of those who welcomed Americans and American rule in California—but unfortunately . . . had his dearest rights invaded and trampled under foot by those scoundrel ruffians found in all our new settled regions, who alike disgrace our nation and a common humanity." The same month that George R. B.'s correspondence was published, a hastily written and sloppily printed romance by an anonymous "Californian" familiar with the history and geography of Monterey and Santa Clara counties was published. Halfway through *The Mysteries and Miseries of San Francisco* the bandit Joaquín appears as a friend to the heroine. He gallops in to rescue her, then takes his leave to attend to a mission of bloody revenge on those who ravaged "his beloved Carmencito." This book is also cited in Gordon, "Joaquin Murieta." See "Californian," *Mysteries and Miseries*, 60–80.

70. Regarding the long beard and false mustache text: as someone who learned Spanish as a second language, I am keenly aware of how and when translation errors are most likely to occur. In conversation especially, it is very easy to think you understand, only to find you misinterpreted a word that, when couched in an unfamiliar phrase, means something else entirely. It is possible that the Spanish phrase which was translated as "a long beard and apparently false mustache" might mean rather, "his beard had grown long enough that something like a mustache showed." But I speculate. The description is what it is.

71. "Latest Account of Joaquin. From our Monterey Correspondent: Monterey, April 16, 1853," *San Francisco Herald*, April 18, 1853. Reprinted in the *Republican*, April 20, 1853.

72. "Latest Account of Joaquin. From our Monterey Correspondent: Monterey, April 16, 1853," *San Francisco Herald*, April 18, 1853.

73. "Latest Account of Joaquin. From our Monterey Correspondent: Monterey, April 16, 1853," *San Francisco Herald*, April 18, 1853.

74. "Latest Account of Joaquin. From our Monterey Correspondent: Monterey, April 16, 1853," *San Francisco Herald*, April 18, 1853.

75. "Latest Account of Joaquin. From our Monterey Correspondent: Monterey, April 16, 1853," *San Francisco Herald*, April 18, 1853.

76. "Latest Account of Joaquin. From our Monterey Correspondent: Monterey, April 16, 1853," *San Francisco Herald*, April 18, 1853.

77. *Republican*, May 7, 1853. Kooser's misspelling of Murrieta reveals an English phonetics applied to Castilian pronunciation in which the Spanish rr is corrupted into a lilting single sound that imitates the English l. In the same way, the a as in "day" is used where the Spanish e makes the same sound, and a short i is used where the Castilian a drops off so lightly after t that it sounds to English ears like the i in "tip."

78. *Alta*, May 11, 1853.

79. *Alta*, May 12, 13, 15, 1853.

80. *Alta*, May 16, 1853.

81. "San Joaquin News," *Alta*, June 6, 1853, quoting the *Republican* extra of the previous day. The paragraph about Harvey was misprinted—minus every other line. See also the *Republican*, June 21, 1853.

82. *Alta*, June 15, 1853. "Raw Head and Bloody Bones" refers to an old nursery "bugbear" or "Bogy-man"—a frightening criminal figure conjured up to scare children into obedience that is mentioned in the works of Rabelais.

83. *Alta*, June 20, 1853.

84. *Alta*, June 24, 1853.

85. *Alta*, July 18, 1853.

86. *Alta*, July 15, 1853.

87. *Republican*, July 16, 1853.

88. *Republican*, July 23, 1853. Sources on the Dawson gang include *Republican*, July 19, 21; correspondence from "Mephistopheles" in the *Republican*, July 26, 1853; *Alta*, July 13, 23, 27, 1853.

89. *Republican*, July 21, 1853. See also Varley, *Legend of Joaquín* 100–101.

90. *Republican*, July 23, 1853.

91. *Republican*, July 28, 1853.

92. *Alta*, July 30, 1853.

93. *Daily Union*, July 30, 1853.

94. *Alta*, August 1, 1853

95. *Republican*, August 2, 1853.

96. *Republican*, August 2, 1853.

97. *Alta*, August 4, 1853.

98. *Alta*, August 2, 1853. The *Stockton Journal* editor was John Tabor, who in June 1854 slandered one of John White's employers—*San Joaquin Republican* proprietor Joseph Mansfield. Mansfield "accosted Tabor upon the street, and after some words, Tabor drew a Derringer pistol from his pocket and fired," wrote Edward C. Kemble in *California Newspapers*, 170–71. Mansfield died and Tabor was tried for murder.

99. *Republican*, August 6, 1853. White knew, through his informants, that Harry Love

and company had been pursuing Joaquín Valenzuela when they came upon a large number of thieves and Indians with their corral of horses near Mission San Juan Bautista. They found the place with help from a prisoner named Jesús whom Harry Love identified as Joaquin's brother-in-law in a letter to the governor, dated July 12, 1853. See "Letter from Capt. Love to Gov. Bigler: July 12, 1853," Joaquín Murrieta Papers.

100. *Republican*, August 6, 1853. A more detailed report was published on August 11—the same day Capt. Harry Love and some of his rangers arrived in Stockton with a preserved head, a three-fingered hand, affidavits collected in Quartzburg and Mariposa, and a statement taken from the prisoner, identifying the head as that of Joaquín Murrieta.

101. *Republican*, August 11, 1853.

102. *Alta*, August 7, 1853. Cites the *Stockton Journal* of the day before.

103. There were at least two other Joaquín Murrietas in gold rush California. During Frank Latta's 1965 interview with Soledad Murrieta, daughter of José Trinidad Mateo Francisco Murrieta Rosas, Soledad said her father was the son of Joaquín Murrieta "but not el bandido famoso." "He went to las placeras [the gold mines] in Alta California and did not come back." See Latta, *Joaquín Murrieta*, 198, 208. I found Soledad's parents in the *International Genealogical Index* 4.01 (Phoenix, Arizona: Intellectual Reserve, Inc., 1997). Soledad's uncle, Manuel de Jesús, was christened in December 1848 and her father in July 1850, so her grandfather, Joaquín, must not have left for California until after the Foreign Miners Tax Law of 1850 was rescinded. Another Joaquín Murrieta from Mexico died in Stockton on Christmas day 1858 at age thirty-five and is buried in the old Catholic cemetery there. See *Gold Rush Days* (Stockton: San Joaquin Genealogical Society, 1979), 2:51.

104. Fr. Dominique Blaive is profiled in Varley, *Legend of Joaquín*, 197n48. Varley mentions that Blaive was posted at St. Mary's, San Francisco in 1856, and founded another parish church there. But Varley also wrote that Blaive's archbishop "had trouble getting him to explain the $30,000 in debts" the San Francisco missions incurred. In the *San Joaquin Republican*, September 24, 1853, a reprint of a clip from the *Alta* reported that it was Rev. Fr. Flovious Fontaine of Mission Dolores in San Francisco, who suddenly departed aboard a steamer and "took with him about $30,000 in Church funds."

105. "Affidavits," Joaquín Murrieta Papers.

106. "Affidavits," Joaquín Murrieta Papers. George Washington Havens was a heavy drinker and, when drunk, tended to start fights, particularly with Mexicans, sometimes with deadly results, as in French Camp near Stockton. See the *Stockton Journal*, June 29, 1852.

107. "Affidavits," Joaquín Murrieta Papers.

108. *Stockton Journal*, August 11, 1853, reprinted in *Alta*, August 13, 1853. In an email to the author, the curator of the Anatomical Archives at the National Museum of Health and Medicine at the U.S. Armed Forces Institute of Pathology, Paul Sledvik, said: "Discoloration of tissue does occur after being fixed in a preservative such as alcohol." He suggested that storing the head in whiskey first and then in medical alcohol with ar-

senic would have caused the tissue to redden and swell in the same way the face of a heavy drinker grows rosy and plump.

109. *Alta*, August 10, 1853.

110. *Republican*, August 11, 1853.

111. *Alta*, August 16, 1853.

112. *Herald*, August 19, 1853. John Foster was killed in May 1850. See Varley, *Legend of Joaquín*, 153–54.

113. Letter to the editor from San Diego, *Alta*, August 18, 1853.

114. For the Mexican perspective of Walker's filibuster campaign in Baja California, see Aguilar, Capítulo XVIII "Filibusterismo e inestabilidad" in *De cueva pintada*. Also of interest is May, "Young American Males," 857–86.

115. Bell, *Reminiscences*, 213–14.

116. *Alta*, August 17, 1853.

117. *Alta*, August 17, 1853.

118. *Alta*, August 17, 1853.

119. *Alta*, August 23, 1853.

120. *Alta*, August 23, 1853.

121. News of Vergara can be found in the *Alta*, July 27, August 18, September 1, 1853, and the *Star*, September 17, 1853. Also see Bell, *Reminiscences*, 151–54.

122. "News from the South," *State Journal*, October 10, 1853.

123. *Star*, October 22, 1853. See also Bell, *Reminiscences*, 147–50; *State Journal*, October 10, 1853; *Republican*, October 13, 1853. One of the outlaws who was hotly pursued in San Luis Obispo, being wounded and fatigued, turned on his pursuers, a revolver in each hand, and fired all twelve shots before he died of multiple wounds.

124. Buck, *Yankee Trader*, 142–43.

125. *Republican*, October 25, 1853; Correspondence from Mokelumne Hill dated October 15 and signed "W. C. P.", *State Journal*, October 17, 1853. See also Doten, *Journal*, 1:313–14.

126. *Republican*, October 27 and November 1, 1853. By the time the head was exhibited in Calaveras and Tuolumne counties, there were no longer any political advantages to stretching the truth. The election results were in, Walker had left San Francisco with his filibuster recruits, and the rangers' term of service had expired.

5. Joaquín Valenzuela and Others in *El Clamor Público*

1. Reprinted in the *Republican*, August 23, 1853.

2. *Republican*, October 1, 1853; *State Journal*, October 4, 1853.

3. *Star*, January 29, 1854, reprinted in *Alta*, February 5, 1854.

4. William B. Secrest, *Lawmen and Desperadoes, a Compendium of Noted, Early California Peace Officers, Badmen and Outlaws, 1850–1900* (Spokane WA: Arthur H. Clark, 1994), 225.

5. *Republican*, March 30, 1855.

6. Howard C. Gardiner, ed., *In pursuit of the Golden Dream, Reminiscences of San Francisco and the Northern and Southern Mines, 1849–1857* (Stoughton MA: Western Hemisphere, 1970), 188–89.

7. *State Journal*, November 2, 1853.

8. *La Estrella*, March 24, 1855.

9. *La Estrella*, May 12, 1855.

10. *El Clamor Público*, August 28, 1855.

11. *El Clamor Público*, June 12, 1858; *San Andreas Independent*, April 24, 1858.

12. *El Clamor Público*, May 31, 1856.

13. *El Clamor Público*, July 19, 1856. When Sr. Cruz Montoya was murdered at San Gabriel, the Spanish-speaking community there called for a vigilante committee meeting to investigate the murder, but no investigation occurred.

14. *El Clamor Público*, July 19, 1856. The Jenkins-Ruíz story was also featured in *El Clamor Público*, July 26, August 2, 9, 16, 23, 1856.

15. *El Clamor Público*, July 26, 1856.

16. *El Clamor Público*, August 2, 1856.

17. To learn more about Jack Powers, see Ross, *Devil on Horseback*.

18. "Opiniones de la Prensa de San Francisco sobre lo que Sucedio en Los Angeles," *El Clamor Público*, August 16, 1856.

19. Editorial, *El Clamor Público*, August 16, 1856. See also *Star*, August 9, 1856.

20. For more about Henry Hamilton see the anonymously authored *An Illustrated History of Los Angeles* (Chicago: Lewis Publishing, 1889), 511–12; Kemble, *California Newspapers*, 182, 234, 247; Newmark, *Sixty Years*, 192, 280, 371; Ayer, *Gold and Sunshine*, 100, 114, 227, 256, 269, 271. See also Robinson, "California Copperhead," 38–51. Robinson's article focuses on Hamilton's politics.

21. The Spanish noun *la manilla* means "bracelet, wristband, or manacle," and, in a colloquial sense, "married."

22. At that time William Walker was in Nicaragua, struggling to keep his second filibuster style "government" together in the face of strong local resistance.

23. Gadsdonia was named for James Gadsden, who negotiated the purchase. For more about Gadsden see Stout, *Liberators*, 133–40.

24. *El Clamor Público*, January 31, 1857.

25. *Star*, January 31, 1857.

26. *El Clamor Público*, February 14, 1857.

27. *El Clamor Público*, January 31, 1857.

28. *El Clamor Público*, January 31, 1857.

29. *El Clamor Público*, February 14, 1857. Van Deusen was one of two San Gabriel constables, and Frank King was one of two El Monte constables, the other El Monte constable, John Ward, also being present. See election results in the *Star*, November 22, 1856.

30. *El Clamor Público*, February 14, 1857.

31. *El Clamor Público*, February 14, 1857.

32. *El Clamor Público*, February 14, 1857.

33. *El Clamor Público*, February 14, 1857; *Star*, February 7, 1857.

34. *El Clamor Público*, February 14, 1857.

35. *El Clamor Público*, February 14, 1857.

36. El Clamor Público, February 21, 1857.

37. El Clamor Público, February 21, 1857. See also Star, February 21, 1857.

38. El Clamor Público, February 21, 1857.

39. El Clamor Público, February 21, 1857.

40. El Clamor Público, February 14, 1857.

41. El Clamor Público, February 21, 1857. The wording of this reminiscence was designed to conjure up images of the innocent Lord Jesus Christ crucified between two robbers.

42. El Clamor Público, February 21, 1857.

43. El Clamor Público, February 28, 1857.

44. El Clamor Público, February 28, 1857.

45. El Clamor Público, February 28, 1857.

46. "Confesión de Espinosa," El Clamor Público, February 21, 1857.

47. "Las Persecuciones de la Família de Berreyesa," El Clamor Público, March 28, 1857.

48. "Carta de Los Angeles," El Clamor Público, March 21, 1857, translated and reprinted from Le Phare, March 4, 1857. According to Horace Bell, the respectable and frank American farmer who saw men playing ninepins with Miguel Soto's head was William "Uncle Bill" Rubottom, Ezekiel Rubottom's older brother. See Bell, Old West Coast, 99–101. Bell confused the fates of Miguel Soto and José "Mexican Joe" Santos in his recollections of a visit with "Uncle Bill" Rubottom.

49. "Carta de Los Angeles," El Clamor Público, March 21, 1857.

50. Editorial y "El Gran Jurado," El Clamor Público, April 4, 1857.

51. Editorial, El Clamor Público, April 11, 1857.

52. Editorial, El Clamor Público, April 11, 1857.

53. San Andreas Independent, June 6, 1857. In this issue Dr. Hernández wrote a letter—in imperfect English—to a Dr. George Hammond, who shared it with the press. This letter and Dr. Hammond's reply caused quite a sensation. The Oroville North Californian (article reprinted in the San Jose Tribune, June 19, 1857) followed the reprinted letters with an "early history of the miscreant Hernández" provided by John C. Frémont or his wife, Jessie Benton Frémont. The Frémonts claimed that Juan Hernández was Pablo Hernández, a Sonoran boy Frémont took under his wing in California in 1841 after Piute Indians murdered the boy's parents. Thirty years later, Frémont's Memoirs, edited by his wife, claimed that when Pablo Hernández grew into a young man, he followed "wrong courses" and became "the Joaquin who for some years was so well known as a robber chief" in California. See John C. Frémont, Memoirs (Chicago: Belford, Clarke, 1887), 370–76, 409. The beheader became the beheaded, memory having held onto the horror of a severed and preserved head but forgetting Henry Crabb and his filibusters.

54. For more about Crabb's filibuster campaign see Stout, Liberators, 143–68, and Forbes, Crabb's Filibustering Expedition.

55. For more about el corrido see Luis Leal's introduction to Paz, Vida y aventuras, 65–79 Spanish edition, lxxvii–xcv English edition.

56. El Clamor Público, May 9, 1857.

57. "Encarnación Berryesa" [sic], *San Jose Tribune*, May 22, 1857.

58. Lorenzo Lopez may have been the same man Teodor Vásquez called "San Lorenzo."

59. Regarding Bernardo Daniel see the *State Journal*, October 26, 1856, and the *Republican*, October 29, 1856. The *San Jose Tribune*, July 9, 1856, reported the brazen act of "Pancho Dormiel."

60. *Republican*, October 5, 11, 1851.

61. "Arrest of a Mexican Desperado," *San Jose Tribune*, November 20, 1857.

62. "Arrest of a Mexican Desperado," *San Jose Tribune*, November 20, 1857.

63. El *Clamor Público*, December 19, 1857, also December 26, 1857; see also the *Star*, February 20, 1858. Hamilton reported that Luciano Tapia "addressed a few words to his countrymen—Sonoranians—advising them to take warning by his fate and to leave this country, as it was no place for them, adding that he was called on to suffer for crimes perpetrated by others."

64. El *Clamor Público*, January 23, 1858; see also "Pancho Daniel," *Star*, January 23, 1858.

65. El *Clamor Público*, December 4, 1858; Newmark, *Sixty Years*, 49, 51, 55.

66. *San Jose Tribune*, April 2, 1858.

67. Photographer O. Henry Mace studied the carte de visite and concluded that the ambrotype or tintype could not have been taken earlier than 1856. See Mace's pamphlet, *Joaquin Murieta*, 15. Historian Manuel Perez Rojas pointed out the similarity in facial features of the young man in the tintype to those of a son of Rafael Murrieta from Sonora in Rojas's book, *Joaquín Murrieta el Patrio*, 90. John Boessenecker and William Secrest date the tintype to the 1860s. To me it looks like it could well be an 1858 tintype carte de visite of Pancho Daniel.

68. Walter Murray thought that "Herrado" was Rafael's surname. *Herrado* is the past perfect tense of the verb *herrar* which means "to forge of iron." El *herrador* is a blacksmith or brander of livestock. Murray reported that Luciano el Mesteño, in his confession, named "Rafael Herrado" as a member of the band, but Luciano was either referring to Rafael's occupation or, figuratively, to his hard-heartedness when he called him "Herrado."

69. The Baratié murder was reported in the *Daily Union*, May 24, 27, 28, June 1, 1858, and in El *Clamor Público*, June 5, 20, July 10, 1857. The *Star*, May 22, 1858, features a correspondence from Santa Barbara, dated May 19, discussing the investigation, and the *San Jose Tribune*, May 28, 1858, reported the murder of Jack Gilkey, the young American farmer Rafael Money shot. Gilkey lived about twenty miles south of the Baratié ranch.

70. "Ocamorenia" could be a conjunction of *ocarina*, meaning "wooden flute," and morriña, meaning "homesick"; or it could be an American corruption of the name "Nacamereño," which El *Clamor Público* reported as Valenzuela's alias. Nacamereño is a Spanish surname, not a nickname. At the time of his execution, Joaquín Valenzuela had been working for David W. Alexander, a former Los Angeles ranger, as a pack mule driver. He was also a gambler. He was seen betting on horses at a race in San Luis Obispo before the Baratié crime occurred. After his arrest he told the vigilantes that

he did not think it fair he should be arrested and tried for old crimes as he had been straight for a year. See El Clamor Público, June 5, 1858. See also "The Fate of Joaquin Valenzuela," a sidebar to Boessenecker, "Pío Linares," 38. A history of the actions of the San Luis Obispo vigilantes, including a rebuttal to the editor of El Clamor Público, can be found in Angel, San Luis Obispo, 294–303.

71. "Desórdenes en Santa Barbara," El Clamor Público, July 12, 1856.

72. Daily Union, May 28, 1858, reprinted in Ross, Devil on Horseback, 138.

73. Walter Murray would, twenty years later, erroneously identify Luciano "el Mesteño" as Luciano Tapia, which afterward became an oft-repeated historical error. Tapia had been dead four months when el Mesteño was hanged. Mesteño is also a word meaning wild—a term used in Spanish and in Mexican California to describe Indians not affiliated with or "civilized by" Catholic missions. For Andrea Baratié's story see the Daily Union, May 24, 1858, the San Jose Tribune, May 28, 1858, the Republican, June 3, 1858, and the San Francisco Bulletin, June 17, 1858. Andrea Baratié later married Alexander Murray, Walter Murray's brother. See Boessenecker, Gold Dust and Gunsmoke, 111.

74. "SAN LUIS OBISPO. Asesinatos—Linchamientos, Atrocidades, &c.," El Clamor Público, June 5, 1858. An excerpt reads: "They formed a Vigilance Committee . . . rabble that calls itself 'THE PEOPLE' and publicly executed . . . an innocent man named Joaquín Valenzuela, widely known by the appellate Nacamereño." A portion of this story was translated and published in the Daily Union, June 16, 1858.

75. El Clamor Público, June 5, 1858.

76. El Clamor Público, June 5, 1858.

77. El Clamor Público, September 11, 1858, reported that "without a doubt he [Jack Powers] has been in Guaymas [Sonora] for the past two and a half months." He was killed in 1860. See San Francisco Daily Evening Bulletin, November 15, 16, 1860, reprinted in Ross, Devil on Horseback, 167–68. For more about Pío Linares, see Boessenecker, "Pío Linares."

78. "Linchamiento de Pancho Daniel," El Clamor Público, December 4, 1858. The history of the Pancho Daniel legal case is traced in El Clamor Público, January 23, March 13, 27, July 24, 31, December 4, 18, 1858. A short summary of the case was published in the Star, December 4, 1858.

79. El Clamor Público, December 18, 1858.

80. El Clamor Público, December 18, 1858.

81. In January 1860 Ramírez moved to Hermosillo, Sonora, and worked on La Estrella de Occidente. In 1862 he returned to California. To learn more about Ramirez see "Dictation of Francisco P. Ramírez," Hubert Howe Bancroft Archives, University of California Library, Berkeley. See also Gutiérrez, "Francisco P. Ramírez, Californio Editor" and Gray, "Francisco P. Ramírez."

6. Of Tiburcio, Procopio, Mariana, and Oral Tradition

1. Joaquin (the Claude Duval of California); or, The Marauder of the Mines. A Romance founded on Truth (New York: Robert M. De Witt, 1865) was published anonymously but has been

attributed to Henry Llewellyn Williams. The story borrows from legend but does not stick to it. In Williams's Claude Duval version, Joaquín is not shot dead: instead he drowns in a lake. Cincinnatus Hines Miller published a lengthy narrative poem about Joaquín Murrieta in a collection of poems titled *Joaquín et al.* (Portland OR: S. J. McCormack, 1869). It was mocked by critics who tauntingly dubbed the author "Joaquín," a name he embraced, becoming known from thence forward as Joaquín Miller.

2. *Monterey Republican*, August 21, 1871.

3. Secrest, *Dangerous Trails*, 122–28.

4. Plummer, *Señor Plummer*, 184–86.

5. Secrest, *California Desperadoes*, 138.

6. Beers, *California Outlaw*; "Crimes and Career of Tiburcio Vásquez," which appeared in the 1874 edition of John Rollin Ridge's *Life and Adventures of Joaquin Murieta* (San Francisco: Fred'k. MacCrellish & Co., 1874). The Tiburcio Vásquez story was later reprinted separately in the pamphlet "Crimes and Career of Tiburcio Vásquez."

7. An article by George Beers which mentions Mariana appeared in the *Chronicle*, May 17, 1874. See also Duke, *Celebrated Criminal Cases*, 189–201. Duke's informant was Sheriff Thomas Cunningham of Stockton, who, like George Beers, was a member of Sheriff Harry Morse's posse when they went in pursuit of Tiburcio Vásquez and met Mariana.

8. Mariana started her own folk legend by claiming in the 1880s that she had been visited by a saint while praying in a cave at Three Rocks, which is also called Joaquin Ridge. It overlooks Cantua Creek and Coalinga. She started a pseudo-Catholic cult at the site with herself as "Prophetess" Mariana Andrada de Murrieta. The cult flourished until a child she was supposed to heal died. She later became known as "Mariana la Loca" (Crazy Mariana). See Wood, *Mariana la Loca*. Mariana also claimed that Murrieta had buried treasure near Three Rocks and that he had been on the point of retrieving it when he was killed. She also said that they had a son whom she named for his father and who was still living in Mexico.

9. See Secrest, "Return of Chávez."

10. *Alta*, November 10, 1879.

11. *Alta*, November 10, 1879.

12. The tt misspelling of the name Murrieta began to appear in newspapers after a Spaniard named Juan Murrieta became postmaster of a town named after him. Juan and his brother Esequiel Murrieta had arrived in California in the early 1850s. They tried mining and various other occupations, then purchased sheep and stayed in the wool, lamb, and lambskin trade for decades. They moved south in 1873 and founded Murietta Hot Springs in what is now Riverside County, south of Los Angeles. Although the town of Murrieta has since changed the spelling back to having two r's and one t, there are still people living there whose mailing address uses the Italian spelling: one r and two t's. Juan Murrieta changed the spelling of his name in an attempt to disassociate himself and his family from the outlaw. It didn't work. Instead, people changed the spelling of the outlaw's name! See Web sites: http://www.oldtemecula.com/history/history1

.htm, http://www.sandiegohistory.org/journal/74winter/temecula.htm, and http://www
.mymurrieta.com/about/juan.php (all URLs accessed August 17, 2010). Juan's brother
Esequiel is listed in the California state census of 1852, Mariposa County, as: white male,
age 23, birth place—Spain, occupation—laborer. I learned this from Joshua Reader.

13. *Marysville Herald*, September 16, 1853. For an interview with Harry Love, see the
September 17, 1853, issue. An interesting story about O. P. Stidger and the duel he had
with Richard Rust, a Southern Democrat editor, is found at the Web site: http://www
.richsamuels.com/nbcmm/snowden/documents/snowden__family_california.pdf., p. 54
(accessed August 17, 2010; the two underscores after "snowden" are essential to the
address).

14. *Alta*, March 28, 1855.

15. *La Estrella*, April 14, 1855.

16. Frank Latta identified the head as that of "Chappo" in *Joaquín Murrieta*, 100–101. I
found a "Chapo" mentioned in the *Herald*, April 13, 1852. One José "Chapo" Valenzuela
was arrested for stealing horses and sentenced to jail time plus a flogging, but he escaped.

17. Thompson, Chap. 2 in *Voices of the Past*. For those interested in knowing more
about Governor John Bigler, see Fredman, "Bigler Regime."

18. *Expositor*, November 12, 1879.

19. William T. Henderson was from Tennessee. He served in the war with Mexico
1846–48, then went to California via the Missouri Trail in the summer of 1848. He was
apparently among the Regulators who settled Quartzburg in Mariposa County. In a reminiscence by Lafayette H. Bunnell, published in *The Pioneer*, March 17, 1899, Henderson
is described as "none too partial to the lower class of Mexicans." Bunnell tried to re-
deem his old friend. Knowing that Henderson regretted having killed Joaquín, Bunnell
shifted the blame, saying it was really ranger John White who killed Joaquín Murrieta
and that Henderson wanted to take him alive. See also Varley, *Legend of Joaquín*, 165–66.

20. Cunningham, *Truth About Joaquin*, 153–54. Cunningham's book is mostly recalled and edited folklore, but in his last chapter he published letters that he had received from various people, including one from Eugenio Plummer. The letter from Gar-
land Ruddle is dated May 22, 1937. For other Ruddle family recollections, see Outcalt,
History of Merced County, 379–80.

21. See Ramey, "Beginnings of Maryville." George R. Smart, great-grandson of Sheriff Buchanan's widow, recounted relevant family history in "Marginalia," *California Historical Society Quarterly* 26, no. 4 (December 1947): 380–83.

22. Latta, "Pioneer."

23. For the Ed Daily story, see Charles Hanley, Sang-Hun Choe, and Martha Mendoza, *Bridge at No Gun Ri* (New York: Henry Holt, 2001). See also "Reliable Sources?" *U.S.
News & World Report*, May 17, 2000, and "The Mystery of No Gun Ri; a soldier's bizarre
recantation," *U.S. News & World Report*, June 5, 2000.

24. Carrillo, *California I Love*, 150.

25. Carrillo, *California I Love*, 152.

26. Carrillo, *California I Love*, 153–54.

27. Carrillo, *California I Love*, 153–54.

28. Carrillo, *California I Love*, 155–57.

29. This story is based on historical events. In 1847 the British-Mexican Reed household at San Miguel Mission was wiped out by bandits, but the culprits were a band of Anglo-Americans and one local Indian. Californio vigilantes pursued the band and caught up with some of them in Santa Barbara, where they were lassoed on the beach and dragged in the surf until they drowned. See Boessenecker, *Gold Dust and Gunsmoke*, 13–22.

Closing Thoughts

1. Frazer, *Bandit Nation*, 58–84.

2. Frazer, *Bandit Nation*, 58–84.

Bibliography

Primary Sources

Bancroft Library, Special Collections, University of California, Berkeley

Perkins, William, "El campo de los Sonoraenses or Three Years Residence in California (1849–1852)," microfilm of his handwritten California diary.

California State Archives, Sacramento, California

Joaquín Murrieta Papers, v, DR. 4.
Military Record Group-Adjutant General's Office, Records of the California Rangers 3A, DR. 33.

Stanford University Libraries Special Collections, Stanford University, California

"El Patrio, The Untold Story of Joaquin Murieta," unpublished and incomplete manuscript and notes, Stan Steiner Papers, m0700, series 3, box 18, folders 10–12.

Secondary Sources

Aguilar, Antonio Ponce. *De cueva pintada a la modernidad: Historia de Baja Califonia.* Segunda Edición. Tijuana, Mexico: Biblioteca Loyola, 2004. http://www.loyola.tij .uia.mx/ebooks/cueva_pintada/index.php (accessed August 16, 2010).
Angel, Myron. *History of San Luis Obispo County.* Oakland CA: Thompson & West, 1883.
Ayer, James. *Gold and Sunshine: Reminiscences of Early California.* Boston: Gorham Press, 1922.
Bancroft, Hubert Howe. *The Works of Hubert Howe Bancroft.* 39 vols. San Francisco: History Company, 1882–90.
———. *California Pastoral.* Vol. 34 in *The Works of Hubert Howe Bancroft.* Published in 1888.
———. *The History of California.* Vols. 18–24 in *The Works of Hubert Howe Bancroft.*
———. *The History of Mexico, 1824–1861.* Vol. 5 in *The Works of Hubert Howe Bancroft.*
———. *Popular Tribunals.* Vols. 36–37 in *The Works of Hubert Howe Bancroft.*

Beers, George. *The California Outlaw: Tiburcio Vásquez*. Mexican American Series. New
    York: Arno Press, 1974. First published as *Vásquez, or the Hunted Bandits of the San
    Joaquin*. New York: Robert DeWitt, 1875.

Bell, Horace. *Reminiscences of a Ranger: Early Times in Southern California*. Los Angeles:
    Yarnell, Caystile & Mathes, 1881. Reprinted with an introduction by John Boesse-
    necker. Norman: University of Oklahoma Press, 1999.

———. *On the Old West Coast*. New York: William Morrow, 1930.

Blanco, Antonio S. *La lengua española en la historia de California*. Madrid: Ediciones Cul-
    turas Hispanica, 1971.

Boessenecker, John. "California Bandidos: Social Bandits or Sociopaths?" *Southern
    California Quarterly* 4 (Winter 1998): 419–34.

———. *Gold Dust and Gunsmoke*. New York: John Wiley & Sons, 1999.

———. "Pío Linares: Californio Bandido." *The Californians* 5, no. 6 (November/De-
    cember 1987): 34–44.

Buck, Franklin. *Yankee Trader in the Gold Rush*. New York: Houghton Mifflin, 1930.

Burns, Walter Noble. *Robin Hood of El Dorado*. New York: Coward-McCann, 1932.

"Californian." *The Mysteries and Miseries of San Francisco*. New York: Garret, 1853.

Carrillo, Leo. *The California I Love*. Englewood Cliffs NJ: Prentice-Hall, 1961.

Castillo, Pedro G., and Albert Camarillo, eds. *Furia y Muerte: Los Bandidos Chicanos*.
    University of California Chicano Studies, Monograph no. 4. Los Angeles: Aztlan
    Publications, 1973.

Christensen, Peter. "Minority Interaction in John Rollin Ridge's *The Life and Times of
    Joaquin Murieta*." *Melus* 17 (Summer 1991): 61–72.

Christman, Enos. *One Man's Gold: Letters and Journals of a Forty-Niner*. New York:
    McGraw-Hill, 1930.

Clappe, Louise K. S. *The Dame Shirley Letters from the California Mines 1851–1852*. With in-
    troduction and notes by Carl I. Wheat. New York: Alfred A. Knopf, 1965.

Coronel, Antonio Franco. *Señor Don Antonio Franco Coronel: Tales of Mexican California*,
    dictated to Mr. Thomas Savage for H. H. Bancroft, 1877. Translated by Diane de Avalle-
    Arce and edited by Doyce B. Nunis Jr. Santa Barbara CA: Bellerophon Books, 1994.

*Crimes and Career of Tiburcio Vásquez, the Bandit of San Benito County and Notorious Early Cal-
    ifornia Outlaw, Compiled from Newspaper Accounts*. Hollister CA: Evening Free Lance,
    1927.

Cunningham, James C. *The Truth About Joaquin Murietta*. Mariposa CA: Mariposa Her-
    itage Press, 1997.

Dakin, Susanna Bryant. *A Scotch Paisano in Old Los Angeles: Hugo Reid's Life in California,
    1832–52*. Berkeley: University of California Press, 1959.

Dary, David. *Red Blood and Black Ink: Journalism in the Old West*. New York: Alfred A.
    Knopf, 1998.

Doten, Alfred. *The Journal of Alfred Doten*. With introduction and notes by Walter Van
    Tilburg Clark. 4 vols. Reno: University of Nevada Press, 1971.

Duke, Thomas. *Celebrated Criminal Cases of America*. San Francisco: James H. Barry, 1910.

Forbes, Robert H. *Crabb's Filibustering Expedition into Sonora, 1857*. Tucson: Arizona Silhouettes, 1952.

Frazer, Chris. *Bandit Nation: A History of Outlaws and Cultural Struggle in Mexico, 1810–1910*. Lincoln: University of Nebraska Press, 2006.

Fredman, Lionel Edward. "The Bigler Regime." Master's thesis, Stanford University, 1959.

Gonzales, Rodolfo "Corky." *I Am Joaquin: An Epic Poem*. New York: Bantam Books, 1972.

Gordon, Thomas. "Joaquin Murieta: Fact, Fiction and Folklore." Master's thesis, Utah State University, 1983.

Gray, Paul Bryan. "Francisco P. Ramírez: a Short Biography." *California History* 84, no. 2 (December 22, 2006): 20–39.

Guinn, James Miller. *History of the State of California and Biographical Records of Coast Counties*. Chicago: Chapman Publishing, 1904.

Gutiérrez, Félix. "Francisco P. Ramírez, Californio Editor and Yanqui Conquest." *Media Studies Journal* (Spring/Summer 2000): 16–23.

Hazera, Lydia D. "Joaquin Murieta: the Making of a Popular Hero." *Studies in Latin American Popular Culture* (1982): 201–13.

Hittell, Theodore H. *History of California*. San Francisco: N. J. Stone, 1898.

Hobsbawm, Eric. *Bandits*. Rev. ed. New York: Pantheon Books, 1981.

Huerta, Alberto. "California: El bandido y el vendido." *Religión y cultura* 35, no. 1/2 (Enero-Marzo 1989): 9–59.

———. "Murieta el Famoso: los mitos no mueran." *Religión y cultura* 31, no. 140 (Mayo-Junio 1985): 283–311.

Jackson, Joseph Henry. *Anybody's Gold*. New York: Appleton-Century, 1941.

———. *Bad Company: The Story of California's Legendary and Actual Stage-Robbers, Bandits, Highwaymen and Outlaws from the Fifties to the Eighties*. Lincoln: University of Nebraska Press, 1977.

The Joaquin Murrieta Scrapbook. Compiled by Joshua Reader. Santa Cruz CA: Cliffside Publishing, 1995.

Johnson, Susan Lee. *Roaring Camp: The Social World of the California Gold Rush*. New York: W. W. Norton, 2000.

Kemble, Edward C. *History of California Newspapers*. Los Gatos CA: Talisman Press, 1962.

Lang, Herbert. *History of Tuolumne County*. San Francisco: B. F. Alley, 1882.

Lang, Margaret Hanna. *Early Justice in Sonora*. Sonora CA: Mother Lode Press, 1963.

Latta, Frank F. *Joaquin Murrieta and his Horse Gangs*. Santa Cruz CA: Bear State Books, 1980.

———. "Pioneer of the San Joaquin." *Fresno Bee*, September 15, 1935.

The Life of Joaquin Murieta, The Brigand Chief of California: the story as it originally appeared in the 1859 "California Police Gazette" with historical notes and illustrations. Fresno CA: Valley Publishers, 1969.

Mace, O. Henry. *Joaquin Murieta: The Legend Begins.* Dramatis Personae Series, no. 2. Sutter Creek CA: Gold Country Enterprises, 1992.

May, Robert E. "Young American Males and Filibustering in the Age of Manifest Destiny: The United States Army as a Cultural Mirror." *Journal of American History* 78, no. 3 (December 1991): 857–86.

Miller, Robert. *Juan Alvarado: Governor of California.* Norman: University of Oklahoma Press, 1998.

Mitchell, Richard Gerald. "Joaquin Murieta: A Study of Social Conditions in Early California." Master's thesis, University of California, Berkeley, 1927.

Mondragon, María. "The '(Safe) White Side of the Line': History and Disguise in John Rollin Ridge's 'The Life and Adventures of Joaquin Murieta'." *The American Transcontinental Quarterly* 8 (September 1994): 173–87.

Morefield, Richard Henry. *The Mexican Adaptation in American California, 1846–1875.* Master's thesis, University of California, Berkeley, 1955. Reprint. San Francisco: R & E Research Assoc., 1971. Page references are to the 1971 publication.

Mullin, Kevin J. *Let Justice be Done: Crime and Politics in Early San Francisco.* Reno: University of Nevada Press, 1989.

Myrick, Thomas. *Letters of Thomas Myrick from California to Jackson, Michigan.* Mount Pleasant MI: Cumming Press, 1971.

Nadeau, Remi. *The Real Joaquin Murieta.* Santa Barbara CA: Crest Publishers, 1974.

Newmark, Harris. *Sixty Years in Southern California, 1853–1913.* 3rd ed. New York: Houghton Mifflin, 1930.

Outcalt, John. *A History of Merced County.* Los Angeles: Historic Record Co., 1925.

Paden, Irene D., and Margaret E. Schlichtmann. *The Big Oak Flat Road: An Account of Freighting from Stockton to Yosemite.* Self-published, 1955. Reprint, Yosemite CA: Yosemite Natural History Association, 1959.

Parins, James W. *John Rollin Ridge: His Life and Works.* Lincoln: University of Nebraska Press, 1991.

Paz, Ireneo. *Vida y aventuras del mas celebre bandido sonorense, Joaquín Murrieta: y sus Grandes Proezas en el Estado de California.* With a introduction and bibliography by Luis Leal. Houston: Arte Público Press, 1999.

———. *Life and adventures of the celebrated bandit Joaquin Murrieta, His exploits in the state of California.* With a introduction and bibliography by Luis Leal. Houston: Arte Público Press, 2001.

Perkins, William. *Three Years in California: William Perkins' Journal of Life at Sonora, 1849–1852.* Notes and introduction by Dale L. Morgan and James R. Scobie. Berkeley: University of California Press, 1964.

Pico, Don Pío. *Historical Narrative.* Translated and with notes by Arthur P. Botello. Glendale CA: Arthur H. Clark, 1973.

Pitt, Leonard. *Decline of the Californios: A Social History of the Spanish-Speaking Califorians, 1846–1890.* Berkeley: University of California, 1966.

Plummer, Don Juan (Eugenio). *Señor Plummer: The Life and Laughter of an Old-Californian.* Los Angeles: E. R. Plummer, 1942.

Ramey, Earl. "The Beginnings of Marysville, Part III." *California Historical Society Quarterly* 25, no. 1 (March 1936): 39–41.

Ramos, Raul A. "Murieta [or Murrieta], Joaquín." *New Encyclopedia of the American West.* New Haven: Yale University Press, 1998.

Rice, William. *The Los Angeles Star, 1851–1864.* Los Angeles: University of California Press, 1947.

Ridge, John Rollin [Yellow Bird, pseud.]. *The Life and Adventures of Joaquin Murieta, The Celebrated California Bandit.* With a introduction by Joseph Henry Jackson. Norman: University of Oklahoma Press, 1986.

Robinson, John W. "A California Copperhead: Henry Hamilton and the Los Angeles Star." *Dogtown Territorial Quarterly* 32 (Winter 1997): 38–51.

Rojas, Manuel. *Joaquín Murrieta: El Patrio, el "Far West" del Mexico cercenado.* Mexicali, Mexico: Gobierno del Estado de Baja California, 1986.

———. "Joaquín Murrieta: Donde la Historia Termina." *Baja California,* El Nacional (December 9, 1976).

———. *Joaquín Murrieta el Patrio: Truthful Focuses for the Chicano Movement.* With an introduction by Alfredo Figueroa. Blythe CA: La Cuna Aztlan, 1996.

Rosenus, Alan. *General M. G. Vallejo and the Advent of the Americans.* Albuquerque: University of New Mexico Press, 1995.

Ross, Dudley T. *Devil on Horseback: A Biography of the "Notorious" Jack Powers.* Fresno CA: Valley Publishers, 1975.

Sanchez, Rosaura. *Telling Identities: The Californios' Testimonios.* Minneapolis: University of Minnesota Press, 1995.

Scanland, J. M. "Joaquin Murrieta: A Californian Fra Diavolo." *Overland Monthly* 26, no. 155 (November 1895): 530–39.

Secrest, William B. *California Desperadoes: Stories of Early California Outlaws in Their Own Words.* Clovis CA: Word Dancer Press, 2000.

———. *Dangerous Trails: Five Desperadoes of the Old West Coast.* Stillwater OK: Barbed Wire Press, 1995.

———. *Joaquín: Bloody Bandit of the Mother Lode.* Fresno CA: Saga-West, 1967.

———. *The Man from the Rio Grande: a Biography of Harry Love.* Spokane WA: Arthur H. Clark Company, 2005.

———. "The Return of Chávez, California Spoiler." *True West* 25, no. 3 (February 1978): 6–12.

———. *The Return of Joaquin: Bloody Bandit of the Mother Lode.* Fresno CA: Saga-West, 1973.

Standard, Sister M. Colette. "The Sonora Migration to Calilfornia, 1848–1856: A Study in Prejudice." *Southern California Quarterly* 58 (Fall 1976): 333–58.

Steiner, Stan. "Murieta or Murrieta, Joaquin, c. 1830–1853 or 1878." *The Reader's Encyclopedia of the American West.* Edited by Howard R. Lamar. New York: Thomas Y. Crowell, 1977.

———. "On the Trail of Joaquin Murieta." *The American West* 18, no. 1 (January/February 1981): 54–56, 66.

———. "In Search of the Legendary Joaquin Murieta." *National Outlaw and Lawman Association Newsletter* 2, no. 3 (1976–77): 6–7.

Stoddart, Thomas Robertson. *Annals of Tuolumne County.* Edited and annotated by Carlo M. De Ferrari. Clovis CA: Word Dancer Press, 1997.

Stout, Joseph Allen, Jr. *The Liberators: Filibustering Expeditions into Mexico, 1848–1862 and the Last Thrust of Manifest Destiny.* Los Angeles: Westernlore Press, 1973.

Taylor, Bayard. *El Dorado, or Adventures in the Path of Empire.* 2 vols. New York: George Putnam, 1850. Facsimile reprint. New York: Time-Life Books, 1980.

Thompson, Paul. *The Voices of the Past: Oral History.* 2nd ed. New York: Oxford University Press, 1988.

Thornton, Bruce. *Searching for Joaquín: Myth, Murieta and History in California.* San Francisco: Encounter Books, 2003.

Varley, James F. *The Legend of Joaquín Murrieta, California's Gold Rush Bandit.* Twin Falls ID: Big Lost River Press, 1995.

Wilkins, Thurman. *Cherokee Tragedy: The Ridge Family and the Decimation of a People.* 2nd ed. Norman: University of Oklahoma Press, 1983.

Wood, Raymund F. *Mariana la Loca: Prophetess of the Cantua and Alleged Spouse of Joaquin Murrieta.* Fresno CA: Fresno County Historical Society, 1970.

———. "New Light on Joaquin Murrieta." *Pacific Historian* 14, no. 1 (Winter 1970): 54–65.

Wood, Richard Coke. *Tales of Old Calaveras.* Angels Camp CA: Calaveras Californian, 1949.

Young, John P. *Journalism in California: Pacific Coast and Exposition Biographies.* San Francisco: Chronicle Publishing, 1915.

INDEX